A Soul has no Gender

TRANSGRESSIONS: CULTURAL STUDIES AND EDUCATION

Scope

Cultural studies provides an analytical toolbox for both making sense of educational practice and extending the insights of educational professionals into their labors. In this context *Transgressions: Cultural Studies and Education* provides a collection of books in the domain that specify this assertion. Crafted for an audience of teachers, teacher educators, scholars and students of cultural studies and others interested in cultural studies and pedagogy, the series documents both the possibilities of and the controversies surrounding the intersection of cultural studies and education. The editors and the authors of this series do not assume that the interaction of cultural studies and education devalues other types of knowledge and analytical forms. Rather the intersection of these knowledge disciplines offers a rejuvenating, optimistic, and positive perspective on education and educational institutions. Some might describe its contribution as democratic, emancipatory, and transformative. The editors and authors maintain that cultural studies helps free educators from sterile, monolithic analyses that have for too long undermined efforts to think of educational practices by providing other words, new languages, and fresh metaphors. Operating in an interdisciplinary cosmos, Transgressions: Cultural Studies and Education is dedicated to exploring the ways cultural studies enhances the study and practice of education. With this in mind the series focuses in a non-exclusive way on popular culture as well as other dimensions of cultural studies including social theory, social justice and positionality, cultural dimensions of technological innovation, new media and media literacy, new forms of oppression emerging in an electronic hyperreality, and postcolonial global concerns. With these concerns in mind cultural studies scholars often argue that the realm of popular culture is the most powerful educational force in contemporary culture. Indeed, in the twenty-first century this pedagogical dynamic is sweeping through the entire world. Educators, they believe, must understand these emerging realities in order to gain an important voice in the pedagogical conversation.

Without an understanding of cultural pedagogy's (education that takes place outside of formal schooling) role in the shaping of individual identity–youth identity in particular–the role educators play in the lives of their students will continue to fade. Why do so many of our students feel that life is incomprehensible and devoid of meaning? What does it mean, teachers wonder, when young people are unable to describe their moods, their affective affiliation to the society around them. Meanings provided young people by mainstream institutions often do little to help them deal with their affective complexity, their difficulty negotiating the rift between meaning and affect. School knowledge and educational expectations seem as anachronistic as a ditto machine, not that learning ways of rational thought and making sense of the world are unimportant.

But school knowledge and educational expectations often have little to offer students about making sense of the way they feel, the way their affective lives are shaped. In no way do we argue that analysis of the production of youth in an electronic mediated world demands some "touchy-feely" educational superficiality. What is needed in this context is a rigorous analysis of the interrelationship between pedagogy, popular culture, meaning making, and youth subjectivity. In an era marked by youth depression, violence, and suicide such insights become extremely important, even life saving. Pessimism about the future is the common sense of many contemporary youth with its concomitant feeling that no one can make a difference.

If affective production can be shaped to reflect these perspectives, then it can be reshaped to lay the groundwork for optimism, passionate commitment, and transformative educational and political activity. In these ways cultural studies adds a dimension to the work of education unfilled by any other sub-discipline. This is what Transgressions: Cultural Studies and Education seeks to produce—literature on these issues that makes a difference. It seeks to publish studies that help those who work with young people, those individuals involved in the disciplines that study children and youth, and young people themselves improve their lives in these bizarre times.

A Soul has no Gender

*Love and Acceptance through the Eyes
of a Mother of Sexual and Gender Minority
Children*

Denise M. Ajeto

Victoria –
It is a privilege to
meet another mother
who is on the journey!
Denise

SENSE PUBLISHERS
ROTTERDAM/BOSTON/TAIPEI

A C.I.P. record for this book is available from the Library of Congress.

ISBN 978-90-8790-896-6 (paperback)
ISBN 978-90-8790-897-3 (hardback)
ISBN 978-90-8790-898-0 (e-book)

Published by: Sense Publishers,
P.O. Box 21858, 3001 AW
Rotterdam, The Netherlands
http://www.sensepublishers.com

Printed on acid-free paper

ABSTRACT

This heuristic inquiry explores my experience as the mother of fraternal twins who are sexual and gender minorities and the process I went through in coming to accept their respective identities. Primary emphasis was directed toward my experience of becoming a more empathic parent to my children as my understanding and acceptance of them increased. Also explored was the impact of this empathic perspective on my relationships with my children and family, with others, and, ultimately, with myself.

This inquiry was initially guided by two primary questions:

(1) How was I able to accept my children and become an empathic parent, given that I didn't start out as one and that research suggests that almost half the parents of sexual minority children reject them?

(2) What is empathic parenting? Why is it important for healthy child development and what happens to children who don't get it?

The concept of *disenfranchised grief*, defined by Lenhardt (1997) as resulting from "experiences that are not or cannot be openly acknowledged by peers or society" (in Bracciale, Canabria & Updyke, 2003, p. 4), was also explored, given disenfranchised grief's proposed role in the parental rejection of their sexual minority children.

Through this heuristic inquiry, another form of disenfranchised grief has been identified that appears to expand Lenhardt's (1997) existing definition. This form of disenfranchised grief is proposed to occur when young children must psychologically defend against the experience of overwhelming pain resulting from a lack of attunement with the mother or failure by the mother to appropriately recognize and regulate her child's distress. It is through the process of attunement that a mother regulates the physical and emotional needs of her child, needs that are expressed as distress. This form of disenfranchised grief is thought to obstruct or interfere with the natural flow of attunement between humans. In particular, this disenfranchised grief is thought to specifically interfere with the *mother's* innate instinct to seek out her distressed child, or to respond empathically when the child seeks her.

It is important to note that fathers also serve a critical role in the regulation of their children. The impact of disenfranchised grief upon a father's ability to respond empathically to his child is thought to be very similar to that of the mother. However, given that this inquiry is based upon the author's experience as a mother and much of the research distinguishes the mother's role in the regulation of children from that of the father, it is written in a mother's voice. The father's voice needs to be heard as well.

The possibility that disenfranchised grief may be operating at a societal level is also proposed, given that it is thought that disenfranchised grief may be transmitted from one generation to the next through the mother-child interaction. However, additional research is needed to further explore this idea. The implications for parents, educators, leadership and society as a whole are addressed, including a call for changes in the educational system that place greater emphasis on both the process of parenting children and on the development of the interpersonal skills that contribute to not only more empathic and attuned parents, but also to greater overall happiness (Noddings, 2003, 2006). Just as Luckman (1978, in Martin, 2005) asserts that "the job of science is to explain everyday life" (p. 212), it is the belief of this author that the job of schools should be to educate for everyday life and for the attainment of happiness in everyday life.

TABLE OF CONTENTS

ACKNOWLEDGEMENTS

When I stand before thee at the day's end, thou shalt see my scars and know
that I had my wounds and also my healing.

-Rabindranath Tagore

While the heuristic journey is a solitary one, I was never alone. There have been many synchronistic events that brought me in contact with remarkable people who have supported me throughout this work and who deserve my thanks.

First, I wish to thank Dr. Margaret Brigham, who gifted me with the awareness that souls have no gender and that Red Roads travel in many directions.

I offer my thanks and gratitude to Dr. Roberto Peña for his willingness to listen and to ask questions, and for truly caring about this journey. My love, gratitude, and thanks go, first, to Dr. Carol Kusche, who provided the empathic witnessing that brought me back from the edge. Also to Taalib-Din Mahdi (rest in peace, my friend), Jean Mavrelis, Dr. Thomas Kochman, Dr. Kenneth Addison, and Dr. Donna Stringer for also being my empathic witnesses and my community. Also deserving of my thanks are Dr. Shirley Steinberg at Lang Publishing, Michel Lokhorst at Sense Publishers, and Rachel Morrison, for her insightful editing. Through their support and encouragement, they helped me to come to the belief that this was an important story that needed telling, that others would benefit from its telling, and that I was the only one who could tell it. Without the support of this amazing community, this book would not have been written.

Finally, my deepest love and gratitude go to my husband and life partner, Renato, my parents, and especially Julian and Kristin for sharing this journey with me. Without your presence in my life, I would not be the person that I am. You have truly shown me what it means to love and to persevere. Each of you has been a "remarkable person" in my life and I am forever indebted.

The stories people tell have a way of taking care of them.

If stories come to you, care for them.

And learn to give them away where they are needed.

Sometimes, a person needs a story more than food to stay alive.

That is why we put these stories in each other's memory.

This is how people care for themselves.

-Barry Lopez

"Crow and Weasel"

INTRODUCTION

It is time for the voice of the mother to be heard in education.

-Nel Noddings

The original intent of my doctoral research, upon which this book is based, had been the exploration of my experience as a mother of sexual and gender minority twins. I wanted to attempt to understand why I chose to struggle with accepting my children's identities when, according to Ryan & Futterman (1998), almost half the parents of lesbian, gay, bisexual, transgender, or questioning (LGBTQ) children do not. I had this term, *disenfranchised grief*, in the back of my mind because it had been suggested as a possible reason that parents might reject their LGBTQ child. Defined by Lenhardt (1997) as a grief or loss that cannot be publicly acknowledged, it made sense to me that disenfranchised grief could be a factor, given how clearly I recalled my own feelings of shame and isolation when my children came out. I thought that if societal stigmatization—due to ignorance—isolated parents of LGBTQ children and led to the rejection of their children, then the solution to this problem had to be better education, specifically better education with respect to human sexuality and the continuum of sexual and gender identities. I still believe that to be true.

However, I now believe there was a larger purpose or intention at work that led me to engage in a deeper exploration of disenfranchised grief. It seemed that the further I delved into the research and compared this research to my own life experience, the more I felt as though an opaque film had been peeled from my eyes. Memories, images, and feelings, long banished to my unconscious, resurfaced with striking clarity and, sometimes, intense pain. But out of what felt like unconscious chaos, three key ideas emerged. First, I began to see how disenfranchised grief had interfered with my ability to be a good mother, as well as my ability to fully experience *being* a mother. Second, I recognized that disenfranchised grief had also been present in my mother and in my grandmother, and likely in many generations of grandmothers before her. A pattern was becoming evident. Finally, I began to see evidence of this pattern in a variety of situations, roles, and relationships. Given the universal nature of the experience of being parented, the idea that disenfranchised grief might be operating at a societal level began to take shape.

A quote by Jonas Salk, *"Evolution is picking yourself up one more time than you fall down,"* provided me with both comfort and a vision as a young woman struggling to accept myself and as a mother struggling to accept my children. Salk's quote also gave me the courage to look more deeply into my own disenfranchised grief. My experience in psychoanalysis has taught me that any pain endured as a result of [re]experiencing my grief is temporary and ultimately worthwhile. Salk's quote, psychoanalysis, and a cancer diagnosis in 2003 taught me that stepping into the experience rather than avoiding it was the only way to move forward. More importantly, I learned that I could do it.

My doctoral research had become a heuristic journey, a search for the meaning of my experience, what Frank (1995) calls a quest story, wherein the question to be answered is: *How did I rise to the occasion?*

> The genesis of the quest is some occasion requiring the person to be more than she has been, and the purpose is becoming one who has risen to that occasion. *This occasion at first appears as an interruption* [italics added] but later comes to be understood as an opening. A woman . . . expresses what is said in almost every quest story: "I would never have *chosen* to be taught this way but I like the changes in me. I guess I had to go to the edge to get there." What started the illness is secondary to the effect of going "to the edge." *[Her] purpose is coming back from that edge to become the person she is, someone who is changed* [italics added]. Illness was an interruption she would not have chosen, but she now accepts it as the cost of changes she likes. *Losses continue to be mourned, but the emphasis is on gains* [italics added]. (Ibid., p. 128)

I, too, would not have willingly chosen to "go to the edge." I would have passed on the "opportunity" to have cancer or be the mother of children who are sexual and gender minorities. I would have passed on spending over 15 years in analysis. But then I consider all that I would have missed. Because, I too, like the changes I see in myself as a result. Initially, I *did* regard having to deal with cancer and with my children's sexual and gender identities as unwelcome interruptions. But I now consider them to be some of my greatest learning experiences. They were what my friend and colleague, Jean Mavrelis, calls *serenity challenges*. More importantly, they were the opening through which I was able to come face-to-face with my own disenfranchised grief, mourn what was lost, and ultimately, begin to integrate this lost part of myself back into the whole. I, too, have come back from the edge to become the person I am. I, too, have been changed. As I continue to learn how to embrace and integrate the disenfranchised part of myself, I am rediscovering my sense of wholeness and attunement. In other words, I am happy. And, according to educator Nel Noddings (2003), happiness is everything.

The question arises, if I was intended to engage in a deeper exploration of disenfranchised grief, why? What purpose did this exploration serve—beyond my own development? Why write this book? The question is particularly relevant for me because this isn't just research, this is *personal*, and it takes a lot for me to place my personal life—and that of my family—out in the public domain. However, like Moustakas (1990), who believes that virtually every question that matters on a personal level can also matter on a social or even universal level, I believe that the best research *is* personal and that some things need to be out in the public domain.

Therefore, while I acknowledge that exploring the nature and meaning of my experience as a parent of sexual and gender minority children is of greatest importance to me personally, I believe that I am also exploring a crucial human experience because as Noddings (2003) notes, parenting is a crucial—and universal—human experience. Parenting is also a crucial human experience given the critical role that parents serve in the development of their child's identity. How well that process unfolds for the child is very much dependent upon "how well the mother[1] is able to recognize her child's needs, her 'wordless inner states,' and how consistently and appropriately she responds to them" (Lewis, Amini & Lannon, 2000, p. 155). In other words, a child's healthy identity development is dependent upon having empathic parents.

Despite the profound influence that parents wield in their child's development, parenting—particularly empathic parenting—is also a "crucial human experience" that is neither understood nor attended to as well as it should be. Noddings (2003) writes,

One of the most important tasks for every human being is that of making a home, *and much of a child's fortune depends on the sort of home into which he or she is born* [italics added]. . . . In addition to making a home, most of us also become parents, and that task is another one that is largely ignored by schools. *If one's home and parents are more important than any other aspect of life in predicting school success or failure* [italics added], it seems odd that schools do not teach something about parenting so that more children can have a better start in life. (p. 95)

If Noddings is correct, then an educational curriculum based upon her concept of an "Ethic of Care"—education that is focused on the attainment of *happiness* in everyday life—could do more for improving school success than anything contained within the policies of "No Child Left Behind." Most of us are not going to live exceptional lives—we will live everyday lives. And I believe that schools should serve the needs of the majority as much as it serves the needs of the exceptional. Further, if more people have the ability to create authentic happiness in their lives, everyone benefits, including the exceptional.

This, I believe, is one of the reasons to write this book, and one of the reasons I came back from the edge. I deeply resonate with Noddings' argument that the greater good is *not* being served by the U.S. educational system's myopic focus on the development of math and science skills that will truly benefit only a limited percentage of the human community. Noddings suggests that the educational system should instead redirect its primary focus, particularly with young children, toward helping students to develop the interpersonal skills that have been shown to be necessary to achieve happiness in everyday life (p. 34), empathy in particular.

It is important to help our children develop these interpersonal skills because researchers are now recognizing that these skills are essential for successful navigation in the social world, and—regardless of gender—essential in the search for good companions. Companionship, according to Noddings, "is *the single greatest factor* [italics added] in producing the subjective sense of well-being" (Ibid.). Lewis, et al. (2000) echo this position in their assertion that, "stability is finding people who regulate you well and sticking to them" (p. 86). Josselson (1996) notes the growing recognition by the psychological community of "relatedness as the central plot of development" (p. 2). In other words, human beings *need* to connect with one another to be happy. Yet, Lewis, et al. also point out that "the world is full of men and women who encounter difficulty in loving or being loved, and whose happiness depends critically upon resolving that situation with the utmost expediency" (p. 9).

It seems clear that many people are suffering. I believe part of the reason there is so much suffering is because our educational system, in its current form, is not teaching our young people how to find people who will regulate them well. Yalom (1989) refers to this suffering as "living pain" (in Josselson, 1996, p. ix), and cites the source of this living pain as being the person's dissatisfaction with their connection to others. Yet, it does not appear that many of our children are learning this critical skill at home, and they aren't learning it at school. Science and technology alone cannot solve these challenges. This is about *relationship*. It is time that we as a society acknowledge this and begin to provide our children with the "other tool kit" they need in order to achieve not only success but also the understanding that success can be defined in emotional, rather than economic, currency.

In addition to education about interpersonal skills, sexuality, and parenting, I now believe that there must *also* be education about disenfranchised grief and the different ways humans utilize, interpret, and manage distress, because such knowledge could positively impact one's ability to respond empathically to expressions of distress. This is not just true for parents of LGBTQ children, who contend with ongoing societal stigmatization, it applies to *every* parent, given the role that parents serve in shaping the emotional lens through which their children will interpret and navigate their way in the larger social world for the rest of their lives. Therefore, it is important for anyone who wishes to parent a child to understand the negative impact that disenfranchised grief can have on a parent's ability to respond empathically—or appropriately—to their child's distress, since distress is the natural way that infants and young children communicate their needs.

I believe that parents dealing with disenfranchised grief become panicked when their children express distress. When operating from this state of panic, those parents can focus only on their own distress. They cannot assist their children in the regulation of their distress because the parents' attention isn't directed toward their children. Their attention is directed inward and focused on managing their own distress. Therefore, the child not only does not get help with her distress, often she isn't even *visible* to her parents.

For a child, I believe the experience of not being seen by one's parents feels like abandonment. Further, if this experience happens often enough, the child's cognitive as well as emotional development is likely to be negatively impacted. As Tronick (1998) noted, "with continued failure and the structuring that that goes on around that failure, affective disorders and pathology may result" (p. 297). One can heal from that pathology and develop a more adaptive personality. I know because I have done it. However, it requires finding an empathic therapist and making a significant investment of both time and money—even *with* health insurance. I was fortunate to have had access to both. Many people are not so lucky. Given that there is information and knowledge about how to help our children to develop appropriately from the beginning, it seems foolish as a society *not* to make a significant shift toward providing the kind of education and experience that will help future parents to be successful at raising healthy and happy children. It is time for us to do so.

In addition to parents—because it is thought that disenfranchised grief is operating at a societal level—it is also essential to educate teachers, doctors, nurses, therapists, ministers, social workers, childcare providers, and anyone who works with those who constitute the most vulnerable members of our society. It could be argued that constant exposure to this vulnerability could trigger or intensify any disenfranchised grief that may be present in the caregiver, resulting in a reduced capacity for empathy on the part of the caregiver and, possibly, further harm being done to those who are entrusted to his or her care. In far too many instances, those entrusted to caregivers with disenfranchised grief (such as terminally ill patients, the elderly in nursing homes, foster children, sexual/gender minority youth, or special needs children in the classroom) become invisible to their caregivers in much the same way that a child is invisible to her unconsciously distressed parents.

It may be that almost every human being carries within them some level of unacknowledged, unresolved grief. To the extent that we do, our ability to be attuned to others is likely to be compromised. If this grief remains unaddressed, it can be the source of much unnecessary chaos and misery (Bracciale, et al., 2003). But if grief can be acknowledged, there then exists the possibility of choice as to how one will respond to it. Acknowledging and then developing an understanding with respect to the source or origin of one's own grief, as well as how children develop healthy identities and the role that parents play in that process, can provide parents with the information they need to make conscious and empathic choices with respect to their children.

Relying upon parents to teach children about *how* to parent and what it *means* to be a parent—as we do currently—leaves much to chance and places those responsibilities in the hands of a significant number of parents who may not have the capacity themselves. Waiting until children are old enough to be parents before we educate them about parenting is a flawed approach because the optimal window of opportunity for the development of empathy is in early childhood. Further, waiting until children are older before educating them about sexuality and parenting creates a situation in which they may become parents before they are truly ready, making it much more difficult for them to achieve happiness.

Of all the insights I bring back from my own experience of going to the edge, the most profound and the most painful is the realization of how much I missed out on the experience of *being* a mother. It was a shock to realize through my research that mothering is intended to be as pleasurable as sex. It makes perfect sense when considered from a survival perspective. Given that human children are utterly dependant upon their parents for both physical survival and emotional regulation, *something* has to be in place to ensure this needed attention is provided. The most effective way to ensure that someone will do something is to make it *feel good*.

As a young mother, that was not my experience. I did not consciously choose to become a mother. I simply got pregnant. I had no idea how to mother my children. I just did the things that I thought mothers were supposed to do, things I remembered my mother doing. It was almost as though I were going through the motions of mothering. I recall holding my daughter when she was about five months old. She had been fed, bathed, diapered, and dressed, and I remember wondering, "Now what do I do with you?" I really did not know. I know now. Recently, I was spending time with my one-year-old granddaughter and we were playing a tickle game. The game was that I would tickle her belly and she would laugh. As we were playing, I wondered whether I could understand what she wanted me to do, even without language. So I stopped tickling her and waited. I was delighted when she pushed her belly up in the air and looked at me with what I swear was an impish smile. I said to her, "Oh, I see, you want me to do it again," and I smiled back at her and tickled her belly until she laughed out loud. God, that was fun! And now I understand *why* it was so much fun.

It has been noted that the phenomenal swimming ability of Michael Phelps, who shattered records at the 2008 Summer Olympics, was the result of a unique set of physical characteristics, life experiences, and choices that were made (both by him and by others on his behalf) at significant moments in his development. I believe he had an attuned mother who recognized what her attention-deficit son needed to develop successfully (swimming) and the rest, as they say, is history. Through a unique combination of characteristics, life experiences, and choices, I, too, have been forged into a sensitive instrument—one capable of recognizing disenfranchised grief in myself and in others.

I have experienced being a young, ignorant, disenfranchised mother. I have also been fortunate enough to have the experience of being an aware, competent, and attuned mother and grandmother. Having experienced both ends of this mothering continuum, I believe that I am in a position to assert that *mothering from a place of awareness and readiness is far better than from a place of ignorance*. I am deeply appreciative to be where I am at this point in my life. I delight in being a grandmother and in having a second chance to observe and participate in the creation of a human being, this time fully aware and fully present. I also enjoy being a mother to my now-adult children. I feel blessed that our relationship not only survived, but that it continues to evolve and deepen. I wish that I could have experienced more of that delight with my children when they were growing up. It is a loss that I attribute to ignorance—and it makes me angry. It is a loss that is so significant to me that it has become another reason to write this book, because I do not believe that I am alone in feeling this loss or this anger. And I want something to change!

I believe, with Noddings, that it is time for the voice of the mother (and the grandmother) to be heard in education because mothers and grandmothers have it in our power to effect change. In fact, I believe mothers and grandmothers can change the world. Mothering is too important to be left to chance. Our daughters deserve to be educated about mothering and what the experience of mothering *can* be. Our daughters also deserve to be taught that they have the right to be happy. They deserve to know that they have the right (and the responsibility) to determine what happens to them—and when. Equipped with this knowledge and support, I believe that more of our daughters will *refuse* to become sexually active until they are ready. I believe that more of our daughters will *refuse* to enter into abusive or unstable relationships because they will have been educated with the goal of happiness in mind and they will possess the skills to connect with people that regulate them well. And I believe that more of our daughters will *refuse* to have children until they are truly ready to mother and are in circumstances that support the best kind of mothering. Our sons deserve the same.

So, it is my intent, in the pages that follow, to take you with me on my journey to the edge, through disenfranchised grief and then back again. By inviting you into my world and speaking to you from a feeling level about the experiences of my life, I hope to kindle in you a desire to use what you learn from my journey to reflect on, understand, and better cope with your own life. By sharing my journey, I hope to instill in you a greater willingness to move into your own serenity challenges and the learning embedded within them. Too many people chose to avoid these challenges outright, or anesthetize themselves with drugs, alcohol, food, shopping, or sex, often with disastrous consequences. I have come back from the edge to become the person that I am, someone who is changed, and I wouldn't change that for anything.

CHAPTER 1

CIRCUMSTANCE

Circumstance does not make the man, it reveals him to himself.

-*James Allen*

Circumstance made me the mother of fraternal twins, both of whom are regarded as sexual or gender minorities; Kristin is lesbian and Julian is female-to-male transgender[2]. Coming to a place of understanding, acceptance, and love for my children for who they are has been as a result of tremendous struggle and ongoing effort. It has also come at a tremendous cost. There was little information and very few resources available to me in 1992, when I was first confronted with the reality of my children's sexual and gender orientations. I felt confused, angry, ashamed, uncomfortable, and alone. I also felt a sense of panic because something like this wasn't supposed to happen and I wasn't prepared to deal with it. I can recall desperately wishing for someone who could help me or tell me what to do.

I had many questions but I didn't know who to ask or how to get information. Publicly acknowledging that you had a gay or transgender child was just not something you did, even in 1992. Most of the people who knew about my children were uncomfortable, and that made me uncomfortable. No one knew how to deal with it, so it became one of those open secrets in the family that we just didn't talk about. I suspect there was a wish that if it wasn't acknowledged, the problem would just go away. As is often the case, the problem didn't go away, no matter how much we tried to ignore it. It became larger and more insistent.

Furthermore, I think we all lost sight of the fact that these "problems" were human beings. They were children, my children—they were children who needed the love, protection, and empathic nurturing of caring parents, family, and community. And they didn't always get it. Like many lesbian, gay, bisexual, transgender, or questioning (LGBTQ) children, they didn't always get what they needed because their identities do not fit the prevailing U.S. mainstream culture's sexual and gender norms (Redmond & Flauto, 2001). Norms represent the majority, but they *do not* represent all. Despite this fact, societal response to deviations from accepted norms is typically negative (Berreby, 2005; Ryan, 2003). This is particularly true with regard to deviations from sexual or gender norms (Berreby, 2005; Rudacille, 2005). As a result, LGBTQ children face a greater risk of low self-esteem, verbal harassment, physical harassment, isolation, mental illness, drug or alcohol abuse, sexual abuse, educational failure, and even death—either through suicide or murder (Capper, 1993; Halverson, 2005; Jeltova & Fish, 2005; Pope, 2003; Ryan, 2003; Yunger, Carver & Perry, 2004).

It cuts through me like a knife when I reflect now upon what it must have been like for Julian and Kristin growing up. How difficult it must have been for them to go through every single day with the knowledge that there was a part of them that people rejected. I imagine what it must have felt like to be a child and hear your parents, family, friends, teachers, ministers, in fact, almost everyone you knew, make hateful, derogatory, or just plain ignorant comments about people with whom you identify. I wonder how many times Julian and Kristin heard those kinds of comments and stayed silent because they didn't feel it was safe to speak up. I try to imagine what it must have felt like to be a child and to have people avoid your gaze or your company. Worse yet, how must it have felt to actually hear them express hatred or disgust? Almost afraid to ask, I wondered what Julian and Kristin saw in my eyes. What words or looks of hate or disgust did I express? My children tell me that, yes, they heard and saw this from their mother, but they also tell me that my expressions have changed.

At times, I have wanted to cry, especially when I understood that such a realization places a child in the terrible position of having to choose between their need for integrity and their need to be loved and to belong. Although this dilemma would be difficult for anyone, it is potentially devastating for children in the midst of their identity formation. Because all children need the care and protection of their parents in order to survive (both physically and psychologically), LGBTQ children learn to hide part of themselves in an attempt to ensure that care and protection. They often do this at the cost of their self-esteem. According to Lifton (1994, in Wood, 2001), "clinicians agree that children cannot form a healthy sense of self if they must disavow reality" (p. 89). Noddings (2003) reinforces this point when she asks, "How can we disavow our daily lives and hope to find happiness?" (p. 56).

Further, if a child is continually required to disavow a part of his or her reality, it seems reasonable to conclude that their ability to determine what is or is not real will also be impaired, thus making it less likely that LGBTQ children will be able to make adaptive choices on their own behalf throughout their lives. Balser (1980) noted, "Kohut is emphatic that all children's potentialities are either developed or thwarted depending on whether or not he/she is the recipient of *empathic parenting*" [italics added] (p. 7). For LGBTQ children, their potentialities are often thwarted—my children included.

Parental Empathy

If empathic parenting is as critical to the development of a child's potentialities as Kohut suggests, it is important to understand what he is talking about, What is empathic parenting? Balser (1980), who uses the term, *parental empathy*, defines it as:

> The capacity of parents to experience, understand, and respond to the psychological needs of their children. It demands that the parents recognize the separateness and complexity of the child; that they actually share and also understand the child's emotional experience, and that they be responsive to

the child on that basis. It is motivated by altruistic rather than narcissistic goals. (Balser, 1980, p. 21)

I was not an empathic parent when my children were young and grappling with their identities. I was young and ignorant. I now believe that my ignorance contributed to Julian's struggles with poor school performance, stealing, lack of social connections, weight issues, lack of self-care, isolation, loneliness, and later on, substance abuse and sexual assault. I believe my ignorance contributed to Julian feeling that he had to emancipate himself from his family when he was just fifteen years old, only to end up living on the streets of Seattle for almost two years. And although Kristin appeared to have adapted well, I didn't realize that she had been keeping a secret that contributed to two suicide attempts by the time she was twenty. I remember feeling so angry with Kristin and wondering what in hell could possibly be so wrong in her life that at age twenty she wanted to die. I had no understanding of the kind of pain she was experiencing. I really had no idea what life was like for either of my children.

I did not respond empathically when my children first attempted to come out to me. I didn't even believe Julian, who came out at age fifteen, when she first told me she was a lesbian. I recall saying something like "Yeah, and last week you were an alcoholic. Do you do this stuff just to drive me crazy?" A few years later when Julian told me "she" wasn't lesbian, rather, "he" was actually transgender, I remember looking up at the sky and wondering what else could God do to me. When I began to realize that Julian was serious, my response was that I didn't want to deal with it. Like many other parents of LGBTQ children, I went through a period of denial and disbelief. I can recall saying, "I don't want to know about your sex life!"

I feel ashamed when I remember the words I said to myself when Kristin told me she was lesbian: "Oh God, not you too." I said those words to myself, but I am sure Kristin saw them in my eyes. I imagine that my children were sad and hurt, but not surprised at my response. Like many people, my understanding of being gay was that "it was all about sex," and that it was morally wrong. I had no concept of sexual orientation or gender identity. It took a while for me to understand what a gay friend of mine meant when he said, "It's not about sex, it's about who we love." It also took a while for me to realize that morality had nothing to do with it.

I am an empathic parent now. Despite many challenges, my children managed to navigate their way into adulthood with their identities and our relationship relatively intact. Although there have been times when we were separated both physically and emotionally, our relationship was never completely broken. There were very difficult times for all of us, and there were times when I wasn't so sure our relationship would survive. But even in those times when the distance between us seemed the greatest, one of us would ultimately make a gesture toward reconciliation and we would try again. And we continue to try. I think Julian and Kristin would agree that it has been well worth the effort. It means a great deal to me now that my children and I didn't give up on each other. I really like that I can say I know Julian, Kristin, and their older brother, Michael, as individuals and that they know me as someone more than "Mom." It feels very authentic to me and

I believe that we are growing toward having deeper, happier, and healthier relationships with each other, with our partners, and with ourselves as a result.

Another gift that is being realized from this effort is the relationship I have with my young grandchildren and the chance to participate in a different kind of childhood experience with them. This time I know what I am doing and it feels like *magic*. The opportunity to experience [grand]mothering with wisdom, confidence, and joy has been healing for me. The opportunity to share that experience with my daughter has been healing for both of us. I believe that as she sees me nurturing her children from this place of wisdom and confidence, she is nurtured as well, and we now share nurturing as a bond. I expect the impact of this bond will play a significant role in shaping the kind of individuals my grandchildren will ultimately become and will contribute to their ability to create happy relationships. I look forward to watching and helping that process unfold.

Evolution

Jonas Salk, discoverer of the polio vaccine, is noted as having said, "Evolution is picking yourself up one more time than you fall down." I can still remember the profound sense of relief that swept through me the first time I read those words over twenty years ago. I was a young woman who believed that I wasn't good enough, as a mother or as a person. It was a revelation to read Salk's words and even contemplate that it was okay if I wasn't perfect and that in order to succeed all that was required of me, or of anyone for that matter, was to try again. I just had to keep picking myself up. In the years since, I have learned that there is a skill, an art, in the ability to determine when I should persevere and when it is best to stop trying and change course. First, however, I had to believe that I was worth the effort. As Maslow (1943) suggested in his hierarchy of human needs theory, it was difficult for me to focus on a higher need for learning or self-actualization when I was questioning whether or not I even deserved to exist.

For as long as I can remember, I felt like I was serving a life sentence, that I was defective in some unnamed way. I just wasn't good enough. I went through my entire childhood, adolescence, and early adulthood this way. Then I stumbled across Salk's perspective. I wasn't defective; I was actually a work-in-progress. As long as I took the next step, the progress would continue. At this point I began to understand that there might be a larger process at work in my life. It was also the first time in my life that I can remember feeling hopeful about myself.

Unfortunately, I was almost thirty years old when I first read Salk's words. I could have used that information a lot sooner. However, to my children's good fortune, I read those words just as I was becoming aware of their sexual and gender orientations. I can recall reciting Salk's quote many times over the next few years as I struggled with how to accept Julian and Kristin and the lives they were trying to create for themselves. It wasn't until some time later that I began to realize that Salk's words weren't just a roadmap to finally accepting my children. They were a roadmap for accepting myself as well—one step at a time. I made many mistakes during this time, but I kept trying because of Salk's words.

I also kept trying because I carried many memories of my own struggles in adolescence with feelings of loneliness and self-doubt. I never felt like I met my family's expectations, or that I was good enough. It seemed that no matter how much I accomplished, there was always something I didn't do, didn't do well enough, or wouldn't be able to repeat. I remember feeling so proud when I showed my father my first straight A report card, and then feeling so defeated when he said that he bet I couldn't do it again next semester. I now understand that he was challenging me. But at the time, I needed him to tell me that he was proud of me. It seemed as though I could never get my parents to respond the way I wanted. I sometimes wondered whether it would have been easier to just feel invisible than to feel like a second-rate player on a first-rate team. When I began acting out in adolescence, it seemed that no one could or would see through my behaviors and notice the little girl underneath who just needed to feel loved and valued for who she was.

I suspect that my long (and for many years, unrecognized) struggle with depression began with the realization that I could not seem to elicit the kind of parental response that I wanted or needed. The only explanation I could come up with in my child's mind was that it must be because I wasn't worth noticing. I have carried that feeling most of my life. I was well into psychoanalysis before I learned that, because children are so dependent upon their parents for their very survival, they often assume blame or responsibility for any perceived problems in the relationship. Being labeled as "bad" was less terrifying than being alone. According to Josselson (2007), one's sense of place in the world depends largely upon the sense of place he or she has been given by others growing up. The danger in not fulfilling the roles that an important person assigns to you is that you risk not being seen by them at all. Josselson further suggests that "the fear of disappearing for another, of no longer existing for them, *is a profound terror* [italics added]. It is better to be a partial self or a false self than not to have meaning for the other at all" (p. 76).

I also learned in psychoanalysis that this belief about myself exacted a high price, as it had had a silent influence upon every choice I made. How do you make good choices for yourself if you believe that you aren't even worth being noticed? I didn't know that getting your parents to respond to you in the way that you needed was what children were supposed to do; otherwise, babies might not get fed, or held, or protected. I was led to believe that this desire was selfish and demanding. I was just the "bad kid." It was not something to be discussed or challenged, and I didn't know why. That was just the way it was.

I believe that my childhood experiences are very similar to what LGBTQ youth experience as they struggle to accept their identity. These experiences may also help explain why I have been able to come to accept my children. I remember how much it hurt to wonder whether I should have even been born, and how painful it was to even ask myself such a question. I remember the loneliness and isolation I felt. I can still feel the *weight* upon my shoulders of carrying around the terrible secret that I wasn't quite good enough—and the fear that people might find out. I can recall many situations in which, if I found myself opening up with someone, at some point I would say to myself, "Yeah, but if they really knew you, they would never like you," and I would find myself shutting back down as though a switch had been flipped. How many lost opportunities in my life could be attributed to my secret contempt for myself? I may never know.

I now understand that there was also this other part of me that was screaming mad because I knew I *was* good enough and I wanted to have good connections and good companionship in my life—and that was denied to me. My internal world was full of very polarizing conflict and I didn't feel like there was anyone to whom I could turn for help or comfort. I felt alone with my pain and I suffered. I did not want my children to ever have to feel that way. But when they came out to me, I found myself struggling. My struggle was not just that I feared that what Julian and Kristin were asking me to accept was beyond my ability, I wasn't sure if it was "normal" and I wasn't sure if I could approve. It is very painful to realize how much hurt I could inflict upon them through ignorance, even with the best of intentions.

I engaged in the struggle to accept Julian and Kristin out of a simultaneous desire to be a good mother and fear that I would be a failure as a mother if I rejected them. To regard myself as such a failure would be a blow to my self-esteem that I could not tolerate. So I felt I had to keep trying, no matter how badly it went at times. I kept hearing an internal voice that said, "You can't quit." I suspect now that the voice was my own internal child, telling me that I could not allow myself to reject my children–as that would also be a rejection of myself and a betrayal of the wounded child I had been. I could not do that to Julian or Kristin, and I no longer wanted to do that to myself. I must have managed to instill that same belief system in my children, because Julian and Kristin kept trying as well.

Learning to Love the Questions

> *Have patience with everything unresolved in your heart and try to love the questions themselves, as if they were locked rooms or books written in a very foreign language. Don't search for the answers, which could not be given to you now because you would not be able to live them. And the point is to live everything. Live the questions now. Perhaps then, someday far in the future, you will gradually, without even noticing it, live your way into the answer.*
>
> *-Rainer Maria Rilke*

As I continued to struggle with my acceptance of Julian and Kristin, other questions, much more difficult to answer, began to emerge. Maybe I could manage to "not reject" Julian and Kristin, but was that really enough? I began to wonder if the real challenge was whether I could learn to like them and love them for who they were. But that would mean putting myself into situations and interacting with people unfamiliar to me, people with whom, quite frankly, I felt very uncomfortable. What if I tried and found out that I couldn't learn to like them for who they were? If they were just too different, what would happen then? Would I be a failure? I had to ask myself whether I was willing to go beyond my own personal comfort zone and experience a little cultural dissonance in order to get to know Julian and Kristin as individuals? Was I willing to meet their friends and invite them into my home? Was I willing to take the chance to find out?

I had to ask myself, wasn't managing to "not reject" my children similar to the concept of tolerating differences in the workplace? In my work as a Diversity educator, I know very well how employees, particularly women and people of color, feel about being "tolerated" in the workplace. They don't like it. They don't want to be tolerated; they want to be valued for who they are. Julian and Kristin were sending me very clear messages that they didn't want to be where they felt unwanted, devalued, or unloved. Would any child want to be in a situation like that? Would any human being? My children were telling me that they were willing to take huge risks to feel safe and wanted, including going it alone. Julian was willing to leave home at fifteen. Kristin considered ending her life. It still hurts when I think about that.

My relationship with each of my children continues to evolve and that brings me a great deal of happiness. My grandchildren—the ones I didn't think I would ever have when my children came out—are a delight to me. The greater joy, however, is the discovery that I enjoy my children in ways I had not been able to appreciate when they were young. I reflect back on all of my earlier questions, particularly the question about whether I was capable of more than just not rejecting my lesbian and transgender children, and I realize that, just as Rilke promised his young poet, I have lived my way into many of the answers. I really do like my kids for who they are. As a result of my experience, I now look forward to learning to love—and live—the questions that remain.

My feelings about my children are not the only things that have undergone a significant transformation. I, too, have been transformed. This transformation, I believe, is a direct result of my willingness to accept and work through the significant life challenges that have been presented to me. I find that each time I work through one of these challenges, I work through something within myself as well. I come away from each experience with a deeper, more defined sense of myself. I find it interesting that I started out working on a "problem" and ended up finding my own Self.

As a result of these challenges and much personal introspection, I believe I have become an empathic parent and have developed an empathic perspective. I see this perspective as the basis for my developing ability to be an empathic witness, not only to my children, but to others as well. I have noted a shift in my ability to "read" Julian and Kristin's unconscious emotional states during an interaction. I have been able to discern how they were feeling, what they unconsciously wanted or needed from me, and most importantly, how to respond. Unlike many times during their childhood when I was not able to be present for them, I have discovered that I can now give them the compassionate support that they always wanted and needed. This has had a healing effect upon Julian and Kristin, and on me.

These experiences and new abilities of reading and responding to my children's unconscious communications, as well as my sense of having developed a more empathic perspective, both reflect and validate Balser's (1980) argument about the importance of empathic parenting. I believe I have developed a greater capacity to "experience, understand, and respond to the psychological needs of my children" (p. 21). I am learning to "recognize the separateness and complexity" (Ibid.) of my children, and developing a better understanding about their emotional experience and how to better respond to them on the basis of that understanding. I have also learned how much better it feels to relate to them in this way—for them and for me.

My observations about my increasing ability to recognize and read my children's unconscious communications also reflect, validate, and underscore the importance of the research on attachment, limbic or mutual regulation, and child identity development. According to Lewis, Amini and Lannon (2000), the quality of limbic or mutual regulation an infant receives from her mother is dependent upon how well the mother is able to recognize her child's needs, her "wordless inner states" (p. 155), and how consistently and appropriately she responds to them. In other words, as Kohut suggested, empathic parenting plays a crucial role.

I believe that I developed in my capacity to become an empathic parent and to hold an empathic perspective because I would not let myself off the hook when confronted with challenges—even those I believed were beyond my capacity, like accepting my children as lesbian and transgender. I remember saying to myself, "This is the hand you've been dealt, now figure out how to deal with it." I would not have willingly chosen to be the mother of a lesbian child or a transgender child, and yet I was. I would not have chosen to have cancer either, but in 2003, I was diagnosed with late stage colon cancer, just two months after being accepted into my doctoral program. Each of these experiences pushed me to the edge. Each of these experiences felt overwhelming at times. Yet, each of these experiences changed me in profound ways.

One of the primary lessons embedded within my experience with cancer—one that was imperative for me to learn—was that I did, in fact, deserve to exist. The experience of having to consciously decide to fight for my life meant that I could no longer hang on to the belief that I was worthless. I learned a great deal about acceptance through having cancer. I learned that fighting to survive meant that I had to decide that I deserved to exist. I carried that learning over to my children when I realized fighting to understand my children meant they deserved to exist as well.

Initially, when confronted with these challenges, my focus was to simply get through them. I did not anticipate that they would be vehicles for growth. I did not expect that out of my struggle for my life and my struggle to accept and love my children would also come acceptance and love for myself—and empathy for the child I used to be. Given the role I believe these life challenges played in the development of my empathic capacity, a brief discussion about these challenges follows.

Serenity Challenges

> *God, give us grace to accept with serenity the things that cannot be changed, courage to change the things that should be changed, and the wisdom to distinguish the one from the other.*
>
> *-Reinhold Niebuhr*

A friend and colleague, Jean Mavrelis, refers to these tests of one's capabilities as *serenity challenges*, in reference to the well-known <u>Serenity Prayer</u>, credited to Reinhold Niebuhr (1892-1971). According to Mavrelis, a cultural anthropologist, serenity challenges are those times in your life when you are confronted with a situation that you are powerless to change. Serenity challenges can also be described as *untenable situations*, wherein you are confronted with having to endure or deal with something that you fear is beyond your capacity. A serenity challenge could be a divorce, catastrophic illness or injury, chronic illness, terminal illness, loss of a job, societal oppression, or the death of a loved one, particularly a spouse, partner, or child (J. Mavrelis, personal communication, August, 2002; See also Bridges, 2001; Montgomery, 2003). I contend that the acceptance of a child's sexual or gender identity that falls outside the accepted norm certainly qualifies as a serenity challenge.

For a long time, I existed in an untenable situation. I was a mother who loved my children but who didn't really know or understand them. I didn't even understand myself. My children were sending me signals that they needed my help, but I did not know how to interpret those signals or how to respond to them. I wanted to be a good mother, but I didn't know how to deal with having children who were lesbian and transgender. I had never had to consider what I thought about gay people, gay issues, or gay culture. I had no experience with individuals who were born one gender but identified as another. Now "they" were my children and I wasn't sure what I thought about "them."

There are those who suggest that serenity challenges such as coming to terms with your child's sexual or gender identity can be a pathway to significant personal growth (Bridges, 2001; Denzin & Lincoln, 2003; Frick, 1990). In his research on the *symbolic growth experience* (SGE), Frick describes one such growth outcome as:

A sudden, dramatic shift in perception, belief, or understanding that alters one's frame of reference or worldview. The internal change or revision is usually connected with an external event but the connection is synchronistic, an intentional or spontaneous happening rather than the result of a cause-effect relationship. The shift in perception and meaning launches in some measure a new attitude, a new process of learning, a character or personality shift in identity and selfhood. (in Moustakas, 1990, p. 99)

Frick notes that the SGE also "serves a corrective function in initiating a resolution to dysfunctional life routines and habits, patterns that repeat themselves in work, *and in relationship to one's own self and others*" [italics added] (Ibid., p. 100). Frick further notes, "in addition to the corrective shift in the resolution of an issue or problem, the symbolic growth experience launches an enhancement of identity and selfhood" (Ibid). In other words, there is a healing or reparative benefit, as well as an increased sense of identity or self, that comes from the willingness to engage in challenges that push or stretch one's boundaries or limitations.

And yet, despite the significant potential benefits that come with accepting the challenge to understand and accept their child's identity, almost half of parents with LGBTQ children do not. Instead, families break apart and LGBTQ children are faced with grim choices. In a recent study, Ryan and Futterman (1998) found that *forty percent* of the youth living on the streets in Seattle identified as gay or lesbian. Many of these children likely became homeless because their families had kicked them out or rejected them emotionally and the home environment had become intolerable. These Seattle youth had no alternative other than living on the streets, partly because only recently have there been any social services available for LGBTQ youth (Ryan, 2003). My own child lived on the streets off and on for almost two years. Although my husband and I never asked Julian to leave our home, it hurts to now understand that he didn't feel like he could be there or that he didn't feel like he belonged.

Teach the Children

It didn't have to be that way for us, and it doesn't have to be this way for other LGBTQ families. I believe there are two fundamental reasons why many parents fail to respond empathically to their LGBTQ child. First, there is an overall societal lack of understanding about parenting, child identity development, and the impact that certain parental behaviors can have on the development of their child's identity. Kochanska, Friesenborg, Lange and Martel's (2004) observations regarding "the dearth of research on personality traits relevant to interpersonal functioning and parenting" (p. 752) provide strong support for this assertion, as does the research of Ryan (2003), who makes reference to the small body of research that is focused on either the parenting of LGBTQ children or to LGBTQ identity development.

Pope (2003) attributes this lack of understanding to the undervaluing by many people and many school systems in the U.S. of what he calls *psycho-affective education*. Pope notes:

> This is not what is being termed "moral education," nor "character education;" it is affective education, psychological education, or psycho-affective education. *Teaching these important affective skills, such as interpersonal, social, and psychological skills, is rarely included in any school curriculum* [italics added] even though such pioneers as Sprinthall (1984) have written about "deliberate psychological education for many years . . . The deliberate psycho-affective education of our children must become a priority. (2003, p. 37)

Noddings (2003) is also critical of the U.S. educational system's lack of emphasis on developing interpersonal skills. She challenges the logic of requiring students to study subjects such as algebra–which the majority of them will never use again once they complete the course–but not the subjects that research suggests will help students to be successful and happy in daily life.

> Algebra and other forms of mathematics are enormously important for some purposes and for some people. But the majority could get by well with knowledge of only a few topics in academic mathematics. In contrast, all of us face the tasks of making a home and finding companionship, and most of

us become parents. When these great tasks are treated at all in schools, they are "add-ons," designed to address a social emergency such as teenage pregnancy, and they never achieve the status of respectability granted to the traditional disciplines. (2003, p. 34)

It is difficult to argue with Noddings' challenge to provide greater emphasis on interpersonal skills development in school curricula when research on subjective well-being has shown that it is the interpersonal factors, such as establishing a home and companionship, that are most closely associated with happiness. Noddings states:

> If today's social scientists are right, *companionship is the single greatest factor in producing the subjective sense of well-being* [italics added]. How well do we prepare children for companionship? If we can believe the figures given to us by Lane and other social scientists, the answer is "not very well," since years of education do not correlate highly with happiness and, thus, presumably not with the satisfactions gained through companionship. (Ibid.)

The second fundamental reason that parents fail to respond empathically to their LGBTQ child is the overall lack of understanding about the diversity and complexity of all the components that constitute our sense of who we are as sexual and gendered human beings. In general, U. S. schools do not educate students about human sexuality (Capper, 1993; Jeltova & Fish, 2005; Noddings, 2003; Pope, 2003). Schools teach students about *sex*, emphasizing the mechanics of reproduction, avoidance of sexually transmitted diseases, prevention of unwanted pregnancy, or, in many instances, simply abstinence. Furthermore, *heterosexism*, or the bias that everyone is heterosexual, is prevalent throughout the curriculum as well as the culture of the educational system itself (Capper, 1993; Chng & Wong, 1998; Wilkinson & Kitzinger, 1994).

Not only is there a lack of education about sexuality in this culture, it is difficult for people to even *talk* about sex. Sex and sexuality in American society are considered taboo subjects (Jeltova & Fish, 2005; Pope, 2003). Pope warns that "the more that homosexuality and sexuality in general is treated as a taboo subject and not discussed openly, the greater the risk of homophobia and misinformation, and the greater the risk of violence to sexual minority youth" (p. 38). Pope also asserts:

> Many of the problems that sexual minority youth face are the direct result of *the abdication of adults who are supposed to love and protect our young and help them develop into healthy and productive citizens* [italics added], who have been entrusted with the care of all of our young people, but instead are turning a deaf ear to the violence that is being perpetrated against one group of our young – our sexual minority youth. *Failing to create a safe environment for all children is criminal and unethical behavior* [italics added]. (p. 44)

When I look back and consider my experience parenting my children, I have to wonder how many times I abdicated my own responsibility to love and protect them. How many times did I turn a deaf ear to their pain? How might I have acted differently if I'd had access to the information I really needed?

I believe I would have benefited from a school curriculum that promoted study and discussion about the critical and controversial issues of sexuality, sexual identity, gender identity, sexual orientation, and interpersonal relationships. Perhaps my first marriage might have lasted or I might have waited until I was older to marry had I been exposed to more education about what it means to be in a relationship, to be sexual, to enter into a marriage or committed relationship, to parent a child. Moreover, I might have had a more positive response to Julian and Kristin's coming out had I not been socialized and educated to believe that there were only two genders and one sexual orientation.

My children and I might have had a very different experience together if I'd had the opportunity to learn about sexuality, parenting, and child development, and to develop the interpersonal skills that are required to parent *well*. Noddings (2003) writes:

> One of the most important tasks for every human being is that of making a home, *and much of a child's fortune depends on the sort of home into which he or she is born* [italics added]. . . . In addition to making a home, most of us also become parents, and that task is another one that is largely ignored by schools. If one's home and parents are more important than any other aspect of life in predicting school success or failure, it seems odd that schools do not teach something about parenting so that more children can have a better start in life. (p. 95)

"So that more children can have a better start in life." That is a powerful statement.

You Need to Tell Your Story

> *You can't write about change without having gone through it.*
> *-Jonathan Diamond*

How was I able to become an empathic parent, particularly given that I didn't start out as one? What is empathic parenting? How does empathy affect the way children develop, and what happens to their development if they don't get it? These questions are important ones for all parents. However, I believe these questions have particular relevance for parents who are faced with the challenge of how to respond when their LGBTQ child comes out to them.

It has required doing a lot of painful work in order for me to get to a place where I am capable of being an empathic parent to my children and able to see and value them for the unique individuals that they are. It has taken me many years, countless hours of psychoanalysis, and much deep reflection to work through all the guilt and shame I experienced as I struggled to understand and accept my children. In an attempt to educate myself, I have read books, attended lectures and conferences, and personally gotten to know many gay, lesbian, bisexual, and transgender individuals, some of whom have become dear friends. It has required a willingness on my part to really look at how I parented and related to my children. It also required that I consider the positive aspects of my parenting as well as the painful ones in order to fully appreciate the meaning of my experience and what it has to teach me. I am still working on it and probably will all my life.

I believe that being confronted with the question about what kind of parent I was going to be to my lesbian and transgender children has shaped me differently than most other parents. For me to really answer that question meant that I would have to look at parenting in general and then at myself as a parent in particular. Therefore, one question turned into many. Did I really know who my children were as individuals? Did I understand myself as an individual? What did I understand about myself as a parent or about how I was parented? What were my values and beliefs and where did they come from? What did I know about sexual or gender identity? Were lesbian, gay, bisexual, and transgender people really normal? Why were my children lesbian and transgender? Had someone or I done something wrong? How was I supposed to respond to them? If I supported my children while they were exploring this identity, was I condoning something that I wasn't sure I accepted? But if I didn't support my children, would they hate me or be irreparably harmed? What was the right thing to do?

These questions were not simply an academic exercise to me. They were—and are—very real. The choices that I have made in response to these questions have had a very real impact in my life and the lives of those I care about, primarily my children. These are also questions that I should have had answers to long before I found myself in the position of having to make these choices, particularly with my children's well-being at risk. The challenge of attempting to search for answers to questions such as these is that the answers cannot be found in the counting of variables. What is needed is a methodology by which to evaluate one's internal experience in order to gain access to the knowledge and wisdom embedded within that experience. Heuristic inquiry is just such a methodology. Heuristic inquiry is a search for the meaning of an experience and the *process* of heuristic inquiry mirrors the natural human learning process, given that humans are meaning-making creatures. The heuristic process also mirrors the process of everyday life, given that, for each of us, believing that we matter is of paramount importance. Therefore, illumination of the heuristic process, through the sharing of my own heuristic journey, might serve to encourage others to also engage in the journey as well.

Heuristic Inquiry

To open the individual path inward is the most exalted of human endeavors.

-James Perkins

Heuristic inquiry is a "process of internal search through which one discovers the nature and meaning of an experience" (Moustakas, 1990, p. 9). The heuristic journey begins with a question or wondering that arises out of one's own experience and requires a "passionate, disciplined commitment to remain with a question intensely and continuously until it is illuminated or answered" (p. 15). Douglas and Moustakas (1985) define heuristic inquiry as a "search for the discovery of meaning and essence in significant human experience. It requires a subjective process of reflecting, exploring, sifting, and elucidating the nature of the phenomenon under investigation" (p. 40).

Adapted from phenomenological inquiry, which seeks to accurately represent the phenomenon being observed, heuristic inquiry explicitly acknowledges the involvement of the researcher to the extent that the lived experience of the researcher becomes the main focus of the research. In fact, the particular focus of heuristic inquiry is the transformative effect of the inquiry on the researcher's own experience. Moustakas (1990) notes:

> Essentially, in the heuristic process, I am creating a story that portrays the qualities, meanings, and essences of universally unique experiences . . . in the process, I am not only lifting out the essential meanings of an experience, but I am actively awakening and transforming my own self. Self-understanding and self-growth occurs simultaneously in heuristic inquiry. (p. 13)

It is the exploration of these "universally unique experiences" (Ibid.) that is of greatest interest to me because, like Moustakas, I believe that the greatest opportunities for learning, growth, and happiness exist within the context of these experiences.

I also share Moustakas' belief that virtually every question that matters on a personal level also matters on a social or even universal level (p. 15). Therefore, while I acknowledge that exploring the nature and meaning of my experience as a parent of sexual and gender minority children is of greatest importance to me personally, I believe that I am also exploring a universally *human* experience. Noddings (2003) validates parenting as a universally human experience when she points out that we have all been parented and most of us will become parents ourselves. Further, she stresses that parenting is a crucial human experience that is neither understood nor attended to as well as it should be.

The Wounded Storyteller

> *Yet once I face death as a life process, what is there possibly left for me to fear? Who can ever really have power over me again?*
>
> *-Audra Lorde*

A different yet equally significant purpose of this inquiry is to witness and tell the story of my experience coming to accept my children on behalf of those who have not been allowed to have a voice and who continue to suffer because the dominant culture denies or demonizes anyone who varies from the heterosexual or gender norm. Frank (1995), who wrote about the experience of illness, particularly serious illness, refers to this witnessing as *wounded storytelling* and suggests that the recovery of one's voice through the telling of one's story can be profoundly healing for the storyteller, for those who hear the story, and for those who are not yet able to speak. Frank writes:

As wounded, people may be cared for, but as storytellers, they care for others. The ill, *and all those who suffer*, [italics added] can also be healers. Their injuries become the source of the potency to their stories. Through their stories, the ill create empathic bonds between themselves and their listeners. These bonds expand as the stories are retold. Those who listen then tell others, and the circle of shared experience widens. . . . In wounded storytelling the physical act becomes the ethical act. Kierkegaard wrote of the ethical person as editor of his life: to tell one's life is to assume responsibility for that life. This responsibility expands. In stories, the teller not only recovers her voice; she becomes a witness to the conditions that rob others of their voices. When any person recovers his voice, many people begin to speak through that story. . . . The wounded storyteller . . . is trying to survive and help others survive in a world that does not immediately make sense. (1995, pp. xii–xiii)

Frank's writing resonates with me because I too am a wounded storyteller. Some of my wounds occurred early in life and profoundly affected my psychological development. I know what it is like to not experience empathy as a child and I struggled as a result. As children often do when their parents cannot recognize their needs, I blamed myself. I was the bad kid, the kid with "defective genes." I saw myself as powerless and unworthy of my parents' love and many of the choices I have made in my life reflected this belief.

Some of my wounds have come as a result of the premature or abrupt termination of my individual development or the loss of close relationships and the grief that comes with such a loss. One of the first abrupt terminations I experienced was the too-early end of my childhood. Initially, I thought this termination of my childhood occurred when I began working on a farm at age nine, because thereafter I recall that my focus was on having a job and being independent, not on being a child. However, during the course of my analysis, I came to understand that my childhood was abruptly terminated much earlier, at age three, when I was molested by a family physician. In my adult life, I have experienced the abrupt and premature termination of marriages through divorce, and of friendships through early death. I don't think circumstances really matter. When you have experienced intimacy or closeness with another human being, the absence of that person's presence in your life causes pain and deep grief. Sometimes that grief is difficult to get over, especially when you feel you have to bear it alone.

I also felt both loss and grief when I finally recognized that I had to acknowledge and then let go of my biased notions about who my children were supposed to be. What is so difficult for me to accept now is that I believe this recognition might have occurred much sooner and the shift might not have felt as catastrophic had I not been taught to believe that there were two genders, one sexual orientation, and that anything else was "abnormal." With that kind of miseducation, it was all I could do to hold it together as I watched Julian and Kristin struggle for reasons I wasn't sure I understood or accepted. For a long time, I didn't even recognize that I wished my children could just be the same as other kids, that they could just be "normal." Even after I was able to recognize the wish, it took even longer before I was able to acknowledge it. Once acknowledged, I spent a great deal of time and energy wishing that it wasn't happening to me. I didn't *want* to have to deal with it and I felt like a horrible person for feeling that way.

This is the critical point at which I believe parents are most vulnerable to potentially rejecting their LGBTQ child. It is also when the right kind of intervention or assistance could help these parents stay engaged with their child rather than reject them. Just because you come to realize that something about your behavior or beliefs is wrong or maladaptive, does not mean that it is easy to change–just consider the experience of anyone who has ever tried to quit smoking. This is particularly true when you are dealing with unconscious and fundamental beliefs about the world that were programmed into your mind before you could even understand language. Given the depth of these beliefs, it makes sense that parents are not likely to be able to do this kind of work on their own and would greatly benefit from assistance or guidance from others who have already been through this experience or who are skilled in empathic witnessing.

Experiencing grief following a loss is natural, and this includes the grief that comes with letting go of an outdated vision of your child. The acknowledgement and expression of this grief is a necessary step towards a return to a sense of normalcy or a shift to a deeper level of awareness or understanding. If one's grief or loss cannot be acknowledged due to societal prohibitions, for example, then it is likely to become what Lenhardt (1997) refers to as *disenfranchised grief,* often resulting in adverse consequences. Consequently, Bracciale, Sanabria and Updyke (2003) have proposed that disenfranchised grief may be one of the reasons why parents reject their LGBTQ children.

Finally, some of my wounds have been physical wounds in the form of a serious illness. I have survived cancer and the experience of having to face my mortality. I endured radiation, chemotherapy, six months managing my bowel activity with an ostomy bag, and multiple surgeries in order to destroy the cancer and save my life. I continue to experience numerous after-effects from my treatment that pose significant challenges for me and likely will for the rest of my life. The body in which I live has significantly changed and I have had to learn to accept that.

I also experienced feelings of shame and embarrassment because my cancer involved bowels and stool and bodily smells and fluids, all things that fall outside the list of topics that may be discussed in polite company. This made it difficult for me to talk about what was going on for me at a time when I really needed emotional support. I remember feeling horrified when I overheard someone mention that people who die of colon cancer emit a particular odor as they are dying. I was terrified that the same thing would happen to me and needed someone with whom I could talk about what I was feeling. I now fully understand why research suggests that cancer patients who participate in therapeutic support groups may have longer survival rates than those who don't (Spiegel, 1992). I know that having my analyst to talk with made all the difference for me.

The experience of confronting my mortality and the limitations of my body has profoundly affected how I view the world and my place in it. I have found that some things that used to be so important to me, like what other people thought of me, are no longer such a big deal. And the pull to give my attention to things that I have been putting off, such as nurturing the relationships with those close to me and listening to my own voice, has become much more urgent. As do many others who survive serious illness or injury, I have found that the experience had unexpected benefits. Frank (1995) shared the perspective of a woman who, like me, had also survived a serious illness. I understood what she meant when she said, "I would have never *chosen* to be taught this way but I like the changes in me. I guess I had to go to the edge to get there" (p. 128). One of the benefits I gained as a result of going to the edge with my illness was the development of the ability to sit with and explore difficult, ambiguous, and uncomfortable issues and to empathically witness others who are going through similar experiences. I understand how important it is to be heard.

I have been very fortunate and privileged in that, despite all the challenges I have had to face, I have had access to resources and support that increased the likelihood I would be successful in overcoming them. I have been fortunate and privileged enough to get a second chance—a second chance at life and a second chance to experience empathic witnessing through the work I have done in psychoanalysis. I use the terms *fortunate* and *privileged* because I have health insurance and access to outstanding medical facilities and doctors, which saved my life. I have also had the financial means, flexibility of time, psychological make-up, and most significantly, the presence of an empathic analyst, which allowed me to be able to fully engage in the analytic relationship, which has saved my soul.

I believe that my ability to engage in this healing work—for as long as I needed it—played a critical role in my development as an empathic individual, as a mother, and as a heuristic researcher. Slesnick (1995) lends support to this belief when she notes, "the therapist's need to come to terms with one's own projections in order to more objectively assess and identify the client's needs and issues…is essential to parents as well" (p. 17). I see my own personal work in analysis as having played a major role in my developing the willingness to engage, rather than run away from, the serenity challenges in my life. It has also contributed to my developing the capacity to tolerate turning the analytic lens inward upon myself such that I can now explore the larger meaning of my experience. I believe that the chance to develop this ability also creates an obligation and a responsibility for me to utilize it and to give back.

Whenever one is able to experience the empathic mirroring that had previously been denied to them (such as through analysis), it creates both the capacity as well as a sense of responsibility to give back or to help others achieve this mirroring as well. Frank (1995) writes:

> People's storytelling is informed by a sense of responsibility to the commonsense world and represents one way of living *for* the other. People tell stories not just to work out their own changing identities, but also to guide others who will follow them. *They seek not to provide a map that can guide others – each must create his own – but rather to witness the experience of reconstructing one's own map* [italics added]. Witnessing is one's duty to the commonsensical and to others. (p. 17)

Initially, I did not want to explore my relationship with my children. The idea of putting my personal life as well as my children's lives on public display is not comfortable for me. The public debate with regard to LGBTQ civil rights continues to be highly charged, divisive, and often violent. Although I have not directly experienced any negative effects as a result of being "out" as a LGBTQ mother and advocate, my children have. Julian and Kristin have been called offensive names and they often have to listen to derogatory comments made about LGBTQ individuals (including comments made by family members) ranging from hateful to just plain ignorant. Every time they hear a comment, they have to make a conscious decision about whether or not it is safe to speak out. They also have to ask themselves whether they want to expend the time and energy to explain or defend the LGBTQ community yet again. It must be exhausting for them.

One of Kristin's co-workers said to her, "People like you should not be allowed to have children." And yet this individual has no idea what kind of parent Kristin is to her children. He has not directly observed how Kristin interacts with her children. If he did take the time to observe them, I believe he would consider my grandsons very lucky little boys because they are growing up with the experience of secure attachment and attunement with their mothers. At the same time, I doubt he would be able to acknowledge that because his social programming likely won't let him get past the fact that there are two mothers rather than a mother and a father.

Julian has been both verbally and physically assaulted. His emotional resiliency has taken a beating, but thankfully, at least he has not been seriously injured or killed. However, I worry about him every day. And I have reason to worry. Some surveys suggest that transgender individuals face *a one in 12* chance of being murdered, as compared to one in 18,000 for the general population. As a mother, that statistic is unacceptable, and it makes me angry, and I will *not* be silent!

It makes me angry enough to speak up even though there are those who will regard both my children and me as morally wrong, or at least morally inferior. But if I am to accept the dual mantles of heuristic researcher and wounded storyteller, and serve my goal of generating deeper understanding and empathy for the life experience of these individuals, then I have an obligation to do this work and do it honestly. I also believe that I am obligated to do this work because I can.

> The heuristic research process . . . demands the total presence, honesty, maturity, and integrity of a researcher who not only strongly desires to know and understand but is willing to commit endless hours of sustained immersion and focused concentration on one central question, to risk the opening of wounds and passionate concerns, and to undergo the personal transformation that exists as a possibility in every heuristic journey. (Moustakas, 1990, p. 14)

This is my journey.

Definition of Terms

Given the small body of LGBTQ research and the ongoing public resistance to engage in discourse regarding LGBTQ issues, many people are likely to be unfamiliar with some of the terms and concepts that will be examined throughout this book. Therefore, defining some of these terms should help to establish a common understanding. The source for the following definitions is the Gay, Lesbian and Straight Education Network (GLSEN) online resource.[3] The GLSEN organization's mission statement is directed toward working to ensure safe, inclusive, and effective schools for all students.

Biological Sex: This can be considered our "packaging" and is determined by our chromosomes (XX for females; XY for males); our hormones (estrogen/progesterone for females, testosterone for males); and our internal and external genitalia (vulva, clitoris, vagina for females, penis and testicles for males). About 1.7 percent of the population can be defined as "intersexual"–born with biological aspects of both sexes to varying degrees. So, in actuality, there are more than two sexes.

Coming Out (of the closet): To be "in the closet" means to hide one's identity. Many LGBT people are "out" in some situations and "closeted" in others. To "come out" is to publicly declare one's identity, sometimes to one person in a conversation, sometimes to a group or in a public setting. Coming out is a lifelong process–in each new situation a person must decide whether or not to come out. Coming out can be difficult for some because reactions vary from complete acceptance and support to disapproval, rejection, and violence.

Gender Expression: This refers to the ways in which people externally communicate their gender identity to others through their behavior, clothing, haircut, voice, and emphasizing, de-emphasizing, or changing their bodies' characteristics. Typically, transgender people seek to make their gender expression match their gender identity, rather than their birth-assigned sex. Gender expression is not necessarily an indication of sexual orientation.

Gender Identity: Our innermost concept of self as "male" or "female"–what we perceive and call ourselves. *Individuals are conscious of this between the ages of eighteen months and three years* [italics added]. Most people develop a gender identity that matches their biological sex. For some, however, their gender identity is different from their biological sex. We sometimes call these people transsexuals, some of whom undergo varying hormonal and surgical procedures in an attempt to change their sex to more fully match their gender identity.

Gender Role: This is the set of roles and behaviors assigned to females and males by society. Our culture recognizes two basic gender roles: masculine (having the qualities attributed to males) and feminine (having the qualities attributed to females). People who step out of their socially assigned gender roles are sometimes referred to as transgender. Though transgender has increasingly become an umbrella term for people who cross gender or sex barriers, many people find any umbrella term problematic because it reduces different identities into one over-simplified category.

Heterosexism: Bias against non-heterosexuals based on a belief in the superiority of heterosexuality. Heterosexism does not imply the same fear and hatred as homophobia. It can describe seemingly innocent statements, such as "She'd drive any man wild" based on the assumption that heterosexuality is the norm.

Homophobia: Refers to a fear or hatred of homosexuality, especially in others, but also in oneself (internalized homophobia).

Queer: Historically a negative term used against people perceived to be LGBT, "queer" has more recently been reclaimed by some people as a positive term describing all those who do not conform to rigid notions of gender and sexuality. Queer is often used in a political context and in academic settings to challenge traditional ideas about identity (queer theory).

Questioning: Refers to people who are uncertain as to their sexual orientation or gender identity. They are often seeking information and support during this stage of their identity development.

Sexual Identity: This is how we perceive and what we call ourselves. Such labels include "lesbian," "gay," "bisexual," "bi," "queer," "questioning," "heterosexual," "straight," and others. Sexual identity evolves through a developmental process that varies depending on the individual. Our sexual behavior and how we define ourselves (identity) can be chosen. Though some people claim their sexual orientation is also a choice, for others this does not seem to be the case.

Sexual Orientation: This is determined by our sexual and emotional attractions. Categories of sexual orientation include homosexuals — gay, lesbian — attracted to some members of the same sex; bisexuals, attracted to some members of more than one sex; and heterosexuals; attracted to some members of another sex. Orientation is influenced by a variety of factors, including genetics and hormones, as well as unknown environmental factors. *Although the origins of sexuality are not completely understood, it is generally believed to be established before the age of five* [italics added].

Transgender: Refers to those whose gender expression at least sometimes runs contrary to what others in the same culture would normally expect. Transgender is a broad term that includes transsexuals, cross-dressers, drag queens/kings, and people who do not identify as either of the two sexes as currently defined. When referring to transgender people, use the pronoun they have designated as appropriate, or the one that is consistent with their presentation of themselves.

Transsexuals: Individuals who do not identity with their birth-assigned genders and sometimes alter their bodies in a variety of surgical and hormonal ways. The transition (formerly called a "sex change") is a complicated, multi-step process that may take years and may include, but is not limited to, Sex Reassignment Surgery.

CHAPTER 2

PREPARING FOR THE JOURNEY

But a person cannot know himself until another knows him.

-Lewis, Amini and Lannon

This inquiry into my parenting experience and what I might have done to better help Julian and Kristin with their identity development led me to explore a number of concepts including *empathy, parental empathy*, and *empathic witnessing*. It also required that I develop a deeper understanding of parenting, the parent-child relationship, and the process of identity development, LGBTQ identity development in particular.

I was interested in the idea of *parental empathic witnessing* and in exploring what impact the intentional and conscious application of such empathic witnessing by parents might have on the development of self-esteem and resiliency in children, particularly for LGBTQ children who face even greater challenges developing and maintaining a healthy sense of identity in a world that stigmatizes them (Capper, 1993; Chng & Wong, 1998; Pope, 2003). It was appropriate to explore the idea of parental empathic witnessing for two reasons. First, self-esteem and resiliency have been strongly linked to healthy identity development (Noddings, 2003), and empathy has been linked to the development of self-esteem and resiliency (Eisenberg-Berg & Mussen, 1978; Montgomery, 2003). Second, parents are, *by design*, the primary source of this empathic witnessing, particularly during the critical periods of infancy and early childhood (Lewis, et al., 2000, Schore, 1994).

Grief Needs a Witness

My thinking about parental empathic witnessing began to develop after reading Montgomery's (2003) dissertation, Grief Needs a Witness. Montgomery argues that grief should be understood as a process of making meaning rather than as an illness that demands relief from unwanted symptoms. She suggests that these symptoms are better viewed as bits of information or messages from which important meaning can be derived, meaning that can contribute to the development of one's spiritual and personal capacities. Montgomery also believes that most people cannot interpret their grief themselves. They need another human being to listen, to hear them, and to help them work it through. They need a witness. "In order to integrate the experience of loss, *no matter what the nature of our loss* [italics added], we want a caring other to see, understand and help us make sense of our experience" (2003, p. 31).

From this perspective, Montgomery explores how and why psychotherapists might better serve their clients by shifting their focus from one of symptom identification and management to one of helping clients to explore, make sense of, and integrate their loss experiences. According to Montgomery, this requires that psychotherapists first recognize that grief is both a process *and* a messenger, and second, develop the ability to be an effective witness to it.

> Depth psychology values symptoms, such as grief, because they are purposeful. Symptoms give us messages of profound personal meaning as well as messages about our spiritual connection to life. *We need to be able to listen to and understand these messages.* In other words, *grief needs a witness* [italics added], and depth psychology embraces the role of the witness. Depth psychology stands in opposition to much of present day psychotherapeutic treatment, which is geared toward changing behavior, eliminating symptoms, and performing other activities that are believed to be objectively curative . . . in short, getting rid of symptoms such as grief without so much as questioning the meaning (2003, p. 1).

Although Montgomery's research is focused on the therapeutic relationship, it could be argued that her assertion that therapists need to become better witnesses to their clients is also relevant for parents within the context of the parent-child relationship. Just as the client in a therapeutic relationship needs the therapist-as-witness to help make sense of his or her grief, children need the parent-as-witness to help them make sense of and integrate their life experiences, particularly those experiences involving distress. How the parent-as-witness responds to these distress experiences has a profound impact on their child's identity development (Davidov & Grusec, 2006; Eisenberg, Schaller, et al., 1988; Leerkes & Crockenberg, 2006).

Like psychotherapists, parents also need to be able "to listen to and understand the messages" (Montgomery, 2003, p. 4) that their children are presenting to them because it is through their interactions—their relationship—with their parents that children will develop a blueprint for understanding themselves, understanding others, and understanding the world in which they live. This process of blueprint building is literally the process through which children learn how to be and requires ongoing interaction with an attuned parent for optimal outcome. Lewis, Amini and Lannon (2000) note, "One of a parent's most important jobs is to remain in tune with her child, because she will focus the eyes he turns toward inner and outer worlds" (p. 156).

However, unlike the therapeutic profession, parents are not required to be trained, supervised, or licensed, and despite the importance of parenting, most people grow up with less-than-attuned parental interaction. As a result, it is likely that the integration of their life experiences, particularly those involving distress, fear, or loss, is also less than optimally adaptive. If true, then it is also likely that most people are carrying around some level of unacknowledged and unresolved grief. As previously noted, Lenhardt (1997) suggests this unresolved grief can impact the clarity of a parent's vision and, ultimately, the developing mind of the child.

If, as Noddings (2003) warns, the educational system remains disengaged from the needs of the larger community and children continue to learn about parenting only through observation of their own parents, it seems unlikely that either the skill or the art of parenting will ever improve. Parents need to understand how to recognize when unresolved grief may be interfering with their ability to appropriately recognize and respond to their child's needs. Once recognized, it is then possible for parents to take steps to work through and integrate their grief so, in turn, they can be better integrators of their child's experience.

Focusing the Eyes of the Child

> *I am not a thing, a noun. I seem to be a verb, an evolutionary process, an integral function of the universe.*
>
> *-Richard Buckminster Fuller*

According to Lewis, Amini and Lannon (2000), an exploration into how and why a child's parents come to "focus the eyes he turns toward inner and outer worlds" (p. 156) begins with evolution and the increase in the size of the human brain. These researchers note that in order for the infant's head to be able to pass through the birth canal, it can only be a fraction of its final size. This means that most of the child's neural development is deferred until after he leaves his mother's womb. This requirement for ongoing post-natal neural programming is a primary reason why human infants remain dependent upon on their parents for a much longer period of time than most other mammals do. A longer period of dependency also means a longer period of vulnerability, so protection and survival also come into consideration. Therefore, an infant's ability to keep his parents close to him helps to ensure his safety and survival as well as optimal neural programming. Lewis, et al. (2000) note:

> A baby's ability to keep his parents beside him has evolved not to serve whim but limbic necessity. *Eons of experience direct his brain to hold open the emotional channel that stabilizes his physiology and shapes his developing mind* [italics added]. (p. 193)

Schore (1994) highlights the similarities of this open emotional regulation channel between the human infant and his or her mother and the concept of imprinting for other mammals. Noting that both processes require "the context of face-to-face dyadic gaze transactions" (p. 75), he suggests that all mothers regulate or imprint information to their babies visually through very specific eye contact. Schore describes this eye contact, which is regarded as the most intense form of human interpersonal communication, as a "visual dialogue between the mother and child" (p. 80) and suggests that this visual link "acts as a crucible for the forging of preverbal affective ties" (Ibid.). Schore's thinking with regard to the existence of preverbal affective ties between mother and infant is also supported by Lewis, et al. (2000) who state:

> In the first years of life, as his brain passes from the generous scaffold to the narrow template, a child extracts patterns from his relationships. Before any glimmerings of event memory appear, he stores an impression of what love *feels* like. (p. 160).

It is this early impression of "what love *feels* like" (Ibid.) that will ultimately guide the child–throughout his life–toward relationships that either regulate him well or poorly. If the child's early experience of love is that it feels good, it is likely that he will be guided toward other relationships that also feel good and serve as good regulators for him. However, if the child's early experience is one of neglect, disinterest, or inconsistency, then love *doesn't* feel so good. But it is still coded as "love," and the likelihood that he will replicate his experience of this "love" in later relationships is quite high.

Therefore, parents focus the eyes of their children by providing the orienting experiences (or programming) that will shape their minds and strongly influence the kind of people they will ultimately become.

> A child is born with the hardware for limbic sensing, but to use it skillfully he needs a guide. Someone must sharpen and calibrate his sonar; *someone must teach him how to sense the emotional world correctly.* [italics added] Nor should this surprise us: experience is a necessary ingredient for normal sensory neurodevelopment. A child's brain will not germinate the neural machinery necessary for depth perception without input from both eyes. Limbic systems also need training on the right experiences to achieve full potential. *These orienting experiences originate from an attuned adult. If a parent can sense her child well – if she can tune into his wordless inner states and know what he feels – then he, too, will become skilled in reading the emotional world* [italics added]. (Lewis, et al., 2000, p. 155)

A mother literally shapes her child's ability to love herself and others through a process of attachment and attunement with her child and by serving as a regulator and model for how her child should behave and interact in the larger world. In order to be a good regulator, a mother has to be attentive or attuned to her child. She needs to know her child's temperament, her needs, and her particular way of expressing those needs.

The degree to which a mother is able to tune in to her child in this way is affected by how much attachment and attunement she herself experienced as a child, and by the extent to which she has been able to resolve and integrate any of her own childhood issues or conflicts. The clarity of her child's vision will be strongly determined by how well the mother is able to recognize her child's needs, her "wordless inner states" (Ibid.), and by how consistently and appropriately she responds to them. Therefore, the greater her integration, the greater the likelihood she will respond to her child consistently and appropriately, resulting in a greater likelihood of healthy regulation for the child.

Bowlby (1988) refers to this regulatory emotional exchange between parent and child as *attachment* and has argued that the attachment relationship is *critical* in the formation of trust. Lewis, et al. (2000) refer to this emotional connection as *limbic resonance* or *limbic regulation.* Tronick (1998) mentions *affective regulation* and *attunement* and notes, "infants must collaborate with others to successfully regulate their physiological and emotional "homeostatic states" (p. 293).

These different researchers suggest that not only is this emotional exchange critical for trust formation and homeostatic regulation in infancy, it remains critical over the entire span of one's life. In other words, humans *never* outgrow the need for relationship. Contrary to the message implied in the American cultural worship of the individual, human beings are not self-contained, self-regulating organisms. Rather, as Lewis, et al., suggest:

> Adults remain social animals; they continue to require a source of stabilization outside themselves. That open-loop design means that in some important ways, people cannot be stable on their own – not should or shouldn't be, but can't be. This process is disconcerting to many, especially in a society that prizes individuality as ours does. Total self-sufficiency turns out to be a daydream whose bubble is burst by the sharp edge of the limbic brain. *Stability means finding people who regulate you well and staying near them.* [italics added] (2000, p. 86)

However, our educational system, in it's current form, is not teaching our young people how to find people who will regulate them well, and it is not likely that many students are learning this critical skill at home.

There are two primary reasons why developing an understanding of this process of open-loop regulation is so important. First, it is important for anyone who wishes to parent a child to understand this process, because parents shape the emotional lens through which their children will interpret and navigate their way in the larger social world for the rest of their lives. Second, it is important for every human being to understand this open-loop process because as Lewis, et al. state, "The world is full of men and women who encounter difficulty in loving or being loved, and whose happiness depends critically upon resolving that situation with the utmost expediency" (2000, p. 9). Given that most people received less-than-attuned parenting, recognition of this fact might influence more people to seek out healthy relationships, including therapeutic relationships, that can serve to re-regulate them in a healthier, more adaptive manner. *"Stability is finding people who regulate you well and sticking to them"* [italics added] (Ibid., p. 86).

It could be argued that almost every human being carries within them some level of unacknowledged, unresolved grief. If that is the case, our ability to be attuned to others is likely to be compromised. If this grief remains unacknowledged, it can be the source of much unnecessary chaos and misery (Bracciale, et al., 2003). But if grief can be acknowledged, there then exists the possibility of choice as to how one will respond to it. Acknowledging and then developing an understanding with respect to the source or origin of one's own grief, as well as how children develop healthy identities and the role that parents play in that process, can provide parents with the information they need to make conscious and empathic choices with respect to their children. In order to begin developing an understanding about the processes of parent-infant regulation and child identity development, the concepts of attachment, limbic or mutual regulation, and limbic resonance will be explored in greater depth, beginning with attachment.

A Bond for Life

> *Whenever I held a newborn baby in my arms, I used to think that what I said and did to him could have an influence not only on him but on all whom he met, not only for a day or a month or a year, but for all eternity – a very challenging and exciting thought for a mother.*

-Rose Kennedy

What is attachment and why is it regarded as so critical for trust formation in infants? Given that human infants are completely dependent upon their parents for survival, Bowlby (1988) believed there had to be some kind of instinctive neurological programming that produced a powerful attraction between mothers and infants in order to ensure the infant's survival. He suggested that this powerful bond also "produces distress when a mother is absent, *as well as the drive for the two to seek each other out when the child is frightened or in pain*" [italics added] (Lewis, et al., 2000, p. 70). This distress response is one that human infants share with other young mammals who also cling to their mothers when danger is present.

However, attachment is not just about the infant's physical survival. It is also the process though which the foundation of the infant's personality will be established. Ainsworth (1978), who studied the interactions between mothers and their infants, found that "the kind of mother a baby has predicts his emotional traits later in life" (in Lewis, et al., 2000, p. 73). From her observations of these mother-infant interactions, particularly interactions involving a separation between mother and infant, Ainsworth identified three distinct classifications of the attachment relationship: *secure attachment, insecure-avoidant attachment,* and *insecure-ambivalent attachment.*

> A mother who had been consistently attentive, responsive, and tender to her infant raised a secure child, who used his mother as a safe haven from which to explore the world. He was upset and fussy when she left him and reassured and joyful when she came back. A cold, resentful, rigid mother produced an insecure-avoidant child, who displayed indifference to her return turning his back or crawling away to a suddenly fascinating toy in the corner. The baby of a mother distracted or erratic in her attentions became an insecure-ambivalent toddler, clutching at his mother when they were together, dissolving into wails and shrieks when the two were separated, and remaining inconsolable after their reunion. (in Lewis, et al., 2000, p. 74)

An infant who is securely attached to her mother will develop a healthy sense of trust and a belief that the world is essentially a safe place. An infant who is securely attached to her mother will also develop a basic fundamental sense of herself as a "good baby" through the pleasure that both she and her mother experience when they are in attunement.

Secure attachment resulted when a child was hugged when he wanted to be hugged and put down when he wanted to be put down. When he was hungry, his mother knew it and fed him; when he began to tire, his mother felt it and eased his transition into sleep by tucking him into his bassinet. Whenever a mother sensed her baby's inarticulate desires and acted on them, not only was their mutual enjoyment greatest, but the outcome was, years later a secure child. (Lewis, et. al., 2000, p. 75)

It could be argued that this is the source of one's self-esteem, particularly if we contrast the mutual enjoyment experienced in an attuned mother-infant bond with the experience of less attuned mother-infant pairings. A less attuned mother-infant bond is likely to be experienced or felt by the infant as frustrating or bad, leading to her developing a sense of herself as a "bad baby."

To illustrate the impact on an infant of having a less attuned mother, Lewis, et al. (2000) described a study in which researchers were able to turn healthy monkeys into poor mothers. Pairs of monkey mothers and infants were situated in an environment where access to food was not predictable; sometimes it was easily found, other times the mother had to search for a considerable time before she found it, and other times she didn't find it at all. These researchers found that the uncertainty of the environment eroded the mother's attentiveness toward her infant. They also found that the young monkeys manifested evidence of emotional vulnerabilities and changes in their brain neurochemistry. However, it was the observation of these infants once they were fully matured that showed the extent of the impact of their mother's inconsistent attention.

Full-grown, these monkeys are living proof of limbic regulation's enduring power: they are timid, clingy, subordinate, and clumsy in their efforts to establish ties to other monkeys. The brains of these animals show lifelong changes in levels of neurotransmitters like serotonin and dopamine. *With their vulnerability to anxiety and depression, their social awkwardness and failures to attach as adults* [italics added], these monkeys exhibit a close animal counterpart to the multifaceted misery that in human beings is labeled neurotic. (Lewis, et al., 2000, p. 90)

These research findings have significant and sobering implications given the number of households in this country that are headed by single mothers with an income below the poverty line. How many of these mothers have experienced the erosion of their ability to be attentive to their children's needs due to the uncertainty of the environment in which they must raise them? How many children, like their monkey counterparts, will also grow up to face a future of anxiety, depression, social awkwardness, and difficulties with establishing meaningful relationships as a result?

From thy Mother's Eyes

The precursor of the mirror is the mother's face.

-*D.W. Winnicott*

What is limbic regulation? How does it relate to attachment and what role does it play in the developing child? In their book, <u>A General Theory of Love</u>, authors Lewis, Amini and Lannon (2000) present compelling evidence that humans are emotional beings who require "mutually responsive interaction" (p. 62) from other humans in order to maintain a healthy existence. They suggest that, as mammals evolved from reptiles, their brains underwent an evolution as well, resulting in a different neural structure referred to as the *limbic brain.*

The limbic brain is another delicate physical apparatus that specializes in detecting and analyzing just one part of the physical world – the internal state of other mammals. *Emotionality is the social sense organ of limbic creatures.* While vision lets us experience the reflected wavelengths of electromagnetic radiation, and hearing gives us information about the pressure waves in the surrounding air, *emotionality enables a mammal to sense the inner states and the motives of the mammals around him* [italics added]. (Lewis, et al., pp. 62–63)

Why would it be important for mammals to be able to detect each other's internal states or motives? What purpose does it serve? And why is emotion the mechanism that is utilized?

From a survival perspective, when a mammal encounters another mammal, the ability to quickly determine the other's state of mind or intent (are they friend or foe?) provides a competitive advantage. For example, in approaching another person, if I am able to read from his face, voice, gaze, posture, and gestures that he intends to do me harm, I can respond by turning around and getting away from him, thereby increasing my odds of continued survival. The faster and more accurately I am able to read those signals, the better my odds. From a mutual regulation perspective, the better I am able to accurately interpret another's state of mind, the more likely I will be successful in finding others who can regulate me well so that I can attach and stick close to them as Lewis, et al (2000) suggest.

One of the primary reasons why one human can "read" the face of another human is because there are particular facial expressions of emotion that have been shown to be universal across all cultures. Citing the research of emotion scientists Paul Ekman and Carroll Izard, Lewis, et al., (2000) note:

Facial expressions are identical – all over the globe, in every culture and every human being ever studied. No society exists wherein people express anger with the corners of the mouth going up, and no person has ever lived who slits his eyes when surprised. An angry person appears angry to everyone worldwide, and likewise a happy person, and a disgusted one. . . *Culture . . . doesn't determine the configuration of facial expressions: they are the universal language of humanity* [italics added]. (p. 39)

The emphasis on facial expressions as a primary means of communication is also evidenced physiologically in that the face is the only place in the human body where muscles connect directly to the skin. Lewis, et al. suggest that "the sole purpose of this arrangement is to enable the transmission of a flurry of expressive signals" (p. 53), signals that inform us as to the emotional state of another and that influence our behavioral responses to that assessment.

The ability to assess the internal state of another human also plays a significant role in another survival strategy: the pooling of resources with others and engagement in reciprocal behavior. Approximately 10,000 years ago when humans were hunter-gatherers and living in family groupings, if one family group had a successful hunt and another family group did not, sharing the food made sense. There was no means of preserving the kill and only so much could be consumed at any one time. Sharing food with another group when they had nothing made it more likely that they would share with your group when your hunt was not successful. Therefore, the ability to *predict* another's behavior, to distinguish those who were likely to share from those who would not, became a very advantageous survival strategy. And certainly, it can be argued that the ability to identify suitable mating partners served to ensure survival through continuation of the species.

From a developmental or evolutionary perspective, interaction with different individuals or groups provides a competitive advantage in that the taking in of new information or experiences can lead to more complex and expanded thinking. Tronick (1998) asserts that the human experience of this more complex, expanded thinking is one of *fulfillment* and, further, that humans *actively seek out* these fulfilling interactions. His dyadic consciousness hypothesis, which is derived from systems theory, states, "open biological systems, such as humans, function to incorporate and integrate increasing amounts of meaningful information into more coherent states" (p. 295). In other words, the reason for human existence is to interact with and integrate their experiences with other humans. Tronick summarized this idea by rephrasing Descartes, "*I interact, therefore I am*" (1998, p. 296).

Human infants are regarded as the most open of all open biological systems, primarily because infancy is considered the "window of opportunity" for neural and socio-cultural programming (Lewis, et al., 2000; Schore, 1994). The period of infancy for humans is of critical importance because it is much more than simply an open window for the imprinting of content (experience) onto an already established neural structure. Rather, it is a period where both structure *and* content are being established at the same time. In fact, it could be said that the structure is formed as a result of the interaction with content (experience). Arey (1962, cited in Schore, 1994) references a "critical period of accelerated growth and differentiation during which it is sensitive to conditions in the external environment" (p. 12). Schore himself notes:

> Any understanding of the ontogeny of autoregulatory systems and indeed of development *per se* must be anchored in the fact *that structure is literally being built on a daily basis* [italics added] during the time of accelerated and continuing brain growth in infancy. (Ibid., p. 10)

The requirement for ongoing neurodevelopmental regulation for the developing infant necessitates having a consistent caretaker to provide that regulation. According to Schore (1994) and a number of other researchers, this consistent caretaker and regulator is the *mother*. Schore notes:

It should be emphasized that the primary caregiver is the most important source and modulator of stimulation in the infant's environment and the primal wellspring of the child's experience. Hinde (1990) articulates the principle that *the most important parts of the environment are the interactions and relationships that the child has with others* [italics added]. Indeed, Scheflen (1981) argues that the neurodevelopmental processes of dendritic proliferation and synaptogenesis which are responsible for postnatal brain growth are *critically* [italics added] influenced by events at the interpersonal and intra-personal levels. Hofer (1983) asserts that *the mother specifically* [italics added] serves as an external regulator of the neurochemistry of the infant's maturing brain. (1994, pp. 12–13)

How does the mother provide this neural programming and regulation for her infant? Hinde's (1990, in Schore, 1994) assertion about the importance of the infant's interactions and relationships with others suggests that the mother provides this regulation through her relationship, or as noted previously, her dyadic connection with her infant (Tronick, 1998). Within that early dyadic connection, mothers and infants communicate wordlessly via the human face and the expression of emotion. "Whether they realize it or not, mothers use universal signals of emotion to teach their babies about the world through an almost limitless array of facial expressions" (Lewis, et al., 2000, p. 60).

One of the most significant and powerful ways that mothers and infants achieve this communication is through eye contact. Referred to as *facial gazing* or the *intent gaze*, this visual communication between mother and infant is regarded as being one of the most intimate forms of human contact and provides the first experience of attunement and mutual recognition. Schore (1994) notes:

Sustained facial gazing mediates the most intense form of interpersonal communication (Tompkins, 1963). Spitz (1958) refers to the importance of visual systems functioning in the "dialogue between mother and child." It is now well established that eye-to-eye contact gives nonverbal advance notice of the other (Reiss, 1978), and that the temporal structure of *gaze, the most immediate and purest form of interrelation* [italics added], provides clues to the readiness or capacity to receive and produce social information. The visual perception of facial expressions has been shown to be the most salient channel of nonverbal communication (Izard, 1971), and visual modes of communication that precede vocal modes of mutual communication (Schaffer, 1984) are dominant in the forging of preverbal affective ties in the first year of life. (p. 72)

As noted previously, the purpose of establishing a state of attunement between mother and infant is homeostatic regulation of the infant, both physiologically and emotionally. Through what Weinberg and Tronick (1994, in Tronick, 1998) refer to as the "exquisite configurations of face, voice, gaze, posture, and gesture" (p. 293), the infant communicates her physical state ("I'm cold") to her mother and her mother's attuned response to the communication (holding the infant closer to her body) both recognizes the infant ("I see that you are cold") and brings the infant back into homeostasis or balance (body temperature is elevated).

In terms of emotional regulation, the infant communicates her inner state ("I'm angry") to her mother and her mother's attuned response to the communication (soothing eye contact and voice, holding close, rocking motion) both recognizes the infant ("I see that you are angry") and brings the infant back into homeostasis or balance (infant is soothed and anger is reduced). Wilson-O'Halloran (1996) noted, "responsive parents provide their children with examples of what to do when problems arise" (p. 4).

Buchholz and Helbraun (1999) argue that there are two other critical aspects of an infant's homeostatic regulation that have been mostly overlooked by researchers. The first aspect that has been overlooked is what is now being recognized as the equal importance of maternal sensitivity to her infant's "alone time" needs as well as her infant's need for connection. Tronick (1998) notes that, contrary to earlier assumptions that an infant's emotions were "disorganized," it is now understood that "infant reactions communicate to the mother his evaluation of the state of the interaction with well-organized emotional displays" (p. 293). Buchholz and Helbraun (1999) maintain:

> While infants do interact with their environment from the beginning and even in utero, in their efforts to manage stimulation, they employ numerous strategies that involve limiting contact and seeking aloneness. Early on, these strategies include not only sleeping and control of gaze, but many actions that regulate sensory input. . . . *Thus insensitivity to infant cues, for either affiliation or disengagement, fosters insecurity. . . . Infants and toddlers are unable to feel secure in attachments that ignore their needs, or in selves that have not mastered some control of behavior and feeling* [italics added]. (pp. 6–7)

Given the importance of the mother's recognition of the needs of her infant, how does a mother know what her baby needs and when? Lewis, et al. (2000), speak very eloquently to this question.

> By the grace of what miraculous intermediary do mothers know when to approach an infant and when to let him be, when a baby needs the warmth of her embrace and when he needs room to breathe? *Limbic resonance gives her the means to that telepathy* [italics added]. By looking into his eyes and becoming attuned to his inner states, a mother can reliably intuit her baby's feeling and needs. *The regular application of that knowledge changes a child's emotional makeup* [italics added]. (pp. 75–76)

The second overlooked critical aspect of homeostatic regulation has to do with what Gianino and Tronick (1985, in Tronick, 1998) refer to as the importance of understanding the impact of mismatches or failures of reciprocity to an infant's development and the necessity for parents to facilitate reparation of the relationship when failures of reciprocity occur. Buchholz and Helbraun (1999) note:

We now know that mismatches and miscoordination are a common experience of infants in interaction with their caregivers. Gianino & Tronick (1985) cite research that estimates mothers and their infants spend roughly 70% of their interaction time in poorly coordinated states. *They suggest that it is the dyad's capacity to repair such ruptures together that ultimately serves development* [italics added] by calling on the infant to develop interactive skills (Stern, 1977; Tronick, Als, & Adamson, 1978), thereby providing *experiences of effectiveness* [italics added] (Tronick, 1980). (p. 5)

A simple example of one of these "experiences of effectiveness" (Ibid.) would be a situation in which a mother and infant are engaged in a playful interaction within close facial proximity to each other. Both mother and infant are maintaining eye contact and engaging in smiling behavior with each other. The infant suddenly reaches out and pulls her mother's hair. The mother is most likely going to pull away from the infant, take on an angry facial expression, look away, or both, and may vocalize her displeasure and pain with a loud "No!"

According to Tronick (1998), the infant is likely to immediately engage in gestures in an attempt to reconnect with her mother, including reaching out for her, attempting to reestablish eye contact, and vocalizing. If the mother understands this and allows her infant to repair the relationship and reconnect with her, the infant's attachment and safety needs are not threatened, and the infant can learn that pulling Mommy's hair does not result in pleasurable feelings, for either Mommy or her. She will have had an experience of effectiveness. However, if this reparation does not take place, over time, the impact on the infant and the bonding relationship can be devastating. Tronick notes:

> When failure occurs development gets derailed and the child's complexity is limited or even reduced (i.e., the child may regress). *The effect is in the child, but the failure is a joint failure* [italics added]. With continued failure *and the structuring that goes on around that failure* [italics added], affective disorders and pathology may result. (p. 297)

It is important to recognize the feelings of loss and grief that inevitably occur when the dyadic relationship breaks down as well as the profound impact this "joint failure" (Ibid.) can have upon both the child and the mother. The tragedy is that this failure is also a preventable failure. With education, mothers could learn to understand the role their children's need for reparation serves in their identity development process. With this knowledge, mothers could better provide their children with experiences that help to develop their children's interactive skills rather than unintentionally contributing to the development of affective disorders. Given the myriad of ways in which grief and loss can affect interpersonal relationships, it would be helpful to briefly review the research on grief and loss.

A State of Estrangement

Modern man is estranged from being, from his own being, from the being of other creatures in the world, from transcendent being. He has lost something –

what, he does not know; he only knows that he is sick unto death with the loss of it.

-*Walter Percy*

Everyone has experienced at least some degree of failure in their ability to experience secure attachment, empathic attunement, or relationship repair and reconnection with their mothers or key attachment figures in childhood. The fact that we have not been socialized in U.S. mainstream culture to acknowledge or deal with emotions, let alone difficult or painful emotions such as grief or anger, contributes to the probability that most people carry some degree of unacknowledged, or disenfranchised, grief into adulthood and parenthood. Given the state of estrangement from one's being as described by Walter Percy (1916-1990) in the opening quotation, should it really be surprising that a parent would disown her LGBTQ child when it is likely that, early on in life, she also had to disown the child in herself? Would it not be difficult to feel empathy for others when you cannot feel empathy for yourself?

Therefore, it is important for parents to explore their experiences of loss and allow themselves to grieve in order to begin to move out of this state of estrangement. It is also important for parents to understand how they have been affected by those loss experiences and to what degree their ability to parent empathically may have been affected. One way that parents might be affected is the way they interpret the *meaning* of their children's needs and behaviors. How a child's need or behavior is interpreted by the parent influences how the parent is likely to respond to the child. According to Eisenberg, et al. (1988), this has potentially significant long-term implications for the child's emotional development. These researchers note:

> Negative parental reactions toward children's emotional responses lead to children's experiencing distress in emotion-eliciting situations (Buck, 1984) *and to the eventual inhibiting or denying of vicariously induced emotional states* [italics added]. These findings are also consistent with prior research indicating that warm, supportive child-rearing practices (that should facilitate the expression of emotion) enhance the development of empathy (Barnett, 1987). (p. 774)

The appropriate understanding and interpretation of loss and grief experiences are important for two reasons. The first reason is that parents perform a function for their children very similar to the function that therapists perform for their clients: the appropriate interpretation of the meaning of the child's interactions in the larger world in such a way that the child ultimately develops the capacity to make appropriate interpretations for him or herself. According to Noddings (2003), when this interpretive role is performed in the context of parental caring, the experience can be transformative for parent and child.

> Genuinely caring can be a magical experience. The one cared for sees the concern, delight, or interest in the eyes of the one caring and feels her warmth in both verbal and body language. To the cared-for no act in his behalf is

quite as important or influential as the attitude of the one caring. . . When the attitude of the one-caring bespeaks caring, the cared-for glows, grows stronger, and feels not so much that he has been given something as that something has been added to him. And this "something" may be hard to specify. Indeed . . . there is no need on either part to specify what sort of transformation has taken place. (pp. 19–20)

However, if this interpretive role is *not* handled within the context of parental caring, a child is likely to experience a sense of shame and the unconscious assumption of a defensive posture in an attempt to defend against it. In his research on attachment, Karen (1994) found that this "negative self-feeling remains, and the fact that it is unconscious gives it tremendous lasting power, if for no other reason than it can never be examined anew, can never be felt, shared, or worked through" (pp. 244–245). In other words, it becomes disenfranchised.

Just because something has been driven underground does not mean that it has gone away. Karen suggests that just the opposite happens, often leading to the beginning of a downward spiral that not only has an adverse affect on the child in that particular situation, but often for years to come.

The defenses that the avoidant child erects — as well as the manipulative and devious ways he develops for getting his needs met – and the anxious displays of dependency to which the ambivalent child is prone are both causes for additional layers of shame, as first family members, then neighbors, and then teachers and schoolmates all begin to react to him as if he were annoying, hateful, inadequate, or odd . . . At some level of consciousness they view themselves as angry, spiteful, unlovable beings. They don't know that they are also sad and desperately hungry for love. Necessity has forced them to disavow such feelings and often to repress the memories that go with them. They thus have little basis for sympathizing with themselves. Meanwhile, the seeds of self-distain are nourished by the punishments, harsh words, and overt exasperation of others. (1994, p. 245)

I believe that parents as well as therapists bear the moral and ethical responsibility to be appropriate interpreters of the experiences brought to them by those entrusted to their care, Therefore, I believe they also bear the moral and ethical obligation to ensure that they develop this capacity in themselves. Therapists are encouraged (and in some instances, required) to undergo their own analysis in order to ensure that their own unresolved issues do not distort the appropriate interpretation of issues or experiences brought to them by their clients. Given that parental interpretations form the *foundation* of the child's personality, it seems not only morally and ethically wrong that we have failed to make the same requirement of parents; it seems *criminal* that we have not done so.

The second reason why the appropriate understanding and interpretation of loss and grief experiences is important is that a sense of grief or loss is frequently reported to be one of the first emotional responses parents experience when their child discloses that he or she is lesbian, gay, bisexual, or transgender (Bracciale, Sanabria, & Updyke, 2003).

One aspect of the grief experience that has particular relevance here is what Lenhardt (1997) calls disenfranchised grief, which is defined as "experiences that are not or cannot be openly acknowledged by peers or society" (in Bracciale, et al., 2003, p. 4). It has been suggested that this unacknowledged grief is one of the reasons parents reject their LGBTQ children. Citing Lenhardt, Briacciale, et al. (2003) note:

> Unlike grief resulting from the death of a loved one, the coming out experience is not recognized by most people as grief; therefore it is difficult for parents to find support or to feel comfortable asking for information regarding homosexuality. The parents may feel that they are alone in their experience and unable to cope with the perceived change in the relationship. *Often parents do not acknowledge their own loss*, or they feel that they do not have the right to feel depressed or angered (Lenhardt, 1997). *Parents may not know how to express their feelings and may believe that their only option is to disown their child.* [italics added] (p. 4)

One significant loss that many parents report when their LGBTQ child first comes out is the loss of their hopes and dreams for their child as well as the loss of the idea of who they imagined their child would be. This loss is significant given that what these parents are challenged to do is nothing less than to let go of all the thoughts and ideas about their child that they had built up over time. Bracciale, et al., (2003) note:

> From the moment a child is born, parents envision the kind of life their child will lead. Most parents dream of having their child grow up to be part of the mainstream culture; a responsible citizen with a respectable job, a wife or husband and children. Yet, once a child "comes out," some parents experience a sense of loss about the image they had developed for their child (PFLAG & Sauerman, 1995). They may experience grief, which may manifest itself as guilt, fear, shock, depression, and/or anxiety (Westberg, 1962). They may also blame themselves for their child's sexual orientation, since historically, it was believed that homosexuality was the result of bad parenting (PFLAG & Sauerman, 1995). (pp. 3–4)

What I was challenged to let go of were all the memories of Julian as my daughter that I had built up over time. What would I do with those memories and how was I supposed to refer to them now that Julian was my son? That is a huge issue to have to wrestle with and a lot to have to let go.

For parents of LGBTQ children who are unable to acknowledge their grief or who lack the empathic societal support to work through it, the process is likely to be extremely difficult. For parents who lack both, it may very well be impossible. Therefore, it should not be surprising to find that these parents believe, as noted previously by Bracciale, et al., (2003), that the only option open to them is to disown their child. Further, as was also previously acknowledged, it is unlikely that one can feel empathic towards another's grief and suffering if one has not been able to experience empathy for one's own.

Empathy and Empathic Parenting

> *To empathize with what a child is feeling when he or she is defenseless, hurt, or humiliated is like suddenly seeing in a mirror the suffering of one's own childhood.*
>
> *-Alice Miller*

Karen (1998), through his work on attachment, identified *first relationships*, or the relationship with one's parents, as one of the major early developmental influences that shape a person's capacity to love throughout their lifetime. Concerning the development of empathy, Karen notes:

> How do you get an empathic child? You get an empathic child not by trying to teach the child and admonish the child to be empathic, you get an empathic child by being empathic with the child. The child's understanding of relationships can only be from the relationships he's experienced (p. 195).

What is empathy and why is it important? What role does empathy play in the healthy development of a child's identity? How do you know if you are empathic? There are numerous definitions or descriptions of empathy. Kohut (1978) has described empathy as "a fundamental mode of human relatedness, the recognition of the self in other; it is the accepting, confirming and understanding human echo" (in McNab & Kavner, 2001, p. 195). Kohut also referred to empathy as "vicarious introspection," stressing that looking into one's own affects and memories is a critical part of the empathic process (in Balser, 1980, p. 19). Kohut sees empathy as a "highly developed faculty" (Ibid., p. 18) and notes that "by it's nature, empathy is a critical tool for parents (and psychoanalysts) since without it one can know nothing of psychological reality" (Ibid.). Kohut also asserts that empathy, along with introspection, defines the psychological field. In other words, Kohut argues that "without empathy, what we observe are actions; with empathy, we observe psychological facts" (Ibid., pp. 18–19). Empathy also holds an important position in Winnicott's (1960) theories of child development and analytic technique. According to Winnicott, it is through empathic maternal care that the infant builds up a "continuity of being" (in Balser, 1980, p. 5).

Gruen and Mendelsohn (1986) suggest that empathy "has become an umbrella term that subsumes a variety of responses (i.e., kindness, compassion, sympathy, and insight, as well as the matching of response of observer and observed)" (p. 609). A number of other researchers have also noted the affective and role-taking aspects of empathy, as well as empathy's fundamental role in defining and shaping patterns of not only the parent-child relationship, but all human interactions (Roe, 1980; Eisenberg-Berg & Mussen, 1978; Barber, Bolitho & Bertrand, 2001; Kochanska, et al., 2004; Aksan, Kochanska & Ortmann, 2006). In addition, Blanck and Blanck (1974, in Balser, 1980) have noted the significance of empathy in long-term development stating that "if development goes smoothly, empathy goes on to mature, and impart an essential quality to many adults who, as a result, *become good parents* [italics added], good therapists, and good lovers" (p. 17).

Wilson-O'Halloran's (1996) definition of empathy seems to be particularly relevant to this inquiry and will be used as the working definition. She conceives of empathy as:

An affective response to the perceived or anticipated emotion of another person, consisting of sharing the emotion and/or experiencing an emotion appropriate to the other person or that person's situation. . . Affective responses to the anticipated emotions of others, such as imagining hypothetical others in hypothetical circumstances, are included in this definition of empathy. (p. 13)

Wilson-O'Halloran's definition of empathy is also preferred because of its similarity to Balser's (1980) concept of parental empathy, which was introduced earlier. Wilson-O'Halloran's work also validates Balser's definition with more recent research. To refresh the reader's memory, Balser (1980) defines parental empathy as:

The capacity of parents to experience, understand, and respond to the psychological needs of their children. It demands that the parents recognize the separateness and complexity of the child; that they actually share and also understand the child's emotional experience, and that they be responsive to the child on that basis. It is motivated by altruistic rather than narcissistic goals. (p. 21)

Balser asserts that parental empathy is a "multi-dimensional construct including affective, cognitive, and behavioral components" (p. iv). She also identifies two types of empathy. The first type of empathy, which Balser refers to as *traditional empathic consciousness*, is defined as "the ability to experience the affect of another person within oneself and to reflect upon it" (pp. iv–v). The second type of empathy, *empathic behavior*, is defined as "the ability to interact in a way that *reflects* [italics added] the sharing and understanding of the other person's experience" (Ibid.). In addition to distinguishing between the two types of empathy, Balser also notes, "the ability to separate self from other as well as the ability to relax ego boundaries are crucial elements of empathy" (Ibid.).

Balser is suggesting that there is an important distinction to be made between the ability to place oneself in another's situation and the ability to act upon that awareness. Developing an awareness of the situation is certainly important, but it is only the first step. The next step is application of your awareness. You take it to an entirely different level when you are able to translate your understanding of another's experience into a behavior or action that makes your understanding visible to the other. It is not enough to just say to the other, "I feel your pain." There is also a need to be willing to share that pain with the other, to try to alleviate it, because, according to Luckmann (1978), *it is the application of such knowledge to the lived experience of our every day life that makes it meaningful* (in Martin, 2005).

Empathy, or the ability to recognize and resonate with another's experience, especially the experience of one's child, is important because, as Kochanska,

Friesenborg, Lange and Martel (2004) suggest, parents must be able to read their children's inner states in order to appropriately regulate them. Empathy, then, plays a supporting role in Lewis, Amini and Lannon's (2000) research on the parent's function as the limbic regulator of their child's developing emotional capacity. Kochanska, et al. (2004) note:

> Parents must read the infant's often-unclear cues and signals and respond to them in a way that addresses the infant's needs (Dix, 1992). The form of empathy that involves taking another person's perspective (David, 1983) may particularly facilitate the parent's ability and willingness to read and respond promptly, sensitively, and appropriately to the child's signals and cues. (p. 745)

A number of researchers are beginning to question why much of the research on the characteristics of parent-child interactions has been focused on the characteristics of either the parent or the child, rather than on the nature or quality of the parent-child interaction or of the relationship itself (Barber, Bolitho & Bertrand, 2001; Fonagy, Steele, Steele, Moran & Higgitt, 1991; Strayer & Roberts, 2004; Tronick, 1998). In other words, these researchers are suggesting that in order to get at the full meaning of the relationship between parent and child, perhaps understanding the whole relationship is of equal or greater importance than attempting to understand its individual components.

Aksan, Kochanska and Ortmann (2006) have written about the presence of a *mutually responsive orientation* (MRO) within the context of the parent-child dyad. They propose that an MRO is composed of "four basic components: coordinated routines, harmonious communication, mutual cooperation, and emotional ambiance" (p. 834), and that these basic components affect the quality or character of these dyadic relationships. Askan, et al. (2006) note:

> Dyads high on MRO are characterized by harmonious communication. *They are proficient in reading each other's signals* [italics added], enjoy the back-and-forth flow of communication, and communication appears to promote their connectedness. In contrast, dyads who have failed to develop MRO communicate less well and often appear disconnected and unable to read each other's cues. (p. 834)

One critical aspect of empathic parenting and this mutually responsive orientation between mother and infant, which is just beginning to be explored, has to do with how the mother responds to her child's expressions of personal distress or less-than-positive emotions, such as fear or anger. Eisenberg, et al. (1988) noted previously that how a parent interprets the meaning of their child's expressions of distress, and how they subsequently respond, can have a tremendous impact on the child's development. Noddings (2003) concurs, noting that "allowing a child to express his misery over a conflict . . . is important for emotional health" (p. 68).

Therefore, parents who are able to appropriately and effectively manage their own personal distress and respond sensitively to their child's distress will likely teach their child to do the same. Given that parents shape the lens through which their children will view the world (Lewis, et al., 2000), the impact of a negative parental response to their distress is that, over time, children will learn to inhibit or vicariously deny their emotional states (Eisenberg, et al., 1988). It seems reasonable to consider that a child's inhibition or denial of her emotions could be a factor in the development of disenfranchised grief.

To bring this discussion about empathy, empathic parenting, and grief to a close, we come full circle back to the place where we began, with Montgomery's (2003) research on empathic witnessing and her idea that "grief needs a witness" (p. 4). Montgomery's conception of empathic witnessing as having to do with the critical experience of "feeling seen and understood by another human being" (p. 63), is consistent with Lewis, et al.'s (2000) and Schore's (1994) research on limbic regulation. In particular, the concepts of empathic witnessing and limbic regulation share a number of elements including that they: (1) have their origin in (but are not limited to) the mother-infant relationship, (2) play a critical role in the emotional development of the child, (3) are ongoing and dynamic interpersonal processes, and (4) play a role in the integration of experience and the ability to self-regulate. Montgomery writes:

> Every child raised in a good enough home with good enough caregivers knows that *grief needs a witness*. It appears to be instinct that sends a child in distress hightailing over to mom, dad, grandma, teacher...whoever is available to listen, understand, empathize, and in so doing, soothe and comfort. This is how we move from a state of fragmentation and chaos into a state of containment. *Empathic responses from another help us integrate painful emotional experience so that we develop the capacity for self-regulation of painful states without needing to defend against them* [italics added] (p. 4).

The concept of empathic witnessing is relevant to this inquiry because it provides a valid theoretical explanation as to what role the empathic and attuned witnessing that I experienced in analysis might have played in my being able to develop into an empathic parent. Secondly, this research supports the idea that this is not an isolated achievement that is unique to me, but instead is a skill that other parents can also cultivate. Therefore, it is possible that other parents can learn from my experience and the process I have gone through in my journey toward developing into an empathic parent. To that end, it is hoped that the sharing of my experience will encourage other parents to be willing to embark on a similar journey so that they too can strive to become better stewards of their children's development.

I want to acknowledge that, while the reader is likely to be far more interested in getting to the results of this inquiry than reviewing a discussion about research methodology or the process through which I came to these results. However, in some instances, a discussion about the process is necessary in order to arrive at a fuller understanding as to the *meaning* of the results. I also feel compelled to include a discussion about the process because I believe that many people, due to their ignorance about the process, have the tendency to want to circumvent it. However, I believe that engagement in the process is *required* to achieve the results, and attempts to circumvent the process will likely yield results very different from those obtained when one is fully engaged. Therefore, a brief discussion about heuristic inquiry and the heuristic process follows.

CHAPTER 3

TELLING A STORY IN THE RIGHT WAY

If the historian will submit himself to his material instead of trying to impose himself on his material, then the material will ultimately speak to him and supply the answers.

-*Barbara Tuchman*

It has come to be recognized that the decision to engage in a process of reflective inquiry often has personal significance for the researcher, whether conscious or unconscious (Etherington, 2004). For some, the personal significance may be a focus on the greater good. For others, myself included, the personal significance *is* the personal, the meaning of one's everyday lived experience. Luckmann (1978, in Martin, 2005) captures the essence of this perspective when he states, "the job of science is to explain everyday life" (p. 212).

Moustakas (1990) regards heuristic inquiry as a methodology, or process, through which the researcher directs her intentional focus on this personal connection for the purpose of "exploring the essence of the person in experience" (p. 39). Etherington (2004) suggests that the researcher's focus on this personal connection "inevitably leads to self examination, significant personal learning and change" (p. 3). Moustakas also makes reference to the "heuristic power of telling a story in the right way and the concurrent shift in one's life and being . . . that in itself enables self-transformation" (p. 13).

This possibility of self-transformation suggests at least one possible explanation as to why I, or anyone for that matter, would willingly and intentionally immerse myself into a process that, according to Roads (1987, in Moustakas, 1990), challenges me to do nothing less than to:

> Let go and fall into the river. Let the river of life sweep you beyond all aid from old and worn concepts. I will support you. Trust me. As you swim from an old consciousness, blind to higher realities beyond your physical world, trust that I will guide you with care and love into a new stream of consciousness. I will open a new world before you. Can you trust me enough to let go of the known and swim into an unknown current? (p. 13)

Denzin and Lincoln (2003) also describe the heuristic journey (which they refer to as autoethnography) as one of considerable difficulty.

> Oh, it's amazingly difficult. It's certainly not something that most people can do well. Most social scientists don't write well enough to carry it off. Or they're not sufficiently introspective about their feelings or motives, or the contradictions they experience. Ironically, many aren't observant enough of

the world around them. The self-questioning autoethnography demands is extremely difficult. So is confronting things about yourself that are less than flattering. Believe me, honest autoethnographic exploration generates a lot of fear and doubts – and emotional pain. Just when you think you can't stand the pain anymore, well, that's when the real work has only begun. Then there's the vulnerability of revealing yourself, not being able to take back what you've written or having any control over how readers interpret it. It's hard not to feel your life is being critiqued as well as your work. It can be humiliating. And the ethical issues . . . just wait until you're writing about family members and loved ones who are part of your story. (p. 207)

This is a lot to ask of a researcher. It is a lot to ask of anyone, which raises the question, why *should* anyone want to undertake such a difficult and painful journey? Denzin and Lincoln believe that there are significant potential rewards for engaging in such a journey. They suggest, "you come to understand yourself in deeper ways. And with understanding yourself, comes understanding others." (Ibid.). In addition, it could be argued that the challenges inherent to heuristic exploration are not unlike the challenges each of us face as we attempt to negotiate the competing agendas that compose our everyday lives. It seems reasonable, then, to suggest that those willing to engage themselves in a heuristic journey are likely to be more successful negotiators in their everyday lives. According to Noddings (2003), this means they are more likely to be happy. This has been the case for me.

There were a number of factors that contributed to my decision to explore the nature of the relationship I share with my children and what it had to teach me about being a parent and about the process of acceptance. One factor was my deep, passionate desire to understand, love, and accept my children as the unique individuals that they are. Second, once I really understood what my children's lives were like, it was important to me that I understand how to provide them with the empathic support and guidance they needed, and to share that understanding with other parents of LGBTQ children. Finally, although it did not become evident to me until much later, my decision was also influenced by my struggle and desire to finally understand, love, accept, and provide empathic support to myself.

This passionate desire to know and understand, which I am realizing is a core aspect of my being, is something that I apparently share with other heuristic researchers (See for example: McNeil, 2005; Pena, Guest, & Matsuda, 2005; Wood, 2001). It was this shared passion, as well as heuristic inquiry's recognition that personal experience and the everyday lived experience are valid sources of data or information, that drew me to this research methodology. Moustakas (1990) notes:

All heuristic inquiry begins with the internal search to discover, with an encompassing puzzlement, a passionate desire to know, a devotion and commitment to pursue a question that is strongly connected to one's own identity and selfhood. The awakening of such a question comes through an inward clearing, and *an intentional readiness and determination to discover a fundamental truth regarding the meaning and essence of one's own experience and that of others* [italics added]. (p. 40)

Another factor that drew me to heuristic inquiry and bonded me with other heuristic researchers was the desire to do research that would not only be of benefit to me personally, but might benefit others as well. I wanted to do research that would encourage compassion and promote dialogue (Martin, 2005; See also Ellis & Bochner, 2000).

It is important to note that my experience with parenting and being parented has taken place over the course of my lifetime of fifty-plus years. For much of that time, I did not really understand what was happening to me or why. I often felt powerless to change anything and internalized a sense of myself as a bad kid, a bad mother, and a bad person. When my children came out to me about their sexual and gender orientations, it was difficult for me not to feel that it must be my fault somehow that they were lesbian and transgender. I certainly *felt* guilty and secretly wondered if it really was my fault. I felt defensive and resentful and told myself that I had done the best I could. I was stuck between the proverbial rock and hard place, which is not a comfortable place to be. The feelings and questions that came up for me are also likely to come up for most parents of LGBTQ children, and they *need* to be acknowledged. My children and I managed to get through it all, but there was so much unnecessary pain. Further, there was much about my experience with my children that felt like unfinished business. We had all carried this unfinished business around for many years. It was time to bring these issues to the surface and complete the process so we could all move forward.

With heuristic inquiry, I had the opportunity to take this tool I had learned about and apply it to my experience as a parent and to my relationship with my children. It had been my hope that this inquiry would lead me toward developing a deeper understanding of my experience at a more holistic level. It has done so. It was also my intention to apply this new understanding in my everyday life. That is happening as well. Through this inquiry, I was provided with the opportunity to "let go and fall into the river," as Roads (1987, in Moustakas, 1990, p. 13) encouraged, and trust that I would be guided "with care and love into a new stream of consciousness" (Ibid.). I have been so guided. As a result of this journey, I have discovered that I like where I now find myself. It was worth letting go.

This journey was a new experience for me, as a researcher and as a person. I felt somewhat apprehensive because adults in my life had not always handled my development with care or concern, and trusting does not come easy for me. There was a risk in taking the leap into heuristic territory because such a leap required me "to experience uncertainty and necessitate[d] living on the edge of creative confusion" (Martin, 2005, p. 207). As a child, I naively took this leap many times and was badly hurt because there was no safety net. I felt like Charles Schulz's cartoon character, Charlie Brown, who time after time was talked into believing that *this* time Lucy would not yank away the football, only to end up again lying on the ground with his breath knocked out of him. It required a great deal of courage for me to be willing to leap once more and trust that, this time, the experience would be different.

A number of researchers (See Denzin & Lincoln, 2003; Etherington, 2004; Martin, 2005) suggest that the risk and the effort, while extremely challenging, are worthwhile. *The potential reward is significant personal growth for the researcher.* Etherington (2004) suggests that it is through the making of a research journey, such as a heuristic inquiry, that the researcher is "helped to re-collect (which is more than remembering) aspects of themselves that had not been previously fully known, thus increasing self-confidence and strengthening their sense of identity" (p. 16). The suggestion that I could come away from this experience significantly changed and with a deeper understanding of myself captured my attention and, in effect, sealed the deal for heuristic inquiry. I knew this was what I had been searching for.

Therefore, I committed to making the heuristic leap into the exploration of my relationship with my children and my experience as a parent. I trusted that what I discovered during this journey would contribute to the possibility of significant personal growth, for myself and for those I cared about. I also believed that what I learned as a result of my willingness to engage in this journey would also prove to be of benefit to any parent who finds themselves in similar circumstances, because the experience of parenting is a universal human experience (Noddings, 2003).

The Purpose

I share Moustakas' (1990) belief that heuristic questions that matter on a personal level, such as exploring the nature of my relationship with my children and what it says about the kind of parent I am, can also matter on societal and even universal levels. This inquiry has relevance on a societal level because sexual and gender norms are understood to be social constructs, constructs that Wilkinson and Kitzinger (1994) state are "socially managed and controlled" (p. 309). These researchers also assert that most people are unaware that the construct of hetero-sexuality is among the most pervasive and coercive of these social constructs. They note:

> For most of those who are *not* heterosexual, the coercive nature of hetero-sexuality is everywhere apparent. But for many heterosexuals, their hetero-sexuality feels 'natural' and 'innate' (e.g. Bartky, 1993) or 'freely chosen' (e.g. Rowland, 1993) . . . The 'compulsory' quality of heterosexuality is differently enforced and *examination of the social control and management of heterosexuality is essential in understanding its functions and meanings.* [italics added] (p. 309)

Therefore, the social purpose of this heuristic inquiry had been to contribute to the essential understanding about these social constructs and how we use these constructs to define and communicate ourselves to ourselves and to those with whom we interact. Further, it was desired that this inquiry might also contribute to the understanding of how social constructs are used by the dominant group to achieve and maintain social control, often at the expense of all those who fall outside the construct.

It is my belief that the exploration of my personal experience as a parent could also be considered an exploration of parenting as a universally human experience given that, as Noddings (2003) argues, parenting is an experience that most humans will ultimately share (p. 34). Although this inquiry was specifically intended to serve as a resource for other parents with children who are questioning or exploring their sexual orientation or gender identities and who desire to help their children develop a healthy sense of identity, from a universal perspective, it is hoped this inquiry will add to the body of knowledge with respect to the appropriate and empathic parenting of *all* children.

Finally, a different yet equally significant purpose of this heuristic inquiry has been to witness, to tell the story of my experience coming to accept my children, on behalf of those who have not been allowed to have a voice and who continue to suffer because the dominant culture denies or demonizes anyone whose identity varies from the heterosexual or gender norms. I know that my experience parenting lesbian and transgender children is not unique to me and that there are many other parents who are struggling with how to love their LGBTQ children. Although too many parents are still reluctant to acknowledge their children's realities, it is hoped that sharing my story will help these parents to understand that they are not alone, that their children are different, not abnormal, and that their children and the relationships they can build with them are worth the effort. Dewey (1916) stated, "any experience, however trivial in its first appearance, is capable of assuming an indefinite richness of significance by extending its range of perceived connections" (p. 225). Parenting is a connection that touches every human being in one aspect or another.

The Journey

Life and narrative are inextricably connected. Life both anticipates telling and draws meaning from it. Narrative is both about living and part of it.

-Art Bochner

In the first chapter, the reader was introduced to the beginning of my story and the stories of my children, as well as the reasons why I chose to focus on exploring the meaning of my experience as a parent and my relationship with my lesbian and transgender children. In Chapter Two, the literature on parenting, the parent-child relationship, LGBTQ identity development, as well as on attachment, attunement, limbic or mutual regulation, limbic resonance, and grief and loss was considered. Through this review, I have attempted to develop a relevant and scholarly framework from which I intend to consider (along with the reader) the meaning of the data that will be presented and analyzed in the remainder of this book.

Consideration of this data (which is the continuation of my story) in this manner is consistent with a trend in social research, noted by Denzin and Lincoln (2003), wherein social scientists are beginning to view themselves as the phenomenon and to write *evocative personal narratives* (p. 213) that focus on the personal as well as the academic. Bochner and Ellis (1999, in Denzin & Lincoln, 2003) describe the evocative personal narrative as a research text in the form of a story. It is a first-person account that expresses vivid, emotional, and often private details about the author's own experience. The primary purpose is to understand a Self or some aspect of a life lived in a cultural context.

> The texts produced under the rubric of . . . narrative inquiry would be stories that create the effect of reality, showing characters embedded in the complexities of lived moments of struggle, resisting the intrusions of chaos, disconnection, fragmentation, marginalization, and incoherence, *trying to preserve or restore the continuity and coherence of life's unity in the face of unexpected blows of fate that call one's meanings and values into question* [italics added]. (Denzin & Lincoln, 2003, p. 217)

The researcher who utilizes evocative personal narrative as a methodology seeks to "write meaningfully and evocatively about topics that matter and may make a difference" (Ibid., p. 213). She hopes to influence the reader rather than simply inform him, to engage the reader in the experience rather than simply explain it to him. The researcher also attempts to "reposition the reader as a coparticipant in dialogue rather than as a passive receiver of knowledge" (Ibid., p. 217). In this more active role, the reader is then "invited into the author's world, evoked into a feeling level about the events being described, and stimulated to use what they learn there to reflect on, understand, and cope with their own lives" (Ibid., p. 213).

In a discussion titled, <u>Why Personal Narratives Matter</u>, Bochner (cited in Denzin & Lincoln, 2003) notes:

> We live within the tensions constituted by our memories of the past and anticipations of the future. Personal narrative, the project of telling a life, is a response to the human problem of authorship, the desire to make sense and preserve coherence over the course of our lives. Our personal identities seem largely contingent on how well we bridge the remembered past with the anticipated future to provide what Danielleen Crites (1971) calls a "continuity of experience over time." (p. 220)

From of a state of fragmentation, the infant's mind is shaped through the regulation of an empathic mother. A therapeutic client's fractured mind is restored through the regulation of an empathic analyst. Similarly, the minds and hearts of both researcher and reader can also be transformed through the healing mutual regulation that is achieved through the sharing of one's story and the witnessing of another's grief (Frank, 1995; Montgomery, 2003). Bochner states:

> The work of self-narration is to produce this sense of continuity: to make a life that sometimes seems to be falling apart come together again, by retelling and restorying the events of one's life. Thus, narrative matters to us because, as David Carr (1986) observes, "coherence seems to be a need imposed on us whether we seek it or not" (p. 97). At stake in our narrative attempts to achieve a coherent sense of ourselves are the very integrity and intelligibility of our selfhood, which rest so tenderly and fallibly on the story we use to link birth to life to death (MacIntyre, 1981). In the final analysis, *the self is*

indistinguishable from the life story it constructs for itself out of what is inherited, what is experienced, and what is desired [italics added] (Freeman, 1993, 1998; Kerby, 1991). (in Denzin & Lincoln, 2003, pp. 220–221)

The life story that I have constructed for myself from what I inherited, what I experienced, and what I desired (Ibid.) is worth sharing because I believe that I am not just speaking to defend the integrity and intelligibility of my selfhood or that of my children, I am speaking for *every* child, *every* mother, and *every* voice that has been silenced.

Before moving to the next phase of the journey, which is the stories themselves, it is important to note two concerns that are sometimes raised with respect to heuristic inquiry. The first concern, generalizability, often comes up when a single case study is used. Denzin and Lincoln (2003) provide a very thoughtful response to this concern. They note:

Our lives are particular, but they also are typical and generalizable, since we all participate in a limited number of cultures and institutions. We want to convey both in our stories. A story's generalizability is constantly being tested by readers as they determine if it speaks to them about their experience or about the lives of others they know. Likewise, does it tell them about unfamiliar people or lives? Does a work have what Stake calls "naturalistic generalization," meaning that it brings "felt" news from one world to another and provides opportunities for the reader to have a vicarious experience of the thing told? (p. 229)

I believe that my particular life story is also "typical and generalizable" and will be tested by those who read it. If, as Denzin and Lincoln suggest, my story is a "naturalistic generalization," that "speaks to the reader about their experience or about the lives of others they know," or informs the reader about "unfamiliar people or lives" (Ibid.), then its validation and value will have been established.

The second concern that needs to be acknowledged is the recognition that attempting this kind of personal exploration carries a risk that family relationships could be affected in profoundly negative ways if not carefully managed. However, from the outset, I believed that the telling of the story, if done with consciousness, competence, and caring, held the possibility of significant potential benefit to my family by creating greater understanding and empathy for all of its members. My family has already experienced tremendous pain and conflict as we have struggled to understand and embrace some of our members. Despite this pain and conflict— or possibly because of it—my family not only remains intact; I believe we are stronger. Just as Jonas Salk predicted, I believe my family has evolved because we keep managing to get up one more time than we fall down. It has not been easy at times, and has not always been very pretty, but we have always hung in there and taken that next step. Therefore, I believe that another purpose of this work is bearing witness to the evolution of a family.

CHAPTER 4

A SYNTHESIS OF FRAGMENTED KNOWLEDGE

Illumination opens the door to a new awareness, a modification of an old understanding, a synthesis of fragmented knowledge, or an altogether new discovery of something that has been present for some time yet beyond immediate awareness . . . In illumination . . . missed, misunderstood, or distorted realities . . . make their appearance and add something essential to the truth of an experience.

-Clark Moustakas

When I began this heuristic inquiry, my intention was to explore the meaning of my experience as a mother coming to understand and accept my sexual minority children. I was also curious as to how the presence or absence of empathy or empathic witnessing influenced the development of identity in children. Finally, I wanted to understand what role the parent-child relationship played in the child's identity development process. I wanted to explore these questions because, as a mother, I had been put into the position of having to radically shift my conceptualizations as to who I understood my children to be. I was successful in making that shift, but it had been an enormously difficult and painful process, and I could just as easily have failed.

Initially, I didn't even recognize that a shift was needed. Given that heterosexuality is the societal norm, I had not been educated about other sexual identities. I was lacking information that might have helped me to recognize that my children were questioning their identities and needed my support. Later on, I realized that I probably didn't *want* to recognize that a shift was needed. The few occasions I can recall sexual orientation being discussed during my youth, it was presented as an aberration, an abnormality, or a character flaw. With respect to gender, I only learned about two classifications: male and female. The transgender identity was never mentioned. My Catholic upbringing reinforced the idea that homosexuality was immoral and that people who engaged in such behaviors were sick, sinners, or both.

With that kind of misinformation, I was not prepared to recognize, understand, or respond appropriately when my children came out to me. In fact, I felt resentment toward them at times for foisting this unasked-for challenge into my life. Yet, as much as I may have resented and resisted the challenges my children were presenting me with, I could not disown them as so many parents of LGBTQ children have done. I was not always able to be supportive to my children in the ways that they needed, but something in me deeply resonated with their need to be recognized. I believe that my unconscious resonance with Julian and Kristin's need to be seen, and my conscious need to not be regarded as a failure as a mother, served as strong motivators to stay connected to my children. As a result, I made a shift. In the process, I found that I not only came to understand and accept my children, I also found a greater level of understanding and acceptance for myself. I had discovered a capacity for empathy. In order to understand *how* I got to this place of empathic acceptance, the next step in the heuristic process was to go back to the beginning of my experience and, in effect, retrace my steps.

In the process of preparing to move into the heuristic process, I mentally sorted through all my different memories, insights, and experiences, searching for the ones that I felt had been pivotal in moving me along my journey toward accepting my children and becoming an empathic parent. I had piles of papers scattered throughout my house that contained notations of different thoughts and memories that came up for me during this time. I found it interesting and also a little scary to pause and take the time to consciously reflect about the experience of parenting my children. Many memories that I hadn't thought about in years came back to me. Some of those memories brought a smile, some of them brought tears, and some brought intense pain. But I felt that the time spent in reflection added a greater sense of depth to my perception of my children and a greater sense of awareness as to how I relate to them now. The depth of understanding and appreciation that I gained from that time of reflection proved to be more than worth the risk that I might have experienced something overwhelming or painful.

In reviewing all my notations, I discovered that many of my key transitional moments could be captured in what have emerged as five different stories. These five stories, which represent the data that will be examined in this inquiry, will be presented to the reader in the same chronological order as they presented themselves to me. They are titled: a) Julian, b) Kristin, c) Re-discovering the voice of my body, d) Where is the voice of the patient?, and e) Where is the voice of the child?. Each of these stories attempts to accurately describe to the reader the pivotal experiences that seemed to have played a significant role in furthering me along in my journey toward becoming an empathic parent. The first story begins with Julian.

Julian

What may have been the first indication that Julian was different was a situation that, in my memory, happened when she[4] was approximately five years old. I remember it being summertime and Julian and I were sitting outside on the grass. I was wearing shorts, sitting cross-legged, and Julian was sitting next to me. At one point, Julian put her hand on my leg and began to massage it in small, circular motions. I remember my head snapping up as though someone had grabbed me by the hair and yanked upward. My full attention was suddenly focused on what was happening on my leg. It felt *sexual* and I was horrified. I don't remember anything else–what I said or what I did–I just remember thinking, "What is wrong with you?"

Reflecting back on that experience years later, I realized that it was very possible that what had occurred with Julian was the Oedipus complex being played out. The Oedipus complex is a concept within psychoanalytic theory referring to a stage of psychosexual development when a child of either gender regards the parent of the same gender as an adversary and competitor for the exclusive love of the parent of the opposite gender. The name derives from the Greek myth of Oedipus, who unwittingly killed his father, Laius, and married his mother, Jacosta (Source: http://en.wikipedia.org). Sigmund Freud, who first proposed the Oedipus complex, considered its successful resolution to be key to the development of gender roles and identity. Given that the Oedipus complex typically takes place between the child and the parent of the opposite sex, Julian's gesture may have been the first indication that he identified as male.

Later, I was shocked to learn that Julian also remembers that experience, but his memory is very different from mine. He told me that he was about ten years old, not five. He said we weren't sitting outside in the summer. We were lying on the couch in our living room watching a football game, and he was giving me a foot massage. Julian told me that this was one of his most painful childhood memories because it was a time when he didn't feel a lot of connection with me, and he very much wanted it. He said that all he was thinking at the time was that it felt so good to be able to feel close to, and to touch, his mother. He said he just wanted to be closer and he touched my leg. He said that I "turned on him in an instant" and he saw a look in my eyes he had never seen before. Julian told me that I said very quietly to him, "You don't touch your mother like that. That's how you touch a lover." He said the tone of my voice was chilling and he felt ashamed. Julian told me that I acted differently towards him after that. It still bothers me that I don't remember this. At this point in time, I don't fully understand why Julian and I have such different memories of the same experience. What I do understand now is that my reaction was likely the result of disenfranchised grief, given that the memory appears to have been blocked out or repressed.

Julian never seemed to have an easy time during childhood. With three children, it seems that there is usually a two-against-one-scenario. With my children, it was usually Julian's twin sister, Kristin, and older brother, Michael, against Julian. From the very beginning, Julian seemed to be different. The family referred to her as an "odd duck." There were all kinds of family theories as to why, but no one really understood Julian. This unnamed difference seemed to play a role in Julian being tagged as more difficult to interact with.

Kristin, on the other hand, was very easy to interact with. People seemed to gravitate more towards Kristin than to Julian. My younger sister, in particular, developed a close bond with Kristin. Their bond was forming at the same time I became a single parent and had to go to work. Because of her relationship with her aunt, I don't believe that Kristin suffered as much attachment loss as Julian may have. I also believe that Kristin's experience of having this extra attachment relationship likely had an influence on the different ways that she and Julian worked through their sexual identity development.

Julian began acting out in kindergarten. It began with stealing little things like paper clips and erasers. By middle school, I was getting calls from grocery stores because Julian had been caught shoplifting. I drove myself crazy trying to figure out what was going on with this child. I could not acknowledge it at the time, but sometimes it was hard for me to like Julian. I seemed to be constantly irritated with her. She just seemed to be so awkward and unmotivated and I constantly had to push her. I recall telling people that this was a period when Julian was so awkward she couldn't even walk down the hallway without bouncing off the walls. During this same period, Julian was also watching television excessively. My attempts to regulate, and then control, the television usage went as far as cutting the plug off the power cord and taking it with me to work. It seemed as though Julian just disappeared into the TV; her body was there but her mind wasn't. It never occurred to me that Julian might be trying to mentally escape her body.

Julian was also gaining weight despite my best efforts to manage her diet. I discovered that Julian was secretly eating in her room when I found candy wrappers stuffed under the floor trim in her bedroom and empty food containers under her bed. On one occasion, I went in the bathroom and found the toilet un-flushed with stool in it and no toilet paper. I remember thinking, "My God, she doesn't even wipe herself!" With evidence that Julian didn't seem to be taking basic care of herself, I became not just frustrated, but concerned. At that time, behaviors such as the ones Julian was exhibiting were often associated with sexual abuse. I could not believe that sexual abuse could be a possibility, but I decided I had better take Julian to a therapist.

I ended up taking Julian to a series of therapists over the next few years. I can't say that any of them really helped and, in my opinion, the last therapist did a great deal of damage. I was referred to this therapist, who held a Masters degree in Counseling, because she'd had experience working with adolescents. She was also somewhat affordable. At the time, my insurance didn't cover mental health providers with less than a Ph.D. or M.D. degree, so I was paying for Julian's therapy myself. The added financial strain and having to take time off from work to take her to appointments created more stress for me. I resented this additional responsibility at times and I am sure Julian saw that in me.

Julian saw this therapist for about a year and a half. While in therapy, Julian began saying that she was alcoholic and needed treatment. She wanted to be placed in a residential treatment facility. At the time, her brother was in alcohol and drug treatment and I thought Julian was just trying to emulate him. I likely said the same thing that a number of family members have often said with respect to Julian, "She's just doing it to get attention." Even if I didn't say it out loud, I know I thought it. I didn't know what Julian wanted from me and I was frustrated. I talked with Julian's therapist and we agreed that it would not be in Julian's best interests to be placed in the residential program. We also agreed to present a united response to Julian.

I had also talked with my own analyst about the situation with Julian. She had strongly advised me that there was a downside to residential treatment programs, particularly for adolescents. She told me that establishing and maintaining their own boundaries was what adolescents needed to learn how to do. Residential programs take over as the container or holding environment for the adolescent rather than the adolescent working to contain or hold herself. If an adolescent who has the capacity to hold it together is allowed to regress, it could have a detrimental effect on her development. I felt that Julian had the capacity to work it through herself.

My understanding and experience with respect to the parenting of adolescents was that the parent had to take a firm stand with them and that it was an adversarial relationship, almost like drawing a line in the sand. As the parent, this meant that, once the line was drawn, I had to be ready to be challenged by my child. It also meant that I really needed to be able to present a united front with other care-giving adults (e.g., the other parent, the therapist, etc.) if I was going to be able to hold the line with my child. I had counted on Julian's therapist to help me hold that line. But she abandoned both Julian and me at the worst possible time and for what I feel were the worst and most unethical of reasons.

Julian's therapist literally dumped her. She told me that she would not be working with Julian anymore because thirty-five dollars a week wasn't worth it. I can imagine that Julian *was* a challenging client. However, I expect that any adolescent in therapy would likely be challenging. This therapist was supposed to have experience with adolescents—that was the reason I took Julian to her in the first place. Furthermore, regardless of how challenging Julian may have been, I believe it is unethical to just abruptly terminate therapy. That therapist should have been able to set aside whatever her issues were with Julian, at least long enough to allow for an appropriate termination. Or, the therapist should have acknowledged her issues and made a referral to another therapist. She did neither of those things and I didn't know to ask her to. Without the therapist's support, Julian got her way and was placed in the treatment program. I still feel very angry and betrayed by the conduct of that therapist.

With residential treatment comes more therapy, including family therapy. Even though we had opposed Julian's placement in the program, we were "strongly encouraged" to participate, and we did. At the same time, we felt like we were being held hostage, and we didn't see Julian putting forth the same level of effort that we were. It was hard not to feel frustrated and resentful. I also didn't have much trust in therapists at that point, given the experience with Julian's last therapist. However, I worried that if we didn't participate in the family therapy, we might be labeled as uncooperative. We were still working with the family therapist when I received notification that Julian had filed a court petition for an Alternative Residential Placement (ARP). Julian was fifteen years old at that time. I was stunned and angry. When I confronted the family therapist about Julian's petition, he expressed surprise and agreed that an ARP was not in Julian's best interests. He wrote a letter to the court strongly recommending that Julian be left with the family. The therapist stated that we were doing our part and Julian needed to do hers. He also noted that any issues that Julian had within our family were issues that she would have regardless of where she was placed. The therapist recommended that the court should leave our family alone and let us work it through. Despite the therapist's letter, and over my objections, Julian was granted the ARP and placed in a foster home.

After the ARP was granted, I had little contact with Julian for almost two years. I didn't know that Julian ran away from a number of foster homes or that she lived on the streets off and on for months. I didn't know whether Julian was alive or dead, and there were times when I said I didn't care. I felt I had been attacked and I was angry. If Julian thought our home was so bad that she'd rather be out on the streets, then that was fine with me! I resented that Julian would attack me in such a public way when I was doing the best I knew how to do. No matter how angry I had been with my parents, I would have never dared to attack them the way I felt Julian had attacked me.

What is interesting to consider now is that, at the time, I didn't remember that my adolescence had been almost as challenging as Julian's. I ran away from home when I was about sixteen because my father had wrongly blamed me for something I had not done and forbade me from attending a concert, the tickets to which I had purchased with my own money. I felt that he was being unjust and I didn't feel that I was going to be heard. So I left and felt righteously justified in doing so. I went to my concert, but afterward I had no place to go. I had wanted to be heard, not homeless. I was scared and in over my head, but too proud to admit it. I stayed with a friend for a week before I finally asked to come home. Actually, the first time I ran away was at age three. My mother told me that I ran away, supposedly because my father would not build me a sandbox. My mother said that I got about four blocks before she caught up with me. I had the advantage because I was small and fast and she was pregnant and had to carry my baby sister. So although I didn't involve the court system, my adolescence was very similar to Julian's. If I believed that my adolescent rebellion had been justified, or at least understandable, why did I respond to Julian's with such resentment and resistance? Why couldn't I remember my own adolescent experience and imagine Julian having similar feelings? I now believe that disenfranchised grief is the reason why.

About a year after Julian was granted her ARP, she came back into my life. She also came out to me that she was lesbian in a rather dramatic fashion. One Sunday morning in 1993, as I was reading *The Seattle Times*, I noticed a feature story about Lambert House, a halfway house and resource center for LGBTQ youth, located on Capitol Hill in Seattle. There was a photograph that accompanied the story, and in that photograph was Julian. I remember I choked on my coffee as I read about my lesbian daughter, looking at the clock and wondering if I had enough time to get to my parents' house in order to steal their newspaper before they got home from church. I was afraid that reading that article would kill my mother. And I was also afraid of what my parents would think about me. I already felt like they considered me their "loser" daughter and I didn't want to provide them with any more evidence. I didn't steal their newspaper, though, and I don't clearly remember my parents' initial reaction. I do know that they and other members of our extended family have struggled to accept that Julian was lesbian. For a long time we just tried not to talk about it.

Shortly after the *Times* article came out, Julian and I met to talk, and slowly we began to reconnect. On one occasion, Julian asked whether I would be willing to meet a woman who had taken her in off the streets and allowed Julian to live with her and her partner. This woman, at that time in her late fifties, was someone Julian considered very important in her life. I was very resistant to meeting her because I saw her as someone who was trying to take my place in my child's life, who, in my child's eyes, was a better mother than me, and I wanted no part of it. I think I was also resistant because I felt like I was being forced or manipulated into doing things I didn't really want to do, but felt I had to do because of what people might think about me. If I refused, I might look like a bad mother and I didn't want to be a bad mother. So I felt I had to agree to the meeting in order to save face.

However, after meeting this woman, I felt a deep sense of gratitude that she was a part of Julian's life. I was moved and amazed to see how warmly she interacted with Julian and that she saw so much potential in her—potential that I had certainly not been able to see. Meeting Arloe and hearing her story affected me, and coming to regard her as a good and decent person changed me. It also marked the beginning point at which my thinking began to change. Questions I had never thought about before began to surface. What *is* normal? Who determines what is or isn't normal? What does it really mean to be a gendered and sexual being? My awareness was beginning to shift, all because I was willing to have a conversation with Arloe.

I met Julian and Arloe together at a coffee shop. Julian introduced us and then walked off to have a cigarette, leaving me alone with Arloe. We sat down and I think Arloe could sense how I was feeling. Her manner was both warm and respectful towards me, which I had not expected. She said it was great to finally meet me and thanked me for agreeing to come. Arloe then looked at me, smiled, and said maybe it would help if she told me a little bit about herself so I would know where she was coming from. Since it meant that I wouldn't have to say anything, I agreed.

Arloe told me that she was lesbian and that she had known that she was different most of her life. She said that, coming of age in the early 1950s, she had realized that there were basically two choices available for someone like her: one choice was to become what was referred to as a biker chick and hang out at bars that catered to masculine women; the other was to marry, have children, and join a "book club." Book clubs were a common social activity for women during the 1950s, and no one ever questioned what went on during those meetings. Noting that a high percentage of the biker chicks ended up as alcoholics, Arloe said she chose the book club option.

Arloe married and gave birth to three sons. What was surprising to me was that she said that her husband went into their marriage aware of her sexual orientation. She told me that they were great friends and loved each other, and she knew he would be a good father to their children. She said that she made it as authentic a life as she could under the circumstances and it worked for them. During the early 1970s, when gays began to come out of the closet, Arloe said that she felt that she had to take the next step to live more authentically and her husband agreed to a divorce. What Arloe told me next not only surprised me, but also convinced me that there was no way that she could possibly be the immoral deviant that I had been taught people like her were supposed to be. Arloe told me that when she and her husband sat down to talk about the divorce, they each asked of the other, "What do you need from me in order to be the best possible parent to our children?"

Upon hearing this, I remember thinking to myself that here were two people who were committed to being honest with each other, who valued the growth and development of their children and each other, who made conscious life choices together, and who could sit down and openly communicate when there was a change in circumstances. Most divorcing heterosexual couples I knew had difficulty managing to be civil to each other, let alone supportive of each other or their children. I was deeply impressed. But I think more importantly, Arloe's story strongly resonated with me. As a young 36-year-old woman and mother who felt powerless to change anything in my life, to hear the story of a woman who had the ability to really consider who she was, the world in which she had to live, and then make a choice that was best for her? Well, to quote a phrase I heard once from Julian, I thought, "You can *do* that? Wow!"

I began to think about this woman whose existence I had been taught to believe was an abomination against God, and yet who seemed to me to be a far more authentic individual and far more competent mother than most of the people I knew, including myself. And Arloe never treated me as any less than Julian's mother. She made it very clear to me that she cared about Julian and saw tremendous potential in her and, more importantly, she let me know that she had no intention of trying to take my place in Julian's life. Arloe said she wanted to provide support for Julian, because she could. She also wanted to help to build a bridge to bring Julian and I back together. When I think about it today, I know I owe Arloe a debt of gratitude that I can never repay for the gift that she was in Julian's life at that time. I believe Julian might not have survived had she not been able to find the kind of positive attachment she experienced with Arloe and her partner. I think it was one of those times when the right intervention came at the right time, and the right intervention did not involve me. It hurt to acknowledge that, but since it was what was best for my child, I needed to manage that hurt.

After meeting Arloe, I began to think that there was much about gender, sexuality, and even my own children that I didn't really understand. I also had to acknowledge that perhaps I had not wanted to understand, that I had been afraid to understand because to do so would thrust me into unfamiliar territory that I wasn't sure I was equipped to handle. I was apprehensive, but I could also sense the beginning of something changing within me. It felt somehow right to me to learn more, and I was intrigued.

I was intrigued, and I was changing, but I was still very much challenged. And Julian kept pushing—at least that's how it felt to me. Shortly after meeting with Arloe, Julian wanted me to come to another meeting, this time to meet a woman named Pauline, who was the executive director of a major LGBT non-profit organization in Washington, DC. Julian had met Pauline when she had been in Seattle speaking about the work her organization was doing for gay rights. Julian had been in the audience and had challenged Pauline about what her organization was doing to help LGBTQ youth. Julian impressed Pauline, and she was invited to come to Washington, DC for six months as their first executive youth leadership intern. The problem was that Julian was under eighteen, which meant that I had to give parental permission for her to go. I felt like I was in a no-win situation. I agonized over the decision, asking myself, if I said yes, was I being untrue to myself, and condoning something I was not sure I could accept? But if I didn't agree, would this decision further damage any hope of having a good relationship with Julian? I didn't know what to do.

It was Pauline who came up with a compromise. I didn't have to give parental permission. I transferred parental authority over to Pauline and she agreed to take responsibility for Julian while she was in Washington. I frankly didn't trust that Pauline would follow through any more than anyone else had, but at least the channels were still open between Julian and I. Besides, I thought, how much say did I really have anyway? However, Pauline did seem to follow through. At the time, I thought that, perhaps once again, Julian had gotten a key intervention at a crucial time by someone who genuinely had her best interests at heart and the ability to be an appropriate mentor.

My impression of Pauline seemed to be confirmed about three months into Julian's internship. I got a call from her informing me that Julian was beginning to make statements that she was homesick and had begun to act out. Pauline told me that instead of sending Julian home, she had wanted to call me and let me know what was going on. Pauline told me that she had invited Julian to come to Washington because she saw a tremendous amount of potential in her. She also let me know that she really liked Julian and wanted her to be successful. Pauline said that she wanted Julian to finish what she started. We talked and decided that together, we would maintain the expectation that Julian needed to finish the internship and be accountable for the commitment she had made.

Remembering Julian's last counselor, I told Pauline that Julian was going to be angry with me, but she would take it out on her. I also told Pauline that enough people had bailed on Julian, and on me, and if she wasn't willing to see it through, she should just put Julian on a plane and send her home now. Pauline committed to follow through and Julian did complete her internship. The experience seemed to have had a profoundly positive affect on Julian because when she came home, I almost didn't recognize her. Julian had lost about eighty pounds and seemed happier and more confident, than I could ever remember seeing her. Julian also spontaneously gave me one of the best shoulder massages I'd ever had. I suddenly realized that it was the first time I could remember saying that I liked something Julian had done. It made me happy and sad at the same time to realize that it was also the first time that I wasn't looking at Julian as my troubled daughter, but as a grown and legitimate person in her own right. I guess it's true that sometimes the mother is the last to know.

Later, I found out that Julian's experience had not been as planned, or as supervised, as I had originally understood. Julian and I never discussed his experience in Washington until I began to write his story for this inquiry. Julian told me that, despite the fact that Pauline had assumed parental responsibility, there had been no formal executive youth leadership intern program. There was also a budget crisis, Pauline had actually resigned as executive director, and no provisions had been made for Julian's housing. Julian told me that the staff had informed him that he needed to find a place to live. He was seventeen years old and in a strange city; it was a sink-or-swim situation. Fortunately, Julian not only learned to swim, he discovered a passion. I asked Julian why Pauline had not told me what was really going on, and he said that Pauline had other stuff on her plate and that Julian's situation was a distraction she didn't have time for. I said, "But she invited you to come to Washington?" Julian replied, "Yeah." I asked what he thought now about his experience in Washington. He said that there were some painful and difficult memories, but also some very good ones. Julian said:

> Mom, there were some amazing parts. I mean, I got to meet Coretta Scott King. I got to work with senators like Ted Kennedy and Patty Murray. That was a lot for a seventeen-year-old who had been living on the streets. Of course, it also turned me off to politics. It was crazy to see all the posturing to insert words in one piece of legislation that would be cancelled out by words in another piece of legislation. It was all so meaningless and yet so all-important. (Julian, personal communication, May 3, 2007)

I had to marvel at this person my child had become.

Julian moved back home for a while after returning from Washington and we negotiated how to be with each other. It was still a challenge for me. I was finding out that accepting Julian as lesbian was one thing, but to actually meet her friends was something else. It was a challenge that I initially resisted, and managed to avoid for quite a while. But one day Julian brought her girlfriend, Meredith, over to the house to meet me and I couldn't avoid it any longer.

I remember that, at first, I didn't want to engage in eye contact with Meredith. Eye contact is a very intimate gesture to me. I have always had difficulty looking directly at someone; particularly if I don't know the person well. However, Meredith was a very friendly and outgoing person and was more than up for keeping the conversation going. When she mentioned that she was a fifth-year student in Women's Studies at the University of Washington, I remember I suddenly looked up at Meredith in surprise and thought, "Wow! You go to college? In Women's Studies? That's pretty cool." We had a great conversation and I ended up liking her a great deal. After Meredith, I began to feel much more open to meeting Julian's friends.

When I reflect back about my initial reluctance to look at Meredith, I know that it was more than about just feeling shy. From the perspective of Lewis, Amini and Lannon's (2000) concept of mutual or limbic regulation, to look directly into another's eyes is to literally be entering into relationship with them. To be in relationship with someone is to have acknowledged the other's humanity. To be in relationship with someone also means that you are open to influencing, and being influenced by, the other (mutual regulation). Therefore, to look at Meredith would mean that I was acknowledging that she was like me, and I had been taught that she wasn't. I find it interesting to consider that here, as in many other aspects of my life, *it was a dialogue that bridged the gap*.

My process of accepting Julian's transition from identifying as lesbian to transgender was another very difficult period for me. It seemed that just when I would get to a place of relative comfort with respect to relating to Julian, he would toss me another curve ball. And this one was tough. I had never considered how deeply the construct of gender is embedded in our society, particularly with respect to language, until Julian began to transition. In Western culture, if there is no word for something, then it doesn't exist. The only words in our culture that describe one's gender identity are "male" or "female." Those are the only choices that are offered when a baby is born. If someone's identity *isn't* captured in one of those two words, we literally do not know what to say. Further, most of the words that have been used to describe someone whose internal sense of their gender is different from the body into which they were born have been either scientific or offensive. When Julian told me he was transitioning, I felt as though the rug had been pulled from beneath me again. I didn't know what to believe, what to feel, or even how to refer to Julian anymore.

It has taken me a long time to understand that Julian's identity is male and that he very much wants and needs me to reflect his identity back to him in a positive manner. In the early attachment relationship, the infant's sense of herself as being a "good baby" or "bad baby" is based upon what she sees reflected back to her in the eyes of her parents. Julian very much wanted me to be able to see *him* as he saw himself and to reflect it back to him as something good. I realized that Julian was still looking to me to help him to work through his identity development process. Julian needed me to help him with holding some of the chaos he was feeling, to perform the parental function of regulation and empathic witnessing, in order to help him to reorganize that chaos into a coherent whole that was his own unique identity. I had not been able to do this the first time Julian needed me. I feel blessed that I was being given a second chance to provide it to him.

One of the interesting developments that took place during this time was that I began getting requests to speak about being the mother of sexual minority twins at my job. As part of my presentation, I shared a photograph of actress, Brooke Shields and her husband that was taken shortly after she had given birth to their first daughter. She had undergone seven in-vitro treatments before she was finally able to become pregnant. There was no question that this baby was a wanted child and it clearly showed in the eyes of her parents. The look of delight in their eyes was obvious and this photograph proved to be an excellent way to make visible to the audience what this positive reflection looks like. This photograph also helped me to communicate to the audience what n*egative* parental reflection looks like by asking them to replace the delighted look on Brooke's face with one of disgust, hatred, neglect, or "you are an abomination against God." I would then ask the audience to imagine the impact of these words on this little infant's sense of herself. The question that I continue to pose to the participants when I speak is this: *Do we really stop and consider what messages we are sending to our children or the impact of those messages on their developing sense of self?*

I don't want to deny or diminish the huge challenge that is presented when a parent is asked to make a shift from knowing their child as one gender and then suddenly being asked to think of them as the other. It is difficult, and initially, it does not feel natural. I didn't know what to do with over twenty years of memories of Julian as my daughter. Those memories weren't going to just disappear and I no longer knew how to talk about them. For a long time, I felt so uncomfortable that I did everything I could to avoid having to say, or not say, "he" when referring to Julian. I remember that I would say Julian's name, or "my child," or "my offspring," or "Hey you!" Any term or phrase that would help me to avoid having to utter the word that caused me to feel so uncomfortable. But the fact that I was experiencing difficulty and dissonance did not negate the reality of what Julian needed from me. Something had to shift. It was an experience with saying a friend's name that finally helped me to make the shift.

I lost my friend and mentor to pancreatic cancer. He was only fifty-nine years old and one of the most brilliant people I ever knew. He was African-American, well over six feet tall, Muslim, and had a Muslim name. When I first met him everyone referred to him by his last name because it was so much easier to pronounce. He had accepted this reality about his name just as he had accepted the reality of being an African-American Muslim man in a Caucasian Christian society. However, he had told me once that his first name held a great deal of meaning to him because it represented his spiritual journey. I had a tremendous amount of respect and regard for him and decided one day that I was going to begin to refer to him by his first name. But when I tried, I found that I just couldn't say it. It didn't *sound* like a name to me. It wasn't Bill or Bob or Joe. It sounded garbled and I felt like I had marbles in my mouth when I tried to say it. I realized that I felt the same way whenever I tried to refer to Julian as "he." It just felt and sounded *wrong*.

But because of the deep regard I had for my friend, I kept trying to say his name. In time, I found that his name became more familiar to me and easier to say. I no longer felt like I was talking with a mouthful of marbles. It had become a name to me. I realized that my struggle learning to feel comfortable saying his unusual name was very similar to my struggle learning to feel comfortable referring to Julian as "he." I understand now that the struggle was more about the integration of something unfamiliar than it was about whether something was right or wrong. It should be noted that, as challenging as it was for me to shift my usage of gender pronouns when referring to Julian, I did not have to also contend with a new name for him as well. It is arguable whether our gender or our name plays a larger role in our identity, but both are certainly *fundamental* elements, and it requires a fundamental shift of perception for those of us who love someone who is transgender.

One last example that illustrates my shift in perspective about Julian, has to do with a meeting that took place between Julian and a Native American colleague of mine, and what I learned about the concept of the *Red Road*. Margaret Brigham, who is a member of the Ojibwa nation, is the creator and presenter of a highly regarded educational program on Native American cultural history and issues. One of the Native cultural concepts Margaret shares with participants is the concept of the Red Road, a concept I will do my best to accurately describe. Within the Ojibwa community, there is a belief that children select their parents prior to birth and are born into the world as complete beings with their Red Road, or life purpose, already determined. The Ojibwa people believe that following one's Red

Road is necessary for one to be in harmony and alignment with the Universe. In other words, there is a belief that you cannot experience happiness or self-esteem if you are not being authentic or if your actions interfere with another's ability to follow their destiny.

This concept underlies the Ojibwa community's practice of what cultural anthropologist, Jean Mavrelis, refers to as an "ethic of non-interference" with respect to the guidance of their children. The Ojibwa believe that when children require information or assistance to further their journey along their Red Road, they will ask the necessary questions. The role of parents and community, then, is one of paying close attention to their children and waiting for the questions (personal communication by M. Brigham, October, 2006). This belief has contributed to a child-centered orientation for both parents and the larger community that places a high priority on the needs of the child. It could be argued that the Ojibwa child's experience of being witnessed and held in this manner by both parent and community is similar to Ainsworth's (1978) concept of secure attachment, which was presented in the second chapter.

Aware of Margaret's cultural philosophy, when the opportunity to invite Julian to meet Margaret and have dinner with us came up, I jumped at the chance. I was still feeling uncomfortable with Julian being transgender and what other people would think of him, and of me. I was very curious to see how Margaret and Julian would relate to each other. I introduced them and then sat back and waited to see what would happen. I was amazed to see how at ease, open and warm Margaret's manner was toward Julian. They seemed to be really enjoying each other, and I found myself relaxing. At the end of the evening, I thanked Margaret for her graciousness with Julian and she looked at me and smiled. She said to me, "Maybe we have a bit of reincarnation in our culture, but to us, *a soul has no gender*" (personal communication by M. Brigham, October, 2006). I remember thinking to myself, "If Margaret can be comfortable with Julian as a male, then maybe I can too."

Margaret's statement, "a soul has no gender," has stayed with me. It has led to my thinking more deeply about souls, masculine identity, feminine identity, authenticity, and, mostly, about Red Roads. It also became the title of this book, as well as my presentation when I speak publicly about my experience. Since that dinner with Margaret, I have reconsidered memories of situations when I had regarded Julian and Kristin's behaviors as acting out, being difficult, or just wrong. I now understand that that these behaviors, when considered from the perspective that my children were trying their best to follow their respective Red Roads, were expressions of their desire and need to be authentic, not difficult. This perspective also made me think about the price that Julian and Kristin have had to pay in order to be true to the people they understand themselves to be. Hadn't I been struggling my entire life to do the same thing? I began to understand that Julian and Kristin each had their own journey to follow. *They* were the ones who were going to answer for how they had lived their lives, not me. Not only do I *not* answer for them, I *should not* answer for them. Their journeys are about their identities, not mine. What I *do* believe I will answer for is how well I have helped my children to stay true to their Red Roads.

I felt a sense of awe, and sadness, when I realized that my children have been willing to put everything on the line, including the love and acceptance of family and friends, their physical and emotional well-being, possibly even their lives, in order to be true to who they know themselves to be—to follow their Red Road. It was difficult for me to acknowledge that Julian and Kristin had wanted and needed my love, acceptance, and support to follow their Red Roads, and hadn't always gotten it. I am their mother and I had not always been there for them. I began to realize that if my children were willing to put themselves at tremendous risk in order to be authentic, then how could I possibly justify *not* doing everything within my ability to support them? I needed to be there for them now.

To bring Julian's story to a close, I would like to share a poem that he wrote a few years ago. Julian is very creative and articulate as a writer and as a public speaker. The impact upon me after reading this poem was that it opened up another way to understand this person who is my child: as a poet. I hope it will have a similar effect on the reader and possibly open up another way to understand the experience of people who are transgender.

I tried to be a girl.
I really mean it.
I tried to want to be graceful,
elegant, and sensual in that stereotypical way.
But like a motivational seminar for a
sugarfied sufferer of ADD,
it had absolutely no hold on me.
I tried to wear dresses.
But flats would not allow for the
recesses of kickball grand slam victory;
booted ball and its tendency to take
my patent leather shoes with it.
My shoulders, always broad
coming from Kansas grain-fed farmer stock
announcing: my soul's in strange housing.
I never cared for make-up.
Unless it was pale face paint and fake blood
and Halloween was on its way.
I craved big, black boots, crew cuts, tattoos,
chaps, choppers, and a winning smile.
I liked the look of dirt and grease under my skin,
in the crevasses between my thumb joint
and the rest of my hand.
Yet I yearn to understand
the tool that I was born with
and the mystery that surrounds it
and hold it differently.
Hold the woman and the man inside me, gently.

Kristen

Parenting Kristin was a very different experience from parenting Julian. Kristin was the child who let me experience most of the traditional milestones that parents are supposed to experience with their kids. She was the only one of my children who graduated from high school, although Michael and Julian went on to earn their GED diplomas. Kristin did well academically, lettered in women's fast-pitch softball, was a member of the Thespian Society, attended her senior prom, and developed a circle of friends with whom she still maintains contact.

Kristin also had a very special one-on-one relationship with her aunt that I think gave her an opportunity for a strong attachment bond with a nurturing female adult in addition to me. After I was divorced, my younger sister lived with me off and on for a couple of years. It was an arrangement that worked out well for me, for my sister, and for my children: my home gave her a place to stay when she was struggling as a young adult and in conflict with our parents, and she was a consistent daily presence in my children's lives when I was working or going to school. I know that she adored Kristin and I suspect that Kristin filled a need in my sister as well. I also suspect that my sister needed a human connection at that time in her life, and Kristin gave that to her. In many ways, it was a win-win situation for both of them. I believe that my sister's warm, positive reflection of her was a significant influence on Kristin's ability to develop better relationship skills than her siblings.

However, for all that she appeared to have going for her on the surface, Kristin had challenges, some of them deeply hidden. One concern was that Kristin's "good girl" role might be more of a reaction to seeing Michael and Julian's struggles than an expression of who she really was. Kristin had a great deal invested in being the good girl because it got her needs met. It probably provided a degree of protection for her as well. Another concern was that taking on the role of the good girl strongly influenced Kristin to internalize her emotions, particularly her anger or distress. It had always been difficult for Kristin to express her anger. Sometimes it would finally erupt and there would be some release for her, but for the most part, I don't think she felt that it was okay, or necessarily even safe, to express it. There were several factors that likely contributed to this. One factor was that Kristin had a very influential role model for internalizing her feelings in her grandmother. My mother tends to be more quiet and a listener by nature, and is somewhat overshadowed by my extroverted and expressive father. However, despite my father's role as head of the family, my mother truly is the matriarch. Therefore, being like Grandma and having Grandma's protection was important.

Kristin may have felt a need for protection for a number of reasons. One primary reason was her relationship with her father and her father's family. I worried about my children's vulnerability with their father and his family after we divorced because the children were associated with me. Their father was brought up in a very tribal family and you were either in or you were out—there was no in-between. Their father also carried an attitude of "you screw them before they screw you," which he modeled to my older son through such routine daily activities as the replacement of a burned out light bulb. He would go to the store and buy a new one, put the burned out bulb in the packaging, return it to the store as defective and get his money back. This kind of behavior was a family practice and I didn't like it, which made me even more of an outsider to them.

Kristin and Julian saw their father essentially every other weekend from the age of three to the age of ten, when he stopped seeing them. I still can't help but feel that his being out of their lives was a good thing, except for the pain that it has caused them. I don't believe that he regarded our children as little human beings that deserved to be raised well and cared for. Rather, our children were an obligation associated with me that he was stuck with and it showed in how he and his family treated them. It seemed that almost every time they came back from a visitation with their father, Kristin or Julian would suddenly start getting hurt at school and it would take days before they would finally tell me that "Daddy said something about you and he told me not to tell you." I would confront their father, but he usually denied it and I felt like there was nothing I could do. So, come the next visitation weekend, they were at their father's again.

It was a different experience for my elder son, Michael. I suspect this was partly because he was born male and partly because I allowed Michael to live with his father when he was eight years old. He had always been close to his father and I thought that maybe little boys needed to be with their dads. I had also thought that if their father had some involvement in the raising of the kids, he might be more supportive of me. My mother was very much against the idea and told me, "You don't split them up." I told her that children were not possessions and maybe Michael would be happier with his father.

This is one decision that I will regret for the rest of my life. My ex-husband was not a good parent. But more importantly, I thought so little of myself that I didn't understand or appreciate that little boys needed their mothers even more than they needed their fathers. I let my son go and the break in our connection has never been fully restored. Because he lived with his father, Michael was one of the tribe. Because they lived with and were associated with their mother, Kristin and Julian were not. Sadly, this familial tribalism has had a negative affect on the relationship between Michael, Julian, and Kristin, and it has created a divide that should not exist between siblings.

Kristin and Julian stopped seeing their father one weekend after an incident when he came up to pick them up at my home. They were late finishing their breakfast and were not ready to go when their father arrived. When they came out of the house about ten minutes later to get into the car, he had thrown their suitcases across the lawn and told them that they were not going to spend the weekend with him. He told Julian and Kristin that it was their fault and that their mother had put them up to it. I remember I walked outside, picked up their suitcases, and took the kids back into the house as their father drove away. I sat them down and told them, "People who love you don't treat you like that." Even though I knew you aren't supposed to say negative things about the other parent, I was afraid that they were going to equate love with abuse.

Neither Kristin nor Julian has any kind of relationship with their father. I don't anticipate that they ever will. It has created a strain between Kristin and Michael, who had always shared a close relationship, because Michael remains fiercely loyal to his father. I carry a tremendous amount of sadness and regret when I consider how difficult navigating between two families must have been for my children. They certainly didn't get much help from many of the so-called adult members of their family. I wish more parents thought about things like this when they consider divorce. If we can't stay together and work it out, then we ought to at least commit to do what is best for our children. Further, we ought to put some accountability into our court system to ensure that this happens.

It is difficult for me to acknowledge that I placed my own needs over the needs of my children. I felt overwhelmed carrying the responsibility for three young children, working, trying to go to school to get a better job, keeping up a household, and also finding time to go out, have fun, and be in a relationship. I *needed* those weekends when my kids went to their father's to recharge, and I sent my children to their father every other weekend so I could have that time. However, I was also compelled to send them to their father's by law. Even when I had reason to suspect that my ex-husband and his family were being abusive to my children and tried to limit visitation, I was told by the judge that, "there was no law against mental abuse," and my petition was denied.

I don't know if Kristin and Julian understood the extent to which I did try to protect them. What I think they *did* know was that not much protection was forthcoming and they had to figure out how to survive those weekends. They way they chose to survive them was to not tell me about what was happening. If they did tell me, the chances were pretty good that I was going to confront their father, and when the next weekend visitation arrived, they would end up back with their father and his family with all hell breaking loose. It was better to just keep your mouth shut. Adding to the complexity, Julian and Kristin's experiences with their father weren't all negative. They loved their father and their brother. And it was fun to be a member of the tribe because there were motorcycles to ride and cousins to play with. But if something went wrong, Julian and Kristin bore the brunt of it.

Kristin spent much of high school hanging out at the local fire department, along with her best friend who shared the same name, but went by the nickname, "Mouse." "The two Kristins," as I referred to them, were very close and spent a great deal of time together. Mouse's dad was a fireman and Kristin wanted to be one too, going as far as beginning training to be an Emergency Medical Technician (EMT). Kristin was so into fire fighting that I always got her something with a fire truck theme as part of her Christmas gift each year.

Kristin's closeness with Mouse was the first signal I noticed that made me wonder about the nature of their relationship. I remember one occasion where I walked into our family room and both girls were sitting on the floor watching television. They were sitting much closer together than one would expect friends to sit, and I noticed it. But I let it go because I had no reason to go any further with it. I wonder now, had I been more educated and aware and understood what "questioning" behavior looked like, whether I would have been able to respond differently when Kristin's behavior began to shift. I wonder if I might have been able to sit down with her and talk about what I noticed, describe questioning behavior to her, and discuss sexuality and sexual identity.

That might also have been an opportunity for me to let Kristin know that I was there for her and that she could come to me for anything. This is a crucial message that *all* parents need to be communicating to their children because research suggests that children who believe they can turn to their parents for assistance have much better developmental outcomes than children who believe they cannot. I did not feel that I could go to my parents for help—particularly not for anything controversial. In my youth, parents were your judges, not your confidants. Because of that belief, I struggled on my own, and the choices I ultimately made were not always in my best interests. How could they be? I was working with erroneous information.

The first changes in Kristin's behavior occurred about the same time that Julian was coming out (very publicly) that she was lesbian. Kristin and Julian had never been particularly close to each other growing up, even though they shared a great deal. They had been very competitive with each other—a family trait that was exacerbated by circumstance. My siblings and I were also competitive with each other, especially the sisters. I used to joke that our family was like the Kennedy family only without the money. To this day, my father still playfully encourages this competition by letting us know who called first on his birthday, who gave the best gift, and who is currently in first position on the will.

Because of my own competitive relationship with my siblings, I didn't understand that the kind of competition I was seeing between Kristin and Julian could also be an indicator that something troubling was going on. I did not understand that one reason people, particularly siblings, compete with each other is over needed resources. If those resources are perceived as limited, the competition can become more serious, and it can get nasty. The limited resource that my children were competing for was their mother. They wanted my time, my attention, and my love, and it seemed as though there was never enough for everyone. It is still very, very hard to acknowledge this. It is very hard to even write the words: my chest is tight, and I am trying not to cry. I have noted previously in this work that I could not imagine how Kristin and Julian must have felt at times. But the fact is that I *do* know how they felt sometimes. I now know that I have felt such despair. It almost kills me to know that I contributed to them feeling that way too. It makes me sad and angry to now understand that my own ignorance and disenfranchised grief got in the way of my being present and attuned to my children, and we all lost out.

There was another aspect of the competition between Kristin and Julian that I missed and it had to do with their differing ways of working through their sexual and gender identities. I believe the competition or conflict between Kristin and Julian centered on differences in temperament, coping or adaptation styles, and a lack of feeling secure. Kristin's coping skills were very much wrapped up in being the good girl and keeping everybody happy. Therefore, I have to believe that Julian's more extroverted and direct way of coping had to have been experienced by Kristin as threatening to her carefully constructed sense of security. Julian was rocking the boat and Kristin was trying hard to keep it afloat.

I also believe that Kristin resented Julian at times because his behaviors often negatively impacted her ability to get her needs met. If I was upset about something going on with Julian, it usually meant there was less of me available for Kristin. And it was easy for me to overlook Kristin because she *was* the good girl. She didn't get as much of my time because Michael and Julian were using it up. I can imagine that she blamed Julian and it likely affected their level of closeness. I don't think there was any way that Kristin could have understood, or even cared, what Julian was going through. She was focused on trying to make it through herself. They were competitors, not allies.

I have to wonder, if I'd had the appropriate knowledge and awareness, whether I would have been able to recognize their competition as a signal that they needed more of my attention. I ask myself whether responding with more attention would have resulted in my either recognizing sooner what was going on with my children or in my creating a more secure relationship with them, such that they might have been able to confide in me sooner and ask for help. It leaves me wondering, if I had been more present to them, would Kristin and Julian have experienced a closer and happier relationship with each other? Or, are they just two very different people with very different lives? I may never know.

As Kristin began her own identity process of moving away from being the good girl to becoming more authentic, she went through a number of phases before she began to acknowledge her sexual orientation. The most challenging of these phases, from my perspective, was her "religion phase," and the most frightening was when she attempted suicide. During her religion phase, she became deeply involved in a church youth group and began avidly listening to Christian music. I remember feeling guarded and uncomfortable because Kristin wanted me to join this church as well. I also felt resentment because I thought that Kristin was putting me in the position in which I had to attend her church functions or risk looking like a bad mother. I felt manipulated and I did not like it.

I didn't understand that hyper-religiosity was a phase some LGBTQ individuals experience in an attempt to "not be gay." This strategy is very similar to the *bargaining* stage in the grief process: "God, I will go to church every Sunday if you will get rid of this feeling in me." This strategy works for a very few, as evidenced by the occasional news story about someone who claims to have been "cured" of their homosexuality. But of greater concern is the possibility that the LGBTQ individual is at risk for additional assaults to their self-esteem and manipulation by counselors or church groups who advertise "anti-homosexuality" treatment programs and are looking for success stories to make their case. Kristin's religious phase lasted for about a year. As is often the case with LGBTQ individuals who engage in hyper-religiosity as a strategy, once she came out, Kristin gradually stopped attending church.

After Kristin graduated from high school, she continued to live at home and worked as a trainer for a local fast food restaurant chain. She had abruptly dropped out of the EMT program with no explanation, she was no longer involved with the church group, and "the two Kristins" were no longer friends. She wouldn't say why, but she seemed happy, so I let it go. I didn't see any reason for worry. Kristin was doing well in her job and had progressed to a lead trainer preparing the crews for store openings. Most of the employees were about the same age as Kristin. She had a way of presenting the information that worked with this group, and her abilities were quickly recognized and rewarded. Everything seemed to be fine, until one weekend when she just seemed to lose it.

Kristin had developed the hobby of making quilts and giving them as gifts, including a beautiful quilt she gave me one year for Christmas. She also had one of her quilts on her own bed. One afternoon I was chilled and not feeling well and I took the quilt off her bed and put it on my bed to try and get warm. My husband came home and got into bed with me and eventually we became intimate. Kristin came home during this time and was furious at me. She was yelling that I had defiled her blanket and was disgusting. I could not figure out what in the hell was going on with her. I remember I responded by lecturing her to show some respect as I was her mother and she was living in my house, and said to her, "For God's sake, it's just a stupid blanket." But it *wasn't* just a stupid blanket to Kristin, and a short time later, she came into the kitchen and tearfully told me that she needed to go to the hospital because she had taken a bottle of ibuprofen.

I was stunned. I was also angry because I felt like I was being manipulated again. My husband and I took Kristin to the emergency room. Her stomach was pumped and we met with a social worker. Kristin was admitted to the psychiatric ward and remained there for almost two months. When she was released, she was transferred to a day program that provided structure and group therapy during the day and allowed patients to go home at night. The program was designed to help patients make a more gradual transition from hospital confinement to resuming daily life. It was while she was in this program that I was first made aware that Kristin had experienced a number of dissociative episodes during group therapy sessions, some lasting up to an hour. I remembered that, during her religious phase, Kristin had had an incident where she almost elbowed a woman who was rubbing her shoulders. I thought that it had something to do with being touched and I told Kristin that she needed to understand why she had reacted as she had. But Kristin wasn't ready. She said, "I know there's something there, Mom, but I don't want to know what it is." I remember telling her that if she didn't look at it, it would affect every relationship she had for the rest of her life. She said she understood, but she just couldn't go there.

I could not understand Kristin's response. I was in analysis at that time and coming to understand that unresolved issues were trouble. I was also vaguely troubled because dissociative disorders were often associated with sexual abuse. Further, I remembered that the weight issues and lack of self-care that I had observed in Julian when he was younger were also indicators of sexual abuse. But I could not fathom how it could possibly be true that they might have been molested, and by who? And how could I not know? I felt troubled because I understood that sexual abuse was often a family legacy affecting multiple generations. But where would this legacy have come from? We were a "good family" and there was no way something like this could have happened. I knew I had some issues, but *nothing* like sexual abuse.

The only memory of that kind I had involved a "touching incident" when I was about ten years old, involving the owner of a produce farm where I worked in the summers. When I first started working there, the farmer had given me the nickname, "Sunshine," and he always called me that. When the incident took place, he asked me if I was his Sunshine as he touched me between my legs. I shook my head no and he left me alone. But as he walked away, he told me that I wasn't his Sunshine anymore. I remembered feeling so bad because I had liked that he had a nickname for me. It made me feel special and I didn't want to lose that special status. It took me two years to finally tell my mother what happened. And when I did, her response was, "Well, what good does it do to tell me now?" I don't have any memory of how I felt at that time, but I am fairly certain that I felt shame. I think that was the last time I went to my mother with something that really troubled me because I didn't want to feel that kind of shame again. I also didn't understand until much later that I wasn't really "special" to that farmer, he was grooming me to accept his sexual advances.

I continued to feel very unsettled. I knew there was a family legacy of not talking about issues, but where was the sexual abuse history that might explain what was going on with my children? It could not have been the result of just this one incident. Besides, nothing had really happened; it had been a touch, not a rape, and he'd walked away when I said no. It just didn't make sense. I knew I'd had boundary issues all through my adolescence and felt like anybody could just walk over me, but I regarded those issues as just more evidence of my character flaws. It never occurred to me that my issues could have been indicators of sexual abuse. So, even though I was suspicious, because neither Kristin nor Julian had made any specific allegations, it seemed more likely that they were just acting out and I let it go. Although I have since come to understand and have had to deal with the fact that I was sexually molested by a doctor as a child, if Julian and Kristin share a similar history, it remains an unresolved issue. I have come to respect their right to determine when and if they ever need to examine their history. My job is to set an example by doing that work myself and showing them how, and to be there to support them if they choose to do so.

One of the first experiences that signaled the beginning of my transition away from being a helpless victim to a powerful and protective mother occurred after Kristin completed her hospitalization and prepared to return to her training job. When she was first hospitalized, we made sure that Kristin submitted a request for Family Leave benefits and provided all the appropriate documentation to her employer. During this time, I was working as an Equal Employment Opportunity (EEO) investigator. I dealt with employee complaints of civil rights harassment and discrimination in the workplace, including disability complaints and medical accommodation issues. Therefore, I was very familiar with the Family Leave law and made sure that Kristin's absence was well documented.

The day that Kristin returned to work, I got a call from her. Her voice was shaking and she said, "Mom, I think I'm getting screwed over." She told me that her manager had taken her into a room and told her that she was no longer a trainer. She was also told that she could either accept a position at one of the stores with a pay cut or she could quit. When Kristin told me this, I remember feeling an explosion of white-hot but controlled fury. I had never felt such anger or such clarity in my entire life. It was the first time I had ever experienced what I now know is the mother lioness rage that says, "If you mess with my baby, I will rip your throat out."

I remember asking Kristin in this very calm voice whether the manager was there. When she told me that he was, I said, "Put him on the phone." When he got on the phone, I introduced myself as Kristin's mother. I told him that I was also an EEO manager for a large corporation, and that his organization was in serious violation of at least nine elements of the federal Family Medical Leave Act (FMLA) that I could think of off the top of my head. I said that unless Kristin was placed back in the job she had held previous to her FMLA leave by the end of that business day, I would be visiting his office first thing Monday morning with Kristin and my attorney. The manager said that he didn't like being threatened. I responded, "I assure you, sir, this is no threat. I know the law better than you do and I know who to call." He then said, "Hold on a minute, I hired Kristin and I had no idea this was going on." I told him that he should have known what his managers were doing because it was illegal and he was ultimately responsible. He asked me to give him a little time to look into the situation and he would get back to me. Kristin called me a couple of hours later and said, "They're scared of you, Mom, and I got my job back." I said, "Good thing for them." Kristin told me later that one of her co-workers had told her that the company had "picked on the wrong person to screw with."

I had never in my life ever felt that kind of rage and I *knew* what it was the moment I felt it. I *felt* like a lioness. I had never in my life felt so full of power. I was amazed to experience anger as a tool that could be used skillfully, that *I* could use skillfully, for good purpose. I had always experienced anger as negative, destructive, or out-of-control, never appropriate. I had always felt helpless to defend against other people's agendas and misuse of anger all my life. But in this moment, powered by anger and seemingly without even thinking, I took in the situation and then acted with clarity and certainty. I can't say I was confident because I wasn't thinking that way. It was like I just moved into high gear and I was focused on one thing—protecting my child.

Afterward, I told my husband what had transpired. He looked at me and shook his head and said, "Don't you think Kristin needs to learn to do that for herself?" And I said, "Yes. But first, she needed to see me do it. She needed to see that her mother thought she was worth fighting for and defending. Now, my task will be to step back and let her do it on her own next time." I wondered why this situation had played out the way it did. Why did I suddenly have the ability to speak up this time? I cannot say for certain. However, my sense is that I had done enough work in analysis, and had a stable relationship, or secure base, to use Bowlby's (1988) terminology, that it was now possible for the good mothering attributes within me to finally be expressed. Regardless of the reason, there is no doubt that this had been a pivotal moment for me.

Kristin saw a therapist for almost two years after her hospitalization. She did not come out as a lesbian during that time to either me or to her therapist, so I still didn't fully understand what was going on for her. But at least she was doing better. Kristin continued to do better and eventually moved into her own apartment later that year. Remembering my own premature emancipation at age eighteen (while still in high school) as well as Michael and Julian's premature separations, I had told Kristin that I wanted her to move out when she was really ready and not before. I also told her that someday she did have to go out on her own. It was my job as her parent to turn up the heat a little at a time, like raising her rent, such that she would become motivated to go out and live her life. But it was important to me that she had an appropriate termination to her childhood. I didn't want her to make the same mistake I did.

Kristin finally came out as a lesbian about a year after she moved out. She told me because she had a girlfriend, Danielle, that she wanted me to meet. When Kristin told me, I remember thinking, "*Oh God, not you too.*" I can imagine that my reaction showed on my face and I can also imagine how much it hurt Kristin. I now understand just how hard it was for her to tell me. She knew that telling me meant that I would be losing my illusion of having a "good child." It was not easy for Kristin to assert herself or to ask for what she needed or wanted, particularly if she believed that it might disappoint someone she cared about. But Kristin had suppressed her needs and desires for the sake of safety, stability, or affection for too long. If she was ever going to move fully into adulthood and become an authentic person, she had to learn to speak up on her own behalf.

Whether or not Kristin consciously realized that she was playing the role of the good girl, I believe she knew unconsciously. The time finally came for the good girl to go, and she was escorted out with a vengeance! Kristin still gets irritated when I describe this time as her "adolescent rebellion" period, but I believe it truly was. Kristin never rebelled against anything as a child or adolescent, and now I saw her trying to learn how to be assertive, to decide things for herself, to have her own opinions, and to live her own life. As common a developmental task as that may sound for most people, Kristin was trying to accomplish this with the additional anxieties of working against long-established defenses of compliance and suppression, and more significantly, fear that she would lose the sense of belonging and acceptance of the family she loved and needed if she revealed that she was lesbian.

That is a lot for a young person to have to manage. I remember how difficult it was for Kristin to tell her grandparents. But it was important to her to tell them, and she did tell them, as well as each member of the family. Kristin said it was one of the hardest things she ever had to do. I think about how *every* LGBTQ young person has to manage this kind of anxiety as they go through the process of deciding when to tell their parents. They go through it again and again with *every* family member that they choose to tell, and with *every* friendship that they'd like to be real or authentic, and with *every* person they think might find out anyway. I feel exhausted just thinking about it. How is there energy for anything else in life? Then I consider that, in addition, LGBTQ individuals have to *always* be on the alert about being "forcibly outed" (when someone discloses your sexual orientation or gender identity without your knowledge or permission), because their safety could be compromised. I am beginning to understand why the suicide rate is three times higher for LGBTQ children than for heterosexual children. That is a burden no heterosexual person *ever* has to think about.

Kristin and Danielle were together for almost nine years, and in that time, became the parents of two young sons. I tried to develop a good relationship with Danielle, but it was not easy for me, or for the family. Danielle came into the relationship with a lot of challenges, both social and emotional, and she was not comfortable around people. Danielle did not experience much of a family life as a child and did not know how to relate to a large, boisterous, and opinionated family such as ours. Her social skills were such that she was awkward, and she often said or did things that alienated or offended someone in the family. Further, Kristin defended Danielle and it put a severe strain on my relationship with her.

I really did not like Danielle at first. I wondered why my daughter would choose a partner who was so socially and emotionally challenged, rather than someone who could stand on her own and who came to the relationship as an equal. I wondered if this was an indication of how Kristin saw herself. Was she looking for someone to take care of? Was she looking for someone who would never leave her and would be loyal to her? Was she punishing me for not being the mother she had wanted? I felt like it was difficult enough that she was lesbian, but did she have to have a wacky girlfriend as well?

Everything seemed to be a battle with Danielle and Kristin. They were committed vegans in a family of meat-eaters, so family or holiday meals became difficult. Danielle exerted a great deal control over Kristin and everything had to be on her terms. It got to a point where no one wanted to invite them to family gatherings. It seemed as though there was no ground upon which we could find some kind of commonality upon which to build a relationship. I felt like I was once again stuck between the rock and the hard place. Either I had to learn to manage my frustration dealing with Danielle, or I might lose my daughter. I didn't have to let it play out to know what Kristin's decision would be if she was forced to make a choice. It seemed like we were in for an endless stalemate.

The stalemate might have remained endless, but then I was diagnosed with cancer in March 2003. I was still reeling from my diagnosis when Kristin announced that she was pregnant. I found out on Mother's Day, when Kristin and Danielle handed me a package containing a silver picture frame inscribed with "I love Grandma" and an ultrasound printout. I remember I was stunned and a little confused because I had no idea that Kristin and Danielle were planning a family. I also remember feeling somewhat disappointed because it meant that my fantasy that Danielle and lesbianism were just a phase was over. Danielle might be here to stay. But I was also deeply moved, especially when Kristin tearfully told me that she was scared that she was going to have this child and I might not be around to share it with her. In that moment, I realized that my daughter could not have given me a greater gift, or a greater reason to live. We had found our common ground. I was not going anywhere with a grandbaby on the way!

But it was still an uneasy situation—and the coming of a grandchild just added to the intensity. I wanted to be in the delivery room at the birth, but Danielle and Kristin said no. They wouldn't tell anyone whether it was a boy or girl. They wouldn't tell anyone the names they were considering. I felt left out of everything and yet I was told they wanted me to be a part of it. I felt useless and frustrated. I was tired from the chemo and didn't have the energy to battle. I was also scared that I might not beat the cancer, and worried about what it would be like for my children if I died. I didn't want them to carry a bunch of emotional baggage throughout their lives and started thinking about how to have a conversation with them about my concerns. That desire began to influence how I interacted with my children.

One afternoon shortly before the birth, Kristin asked me to meet her and Danielle for coffee. I don't recall whether the purpose of meeting was to talk seriously or whether it just came up, but in an open moment, Danielle looked at me and said, "Do you know what I'm most afraid of? I'm afraid that if something were to happen to Kristin, you would come and try to take the baby away from me." I remember that I instinctively reached out and took Danielle's hand and said, "I would never do that to you, unless you gave me a reason to. I don't want to be this baby's mother, I want to be the grandmother." It was the first time that I had an interaction with Danielle when I felt like she had been able to be open and direct about what she was feeling. It made a huge difference for me, possibly because I caught a glimpse of the person behind the defenses.

When my grandson, Joshua, was born, I didn't find out until after he had arrived. I was a little hurt that they didn't call me on the way to the hospital, but I had to let that go. I decided to rally a family response and called my parents, Michael, and Julian and asked if they wanted to go to the hospital to see the baby. I was pleased when they all agreed. I held my new grandson for a few minutes, marveling at how much he looked like Kristin. I then handed Joshua to my mother. I knew what a difficult time my parents were having with the acceptance process. I also knew my mother and I shared a deep love of babies. I had a feeling that if she held the baby, the ice would be broken and her connection to Kristin could begin to be reestablished. I was right and it was lovely to watch my mother fall in love with her great-grandson. I remember smiling to myself, and feeling proud for sublimating the almost overwhelming urge to keep that baby to myself so that his place in the family could be established.

Kristin looked tired. Joshua's birth had been a difficult experience for both her and Danielle. They had planned the entire birth experience and wanted certain things to happen: they wanted to have soft music playing during the birth, Danielle was supposed to cut the baby's cord, and they had planned to have everyone leave them alone for a time after the birth so they could have some quiet bonding time with the baby. It didn't happen. Kristin went into labor during a severe rainstorm. Then Kristin's labor just stalled out and Danielle starting worrying that the baby wasn't going to come out. The baby began to go into distress and an emergency Csection was performed. There was no soft music, there was no quiet bonding time, and the doctor cut the cord. I remember Kristin and Danielle both saying how difficult the experience was. I looked at them, smiled and said, "You are young, Grasshopper, but you will learn. Sometimes it is good to have Grandmother in the delivery room!"

One of the many gifts that has come from Joshua' birth, and, eighteen months later, the birth of Danielle's son, Logan, is that their existence provided the opportunity for me to strengthen my connection with Kristin, and to also work toward developing a sense of compassion for Danielle. It happened because I got to see Danielle in a different way than I had seen her before, as a mother. One of the things I was amazed to learn from Kristin was the process that she and Danielle went through in order to have their children, particularly as it compares to the "normal" means through which people come to have children.

The State of Washington, currently one of only a few states to recognize same-sex families and same-sex adoption rights, recently passed a law with respect to parental rights and artificial insemination. The law states something to the effect that if it could be established that an individual had no intention of being a parent, then there were no parental rights for them to relinquish. Kristin and Danielle each used artificial insemination to get pregnant. In order to establish that there was no intent on the part of the sperm donors to parent, they paid the donors five dollars and got a receipt! They also formally adopted each other's biological child in order to establish and protect their legal right to be a family. I remember thinking that Kristin and Danielle had put more thought into having children than probably ninety percent of the population, including me. They had carefully researched the options available to them, they laid out their plan, and now they had two beautiful sons. I was impressed.

I continued to have challenges with Danielle. Some of the challenges had to do with Danielle being the stay-at-home "Mommy" and Kristin being the going-to-work "Mama." I felt like the paternal rather than maternal grandmother. Danielle made all the rules with respect to the baby and it seemed like I couldn't do anything right. I didn't wash my hands enough. I let the baby put his fingers in my mouth. I bought the wrong kinds of toys. I even bought the wrong kind of baby shampoo! I felt frustrated and wondered if Joshua would even know who I was or whether I really would have a place in his life. I was fortunate in that a good friend told me that her daughter-in-law was just like Danielle. She said that if I wanted to have a relationship with my grandson, I needed to do the opposite of what Danielle, unconsciously, was trying to get me to do, which was reject her. Danielle was used to people rejecting her and her defenses were set up to manage rejection. Therefore, rejection was familiar to her, and familiarity provides some measure of comfort. If something is comforting, the chances are pretty good that it will get repeated, particularly under conditions of stress. I can imagine that the experience of trying to find a place for yourself in a strong-willed family when you had no experience with families felt very stressful to Danielle.

I started thinking about the situation and what I wanted from it. I knew I wanted a good relationship with my daughter and I knew I wanted to be a part of my grandsons' lives. I was also tired of everything being a fight in my life. I thought if it was important to me that Danielle be a good mother, then shouldn't I be trying to help her, rather than criticize her? I decided that I was going to focus more on what Danielle did well, rather than what I didn't like. One other commitment I made to myself was that I would never distinguish between Kristin and Danielle's children. They are *both* my grandsons. I made it a point that Logan and Joshua both got my attention. I did that for Logan, primarily, but also for Danielle, so that she might see that I valued her child, and therefore her, as much as I valued my own child. I think Danielle has been searching for acceptance for a very long time. Unfortunately, the rigid and controlling aspects of her personality defenses are such that she often drives people away, rather than toward her. I thought that working on establishing a good relationship with Danielle might help her to let go of some of that rigidity. I thought it was at least worth a try.

One example of this strategy occurred on Danielle's birthday. I had noted it on my calendar from the previous year because Kristin had reminded me to remember her birthday. I decided to send Danielle a card and a little gift. I also didn't tell Kristin what I had done. Instead, I decided to just wait and see if there was any response from either Kristin or Danielle. I waited for about a month, but one day, Danielle made a comment about being surprised that I remembered her birthday. She said she had accused Kristin of reminding me about her birthday, but Kristin said that she was surprised as well. I smiled to myself because this was validation that my strategy had been effective. If I was willing to make the effort, as challenging as that could be at times, there was a possibility that I might be able to have a positive effect on Danielle. For the sake of my daughter and my grandsons, I was willing to make the effort.

The result of this effort is the deep bond that I have with my daughter and my grandchildren. However, the relationship between Kristin and Danielle did not last. After what I know was a great deal of soul-searching, Kristin ended her relationship with Danielle. I believe it was the right decision. I learned from Kristin that during the course of their relationship, Danielle had engaged in both physical and emotional intimidation in her efforts to exert control over Kristin, and with her history of being compliant, Kristin slowly lost her own voice. I have to acknowledge that it has been deeply gratifying to see my daughter re-discover her voice and her authority and stand up for both herself and her children. Kristin now has primary custody of Joshua and Logan, and Danielle has regular visitation with them. Kristin has also entered into a new relationship. Her partner, a county sheriff, and her young daughter have quickly become members of the family. It looks and feels to me like a happy relationship. I can see it in my daughter, and in my grandsons.

Sometimes when I reflect upon the evolution of my relationship with Kristin, I can't help but feel a sense of amazement about what I have been privileged to learn from this person who is my daughter, and just how profoundly she has influenced who I am at this point in my life. I have come to respect Kristin even more deeply and admire the integrity with which she tries to live her life. I know that this integrity has been hard won. It was a difficult journey at times, but we all came through to the other side, stronger and closer than we were before. I am looking forward to the next phase of the journey.

Re-Discovering the Voice of my Body

Frankly, for most of my life I regarded my body not as the sacred housing for my soul, but as an enemy—a willful enemy that could not be trusted and therefore required constant vigilance and discipline. Although I had been a skinny kid, I was born into a family of big eaters. My mother is an excellent cook. She made homemade bread, butter, jams, and countless preserved fruits and vegetables as I was growing up and I learned how to cook from her. I didn't appreciate physical activity nearly as much as I did eating. I was somewhat introverted and curling up in front of the electric wall heater with a good book was far more appealing to me than going outside and playing with other kids. By adolescence, I wasn't a skinny kid anymore and I became self-conscious about my body. I often looked at myself in the mirror with disgust and wished I could just be smaller.

Like many adolescent girls, my self-esteem was strongly associated with my body size. I struggled with my weight and self-esteem all through high school. By age twenty, I had married, given birth to three babies, and weighed over two hundred pounds. My then-husband's response was that he didn't care if I weighed three hundred pounds. But that wasn't particularly comforting to me. I realize now that his comment was another example of people responding to me out of their own needs, not mine. He didn't really see me, and he certainly wasn't empathic to what I was feeling. He was thinking about his own sense of security. He was a long-haul truck driver and was sometimes on the road for three weeks at a time. If his wife was fat, he didn't have to worry about other men. What he should have worried about was his wife's happiness. I was twenty-two years old when my children's father and I were divorced. Suddenly I was an overweight single mother with three children and a high school education.

I was also just twenty-two years old when I had a hysterectomy in December 1980. I had been fortunate to be one of those women who'd had a relatively easy time with my periods all through adolescence. But I had recently begun to bleed heavily and went to a doctor. The doctor was an older man; I recall him as being in his late sixties. He ran a few tests and tried several different treatments, but nothing seemed to work. He finally told me that, as I had three children and had said I didn't want any more, my uterus had served its purpose and was now, in effect, useless and I should "just get rid of it." I was only twenty-two and he was a doctor. I did as he said. I didn't question him and I didn't ask for a second opinion. I didn't stop to consider that this procedure was a traumatic invasion of my body and I should not allow such an invasion unless it was absolutely necessary. But doctors had been invading my body since I was three years old. I was only twenty-two years old, he was the authority, and I did as I was told.

When I lost my uterus, I also lost all connection to the rhythms and cycles of my body because I no longer had a menstrual period each month. At the time I thought it was great that I wouldn't have to deal with the monthly hassle, but I had no idea then of what I was actually losing. I had been disconnected from my inner voice earlier in childhood and now I had become disconnected from my embodied voice as well. I was, in effect, completely detached from myself, clueless and voiceless. I existed like that for over twenty-five years, until I was diagnosed with colon cancer in 2003. I had been in tremendous emotional pain for a long, but it had gone unrecognized. Now, my unconscious was turning up the volume and it was time for me to pay attention. Since my diagnosis, as I have come to terms dealing with and, ultimately, surviving cancer, I have also come to find a sense of peace with respect to my body. In the process, I also began to rediscover my voice, and in the most unlikely of ways—through an ostomy bag.

It was a co-worker whose husband had a similar surgery, not the medical professionals, who provided me with the information I needed to manage life with an ostomy. An ostomy is a surgical procedure in which stool is diverted to a bag on the outside of the body to allow the bowel sufficient time to heal from surgery and additional chemotherapy. My co-worker came into my office one day shortly before my surgery with an ostomy bag and some literature. She showed me what an ostomy bag looked like, what to do, and talked about what it was like to live with one. She, not the medical professionals, gave me what was perhaps the best piece of advice for how to live with an ostomy. She said to me, "You just make up your mind to deal with it, and you don't look back." I deeply valued that advice because, despite the assistance of an ostomy nurse, I never did have an easy time during the six months I had the ostomy, and that bit of advice helped me get through it.

There were many occurrences of what I came to call "bag failures" that sometimes pushed me to the edge of my ability to cope. Every four to five days the bag had to be changed, which involved replacing a patch that connects the bag to your body. No matter how careful I was, I could never seem to consistently get a good seal when I applied that patch and the seal would often rupture, sometimes at the most inconvenient times. Because I never knew when it was going to fail, it got to a point at which I was apprehensive about attending meetings, or being too far away from home, because I lived almost two hours from my work location. I learned to carry my version of a diaper bag with extra supplies in case the bag leaked. I carried at least three complete sets of bags and seals, diaper wipes, and a change of clothes because I had to be prepared. On one occasion, I had three bag failures in one day, ran out of supplies, and had to drive for two hours with acidic stool blistering my skin until I could get home, clean up, and change the bag. Another time I was stuck in a Starbucks bathroom, with people pounding on the door, while I frantically tried to get myself put back together. Yet another time, I was stuck in a bathroom at work because the bag failed and I had left my supplies in my car. I remember sitting in one of the bathroom stalls with my cell phone and my keys, wondering if I was desperate enough to slide the keys under the stall and ask the next person who walked in to go to my car and get my bag. You get to the point where you have to laugh about it or you will go crazy.

I find it sad, ironic, and particularly relevant to this inquiry to note that much of the difficulty I experienced with bag failures was, I believe, largely due to the fact that the adhesives used to secure the bag to the ostomy site were designed for placement on an abdomen that is flat and firm. I learned from my ostomy nurse that bag failures were a common problem, which is why there was a need for ostomy nurses. She had all sorts of creative fixes to help me try to get a better fit and seal, but with limited success. I believe this was because the real problem, a mismatch between reality and design, was not even being addressed.

It has been my observation that most people do not have a firm, flat abdomen, particularly those who are of the age that they are dealing with colon cancer. Given that cancer treatment is challenging enough, it is very puzzling to me why there isn't a greater emphasis to create products that really fit the conditions of the need, and which could help make a difficult experience much less difficult. The relevancy to this inquiry is that I suspect that the reason this does not occur is due to a lack of empathy associated with disenfranchised grief. I don't believe that the medical professionals who develop products such as ostomy bags really consider the *human beings* who have to use the products they design. Because if they *did* actually put themselves in the place of the patient, and thought about how *they* would feel if *they* were having a romantic dinner with the love of their life, or presenting at an important meeting, or trying to carry a small child and a bag of groceries, or driving on the freeway during rush hour when the bag suddenly ruptures, at the very least, there would be better-designed ostomy bags. This consequence of disenfranchised grief needs to be recognized and addressed.

However, my ostomy bag experience was also a gift, because it was the means by which I began to rediscover my lost voices. In a unique way, that ostomy bag was a "window to my soul." It became the access point (which had been lost to me when I stopped menstruating) through which I was able to once again see the physical rhythms and cycles of my body, and reconnect to my embodied voice. It happened because of a mix-up on an order of ostomy supplies. One of the services the ostomy nurse provides for the patient is education on how to order the necessary supplies, including the ostomy bag itself. The supplier provides a large and somewhat overwhelming array of choices in ostomy bags. One choice is an opaque bag, which is designed to hide the contents. Given that I was not particularly interested in having to look at the contents, I ordered the opaque bags. However, when the package arrived, the bags were not opaque, they were clear.

I could not believe it when I realized the mistake. I was in the middle of chemotherapy and wasn't feeling very good. Because of the high number of bag failures, I was going through my supplies quickly, and had placed a large order. The thought of having to re-package the order, drive to the post office, reorder, and wait for a new delivery of supplies was just too overwhelming. So I kept the clear bags. At first, I was just disgusted. I knew I had issues with shit and having to look at it was repelling to me in the beginning. I also had issues with the reality of having a bag attached to my abdomen and it was difficult to look at myself in the mirror.

One time I caught a glimpse of my body in the mirror as I was getting into the bathtub, and recall that I cringed and said, "Oh my God, I have a Ziploc hanging off my belly." However, I had started reading a book called <u>Full Catastrophe</u>

Living. The author, Jon Kabat-Zinn, is founder and director of a stress and pain reduction program at the University of Massachusetts Medical Center which teaches "practiced mindfulness" to control and calm the patient's responses to stressors, particularly to pain. The program is also intended to help the patient develop a deeper awareness and ability to sit with and accept their inner states and feelings, as opposed to resisting them. The belief is that this resistance is the source of the pain. The program has been particularly effective for patients suffering from chronic pain.

Kabot-Zinn (1990) suggests that your physical body in any given moment reflects the sum total of every choice you have made up to that point in time. He states that if you refuse to even be present to your body, to take it in fully, in that moment, as it is, then it is less likely that you will make the changes you need and desire to make. He suggests that if you can learn to be fully present to your body, it will affect you, which will affect the decisions you make, and the changes will occur naturally.

In that moment, just as I caught myself expressing my disgust for my body, I remembered Kabot-Zinn's words, and I stopped. I remember thinking, "Listen to the way you talk to yourself. What message are you giving to yourself?" I realized that if I was going to beat this cancer and survive, I had to start to regard my body as an ally, not an enemy. I turned and faced the mirror and took a good look at my naked body, ostomy bag and all. As I looked at myself, I said, "From now on, we are in this together and we are going to make it together." After that night, I started to pay attention to the words I said to myself. My analyst even caught me one time referring to myself as a "piece of shit" and she asked me, "What kind of cancer do you have?" Since that time, I have been working on removing the word "shit" from my vocabulary.

After that moment of truth in the bathroom, I gradually found that I was more attentive to myself. The ostomy helped to facilitate that process, because I had to pay attention to my body's cycles in order to determine the best time to change the ostomy bag. The optimal time to change the bag is in the morning before you get up, become active, and eat breakfast. Since I was working with technology that was not designed for the kind of abdomen I had, I can't even count the number of times I changed the bag according to instructions, got up, ate breakfast, and suddenly realized the bag was leaking just as my body was swinging into high gear to process the meal. It was always frustrating. Sometimes it was overwhelming. I would just lie on the bed and cry while my poor husband ran to find more washcloths so I could clean myself up and get another bag on. But just as a surgeon operating in a field hospital under conditions of war learns to adapt to the situation, I also learned how to adapt, and I learned how to handle that damn bag.

I even learned to laugh about it. One of my favorite jokes was to go up to my husband and say, "Hey honey, do you want to see what I had for lunch?" But the biggest gift that came from living with that ostomy bag was the realization one day that those clear bags, which had forced me to look at this part of my body that I didn't want to see, had also provided me with a window to my body. Through that clear ostomy bag, I began to learn to associate what I was observing in the bag with what it felt like when my body was active and when it was quiet. I realized that I was learning to read the sensations that were the language of my body and that had been lost to me for many years. Later, after several bowel reconstructive surgeries, when my body had to literally relearn how to function (an agonizing process), I again learned to quiet down, listen, and wait for my body to tell me what was going on. I was amazed when I realized I had rediscovered the voice of my body.

Where is the Voice of the Patient?

A colleague invited me to attend a conference for hospice caregivers and other healthcare professionals whose work involves care of the dying. I thought the event might be worthwhile, as the stated purpose of the conference was to explore the implications of Ernest Becker's thoughts regarding the care of the dying and to deepen the caregiver's understanding of the spiritual and resource needs of this special population. There were a number of highly regarded keynote speakers on the agenda and I was curious to hear what they had to say about the care of the patient.

I was curious because during my own illness with colon cancer, there had been situations in which I felt like the medical staff only saw me as a body going through the process of treatment, not a human being. There were a number of times when my needs as the patient, which were supposed to be the highest priority, were set aside in the interest of compliance. I want to use the word *abandoned*, because that was how I experienced it. However, I don't really know the state of mind or intent of my care providers. Therefore, *set aside* is the more accurate term. But abandoned is how I felt.

In one instance about midway through my treatment, I experienced an episode of rectal bleeding. Rectal bleeding, one of the primary warning signs for colon cancer, had also been my primary symptom, but it had been misdiagnosed. Therefore, I was frightened when that symptom reappeared and I consulted my cancer surgeon. He told me I would be scheduled for a CT scan, but I was also instructed to complete the bowel cleansing procedure that is typically done prior to a colonoscopy. Although I was surprised by the instructions, it didn't occur to me to question them because I thought I could trust my doctor. When I arrived for my appointment, I was led into a procedure room equipped with an examination table and an enema bag that looked large enough for an elephant. I assume the technician saw the look on my face because I remember he said, "They didn't tell you what we're going to do, did they?" No, "they" hadn't. The technician did put all that fluid into me and it was as uncomfortable as one might expect. I had an appointment with my oncologist right after that procedure. When he walked into the examination room, he was looking at my chart and he looked up at me and said, "I hear Dr. 'M' pulled a fast one on you, huh?" I remember that I responded, "Yes, he did, and it wasn't funny."

Another experience took place after the first surgery, during which the tumor and about twenty inches of my colon were removed. I knew when I awoke after the surgery I would have the ostomy bag and that I would have to learn how to manage for the next six months as I completed another four rounds of chemotherapy. I was very scared at that time because my cancer was stage three and the long-term survival rate was not impressive. However, I was being treated with a regimen of radiation, chemotherapy, and surgery, which was then in the final phase of clinical trials (and is now established as the new standard of treatment) and my prognosis looked promising.

But as I prepared for what proved to be the first of the six surgeries that I would eventually undergo, I really wanted and needed to know what to expect so that I could get myself prepared. I wanted to be prepared because I was entering into a challenging period of my life and my cancer treatment was only a part of it. I was also preparing to begin four weeks of "doctoral boot camp" in July, just a few weeks after the surgery. My parents, and occasionally my husband, thought I was crazy to not postpone my doctoral program until I after I finished treatment. But my doctors were supportive because, as my surgeon told me, "You having some place where you want to be on July ninth is as good a way to motivate you to do the things I need you to do as anything else I can think of. Go for it." At the time, I appreciated his support, but I now believe that his *primary* thought was that this was a great tool for patient compliance.

I remember the night before the surgery, which took place in early June. It was a lovely evening. I went outside and walked in my garden and just took in the sights, smells, and sounds of this garden that I had spent so much effort creating. As I listened to the early evening birdsongs, I said a silent prayer and marked the moment. I told myself that things were going to change very dramatically when I awoke from surgery. I said good-bye and thank you to the part of my body I knew I was going to lose and set my mind to accept and deal with what was to come. With that, I felt *ready* to face the next phase. The surgery went well, no complications. When I woke up in my room, my husband and parents were there. I wasn't feeling any pain, thanks to an epidural and a morphine drip, and I drifted back to sleep. I remember thinking, "*Everything was going to be okay.*" The day following surgery, I was more awake and felt pretty good. My doctors believed they had gotten all the cancer. There was no evidence that it had metastasized and my family was with me. I felt really, really blessed.

The second day after surgery, I wasn't feeling so blessed. I woke up with severe abdominal pain and it wouldn't let up. I remember I was in so much pain I was squirming in my bed trying to find a position where I could get some relief. I thought something must have happened with my pain epidural and called the nurse. After I explained to her what I was experiencing, she looked at me and said, "Oh didn't anyone tell you? When the anesthesia wears off and your intestines start to wake up there is one day that you will be in a lot of pain. The pain meds don't work on smooth muscle and all you can do is roll your body from side to side or get up and walk around. Sorry about that." I felt like I'd just been pushed off a cliff. I remember I was so stunned that I couldn't even speak. I just looked at her.

During all the preparations for surgery, I was told repeatedly—by doctors, nurses, nurses' aides, and technicians—that there were all kinds of medications and remedies for pain. They told me, "These days the patient doesn't have to suffer.

You just have to let someone know that you're hurting." In fact, all around my hospital room there were posters with a series of faces and corresponding numbers, ranging from one to 10, with the happy face being number one and the very unhappy face assigned to number ten. The posters were even printed in several languages. The creator of this simple chart had done everything possible to ensure that *everyone* understood that they didn't have to suffer. Heck, you didn't even have to speak, just point to the appropriate face and number. Yet, when actually *in* pain, despite pointing most emphatically to the number ten, very unhappy face, I was told that there was nothing they could do and that in this instance, I *did* have to suffer. I felt *betrayed*. And, to me, it was so unbelievably insensitive. The best time to find out that nothing will help alleviate your pain is not when you are in the middle of experiencing it, particularly when you had been specifically told otherwise. At that point, what are you going to do? You just have to get through it. I think the doctors and nurses know that, too.

Another hospital experience that proved to be a cultural learning moment for me involved a nurse originally from India. I experienced complications from my treatment that resulted in several emergency surgeries due to bowel obstructions. I was throwing up and in severe pain and my doctor wanted to put in a nasogastric (NG) tube to alleviate the vomiting. I did not want one. I had heard that they were very uncomfortable and I was uncomfortable enough already. My surgeon had previously threatened me with the NG tube when I'd been throwing up and I had always managed to make myself stop because I did not want that tube down my throat. This time, he told me that he really thought it would help. He said that if I didn't like it, I could have it taken out. I took him at his word and agreed to try the NG tube. I should have remembered my experience with the elephant-sized enema bag.

That NG tube was as awful as I had heard. It hurt. I couldn't move my head without the tube irritating my nose and throat. I couldn't sleep. I was miserable. Having been raised in polite female culture, I waited until 7:00 a.m. before I finally asked that the tube be taken out. The nurse who responded to the call button was a woman from India. I asked her to get my doctor so I could get the tube removed. She said, "Oh, I cannot do that. He is very busy right now." I remember saying, "I don't care. He said I could take this out if I didn't like it and I can't stand it anymore. I want it out now!" At that point, my husband, who had been sleeping in a cot by my bed, made the mistake of saying, "Maybe you're making too big a deal out of this." In that moment, if my hand had been able to reach his throat, I think I could have crushed it. I said to him, "Let's shove a tube up your nose for twenty-four hours and see how perky you are!" The nurse left the room and I did not see her, or the doctor, until 10:00 a.m., when he came in and finally removed the tube.

Later, I asked myself what had gone wrong with that situation? I was supposed to be some kind of cultural expert in my job, and this situation had been a total disaster. I realized that I was dealing with someone from a hierarchical culture where people, particularly women, do not challenge those in a position of higher authority. It would be almost unthinkable for her to "summon" a doctor. I could imagine that, to her, I was a selfish American woman who went around issuing demands. I imagine she didn't like me as much as I had not liked her. Later that day, as I was walking around the hallway, and I heard a young Caucasian nurse's aide brightly ask this same nurse, "So, how are *you* doing today?" The Indian nurse replied, "Oh, it is not for me to say how I am." I remember thinking to myself, "Oh, that explains a lot."

When I thought about how I might have better handled that situation, I realized that, if my husband had been the one to make the request, the nurse might have been more likely to comply, because he is male and regarded as the head of the family. In other words, the nurse would have been transmitting the request of another authority figure, not a lower status female patient. It didn't matter that this played out in a U.S. hospital in 2004; culture dies hard. As for my husband's near escape from death at my hands: later on, I was able to tell him, "What I did not need was for you to be one more person telling me that I didn't know what I was talking about. I needed you to be my ally and to help me get what I need." But my husband is Filipino, and from his cultural perspective, the individual does not make demands, you suffer in silence. Culture dies hard.

In reflecting about these different experiences, I realized that in each one of them, I had been in a very vulnerable position. And in that place of vulnerability, I might have held certain unchecked expectations as to what was supposed to happen during my treatment. In other instances, though, I realized that my expectations were likely being "managed" through the providing, censoring, or withholding of information about the process. My sense was that the intent behind the management of this information was, again, patient compliance.

I do not for a second believe that it was anyone's conscious intent that I suffer. In fact, those doctors, nurses, technicians, and other professionals were all sincerely dedicated to destroying the cancer and saving my life, and they directed all of their technical expertise toward that end. They were successful and I am deeply grateful to still be alive. However, when I think back on my experience, I don't think it occurred to most of these caregivers to consider what might be going on for me emotionally. I suspect that some others, doctors in particular, *do* think about it, but don't really know, or want to know, how to deal with the emotional aspect of their work. They just want to concentrate on the technical side. I just don't believe they really think about the impact of their words and actions on someone who is frightened, overwhelmed, panicked, in pain, and looking to them for help or hope. I don't believe that they really put themselves in the place of their patients. I believe that disenfranchised grief is one reason why.

At the end of this self-analysis, I came to the conclusion that I was going to have to learn how to be my own advocate. I said to myself:

> Sister, if you aren't willing to be an active participant in your treatment, do your own research, ask questions and demand answers, and keep asking until you get the information you need, at the end of the day, the only person who's hurting is you.

I realized that I had handed over my entire being to them for healing, and the only thing they were trained to heal was my body. I had to step up and protect my own soul. In that moment, I took responsibility for my life. What made me sad and angry was that most of the people on that oncology ward with me were much older than me, likely had the same expectations as me, and did not have the same ability as me to advocate for themselves or protect themselves. They were abandoned too.

I carried all those experiences with me to the conference I attended, "Finitude, Medical Futility, and Faithful Care of the Dying." I was curious about what these presenters might have to say about empathy for the patient. I was there with an open mind and hoped that it would be a good experience. It was actually a profound experience, but not in the way that I had imagined. It was profound because I was deeply shaken to my core.

As I listened to the first keynote speaker, I was surprised to find myself shutting down emotionally. The speaker literally started talking about how noble the work of caring for the dying was and how wonderful they all were for doing it. He said that they all needed to make sure and take care of themselves so they wouldn't burn out and have to stop doing this noble work that was so badly needed. I looked around the room and everyone looked very happy with themselves and with each other. I didn't feel good about what I was hearing, but I didn't know why at the time. I chalked it up to having an attitude, and set the feeling aside.

That evening, the film, Wit (2001), featuring British actress Emma Thompson, was presented and I attended with a colleague. In the film, Thompson's character is a brilliant but emotionally isolated professor of seventeenth century English literature who is diagnosed with ovarian cancer. Throughout the film, Thompson's character speaks directly to the camera as it follows her from the day of her diagnosis to the day of her death. The film was an unrelentingly vivid, stark, and poignant portrayal of the experience of illness and dying in this society, and how dehumanizing and undignified it has become. It also hit a too little close to home. By the end of the film, I was shaking so badly, I said to my colleague, "Please get me out of here." I felt bad that I was going to miss the discussion, but, as we were leaving, the moderator thanked the group for attending, wished them a nice evening, and said the conference would start up again at 8:00 am. I was a little surprised, but also relieved that I wouldn't miss the discussion after all. I assumed it would take place in the morning.

However, the following morning, nothing was said about the film. There was no debrief or discussion. No one asked, "What can we learn from this person's experience that can help us to be more present to the patient? What was done well in the film? Where do we fall short? What needs to be different?" Instead, the presenters immediately moved into a closing small group activity where the participants were asked to discuss what they had learned and would take away from the conference. Afterward, the group would come back together and share some of the learning.

I sat and listened to the different comments people in my small group made about how rejuvenated and recommitted they were feeling. As I listened, I couldn't help thinking that, for a conference whose stated focus was to "deepen the understanding of the spiritual and resource needs of the dying," I had not seen a single workshop dedicated to the experience or perspective of the patients, whose needs they were supposedly there to understand. The workshops tended to focus more on either the theory or the mechanics of caring for the dying, or on self-care for the caregivers. The only material that presented the perspective of the patient was the film, and it had not even been debriefed. I noted that I had begun to feel angry again as the large group reconvened.

When the facilitator asked for people to share their thoughts, I made the decision to say something and raised my hand. When the facilitator called on me, I was shaking as I stood up and started to speak.

> You know, I have been at this conference for the last two days and as this event comes to a close and people prepare to go back to their daily lives, I find myself asking: "Where is the voice of the patient in this dialogue? Well, at least one voice is sitting right here, and I would like to share a few things with you. First of all, please don't get me wrong, I am very grateful for the work that you do and for saving my life. But you did some things to me while you were saving my life and I'd like to let you know how it made me feel. You sometimes lied to me. You sometimes withheld information from me because you anticipated that I wouldn't like it, wouldn't be able to handle it, you didn't want to be bothered, or maybe, it just never occurred to you.
>
> I wonder if you ever really stop and think about what it's like to be in my place. Do you ever stop and think about what kind of message your actions are sending to me with respect to how much importance the voice of the patient has for you? You showed a film that very powerfully showed the experience of the dying patient and how she was treated. But you showed it at the end of a long day when people were tired and just wanted to go relax. And when the movie ended, you didn't debrief it. And you didn't even mention it the following day. You didn't ask the important existential questions: what might we learn from this story? Was this patient served with care, concern, dignity, compassion, and empathy? Or did we fail her? You didn't ask the question, what might we need to do differently? I haven't heard anyone talk about asking the patient, what do you need from us? How can we help make this easier for you or more meaningful for you? What message does this send to those of us who look to you for compassion and empathy as we go through this challenging experience in our lives? (July 27, 2006, Seattle, WA)

I was still shaking as I sat down, but I felt *good*. This time, I had not remained silent. After the conference ended, a couple of women who were training to be chaplains came up to me and said, "We could have used you in our class a couple of months ago." I smiled and said, "Yes, you could have."

My experience at this conference brought back memories of a close friend, Nashid, who had died of pancreatic cancer the previous spring. I had flown back to Chicago with some friends to say goodbye to him at the facility where he had been getting treatment. This particular organization's marketing emphasis was the "integrated team approach." The facility itself and the grounds were beautifully laid out and appeared to be state-of-the-art. Each patient had a treatment team consisting of a primary physician, nurse, nutritionist, social worker, psychologist, pain management specialist, physical therapist, and others as determined by the primary physician.

I remember sitting with Nashid two days before his death with a group of colleagues who had come to say goodbye. At this point, Nashid was being given large doses of morphine and other drugs to manage his pain and, therefore, was in and out of consciousness much of the time. Sometimes he was with us and sometimes he was somewhere else. But that didn't matter. We were Nashid's community. We were there to witness him and help him transition to the next phase of his journey. The family and friends gathered in his room had been taking turns playing the jazz he loved and reading poetry out loud. I believe that is exactly as he wanted it to be. However, the peacefulness of the environment was broken when the integrated team of caregivers burst into Nashid's room to check on how he was doing. With big smiles and cheerful voices, they exhorted him to "hang in there and not give up because miracles do happen!" I watched as Nashid mustered all the strength he had in order to give them a "thumbs up" sign in response. The team then all filed out of his room, continuing to smile brightly and hopefully as they left.

I remember being filled at that moment with absolute rage. I wanted to go up and slap each one of those people in the face. Could they not see that he was dying? Couldn't they have just quietly asked if there was any way they could be of help to Nashid or his family? It felt like they weren't present to him at all. Rather, it was all about preserving their image of themselves as healers. Were these people really so narcissistic that they would eat up a portion of a dying man's waning life force to fill their need to be regarded as "a good integrated team?" I was so angry I went down the hallway and broke down. It could just as easily have been me laying there dying and I was horrified at the what I had witnessed.

Later that afternoon, another friend, Ken, noticed Nashid just quietly looking at him. There was an expression in Nashid's eyes that caused Ken to get up and move his chair closer to the bed. Ken later wrote a moving letter describing the conversation that took place between them. Ken wrote that Nashid whispered to him, "So, what do you think?" Ken looked at him and gently said, "My brother, you are dying and you need to prepare yourself. Forget about the past. Forget about the future. You need to focus on the task at hand. We are here with you and we will see you over to the other side" [K. Addison, personal communication, 2006]. Ken, who has been a practicing Buddhist for over thirty years, could sense that Nashid was frightened and asked him if he would like Ken to teach him a chant that would help him to relax. Nashid nodded and Ken taught him how to meditate using a particular chant as his focus point. Ken promised Nashid that from then on, he would also use that same chant to keep the channel open if Nashid wanted to communicate with him. I will never forget the glow in Nashid's eyes when Ken told him that.

The difference between the integrated medical team and Ken was that Ken was empathic. Because he was empathic, he was able to be fully present to Nashid. Being fully present, Ken was able to recognize and respond with what Nashid needed in order to help him through his death. Like the mother who needs to be able to recognize and respond to the needs of her infant, caregivers to a dying person also need to be able to recognize and respond to the needs of our fellow human beings at the end of life. We need to be able to recognize, respond, and be present to these needs because I believe that humans need their deaths to be witnessed just as much as their grief. Just as Montgomery (2003) believes that therapists need to help clients to explore, make sense of, and integrate their loss experiences, care of the dying person also needs to include helping him to explore, make sense of, and integrate his death. There is more to the death process than simply the care of the physical body.

That evening, when it was time to leave and say our last goodbyes, everyone in the room stood in a circle around Nashid's bed and held hands. We all waited for someone to speak, assuming it would be Tom, the patriarch of our little community. However, it was not Tom who spoke. It was Nashid. He looked us and lifted his hand, pointing his index finger and moving it to indicate a circle. Nashid whispered that Ken had asked him what dying meant to him. He told us that, at the time Ken asked the question, he didn't have an answer and he was confused and frightened. But now, he said he knew that his life had come full circle and he had learned that what mattered most was family and friends. Nashid then said to us, "Go in peace." No one spoke for several minutes. Then each one of us took turns saying a private goodbye and we walked out of his room. Nashid passed away the following day.

The experience of being part of a community that came together in love and respect to witness the passing of one of our own profoundly changed me in ways that I am still processing. There are so many things I learned from that experience. I learned about what it means to have a "good death," and I now know that I want one. I learned what it means to be a community as well as a member of a community. I learned what it means to be fully present to someone for the sole purpose of being there as their witness. It was a privilege to be a part of such an experience. I also learned that something very powerful happens when you witness someone, whether in grief or in death. My sense is that it is another validation of Lewis, Amini and Lannon's (2000) limbic mantra, "Stability is finding people who regulate you well and sticking to them" (p. 86). The need for being surrounded by people who are attuned and present to someone in the process of their death is just as powerful as the original limbic regulation that occurs between mother and infant. Most of us miss out because we are so terrified of our mortality that we turn away from anything relating to death or dying. Because I was gifted with the opportunity to witness my friend's death, I now have hope that I will also be able to achieve a good death. I hope that *my* community, those individuals who have shared and shaped the meaningful moments that have made up my life, will also be surrounding me as I move through the transition of death.

One of the most precious gifts I ever received from Nashid came in the form of a question he once posed to me. At the time, I really didn't have an answer to Nashid's question. However, my presence at his passing was my way of letting him know that I had figured out the answer. The question Nashid had asked of me was, "Do you really know what it means to be a friend on the deepest level?" His question upset me, because the implication was that I did not know, and it felt like a challenge. That was the nature and gift of Nashid's friendship. He had truly been present to me, and I learned from him how to be present to others. Nashid was a philosopher and he recognized and delighted in the philosopher in me. I still grieve the loss of his friendship every day. But I keep him alive in me and honor him through the question that he cared enough to ask me. It is the standard by which I now measure myself, and how I try to live my life.

Where is the Voice of the Child?

When you are eight years old, nothing is your business.

-Lenny Bruce

The last story to be shared in this work is also the most recent to occur. I believe it illustrates that moment, noted earlier by Roads (1987, in Moustakas, 1990), wherein the researcher is asked to decide, "Can you trust me enough to let go of the known and swim into an unknown current?" (p. 13). This story is about my particular experience with how heuristic inquiry can take the researcher in directions not previously imagined, if the researcher is willing to let go and trust where the current will go.

A few years ago, I came across a magazine article about a cooperative project between a number of well-known fashion photographers in New York and a New Jersey non-profit agency whose mission was to find adoptive homes for hard-to-place children. The idea was that the photographers would work with each child to create an image of the child that captured the essence of the child's personality in such a way as to appeal to potential adoptive parents.

One of the photos was of an eight-year-old African-American boy named Jessie. Jessie's photo showed him leaping in the air like a dancer. His arms were extended upwards and he had his head thrown back. His eyes were closed and the expression on his face was simply beautiful to me. Each child's photograph included a caption that contained a quote from the child. Jessie's quote read, "*I just want to have a family, a real family. I just want to be somebody's son.*" Those words just grabbed at my heart. I remember looking at his photo and whispering to myself, "Jessie, do you want to be *my* son?" But at that time, I was just finishing my cancer treatment and wasn't sure that I was really in a position to consider another child, so I let Jessie go. That little boy haunted me and was the catalyst for my beginning to consider whether I might want to parent another child.

I thought about Jessie from time to time and wondered if he ever found a family. I wondered if I should have pursued the possibility of adopting him. But I wasn't sure whether taking on a second family was the right thing for me to do. My husband, Ren, and I have five children between us, but never had a child together. In the last few years, as we have gotten closer to the age when we can think seriously about retirement, we have talked about how we might engage in more meaningful rather than moneymaking work. How could we give back and serve the larger community? What skills or talents did we have to offer? What would we find truly meaningful and make us happy? What were we meant to do?

After our children were grown, Ren and I had the opportunity to build a beautiful home that we designed ourselves on our seven acres. We are both avid gardeners and have often joked that we built our home because we landscaped ourselves out of our last house. Our vision had been to find some property where, when we were finished, we would be there to watch our efforts mature. We once talked about working with children in our gardens and creating opportunities to bring them in contact with the earth. I had heard about research that supported the idea that gardening could be a healing experience for children in the same way that communal gardens or pea patches bring people from inner city neighborhoods in contact with nature, the earth, and a sense of healing or balance.

There have been times when I have felt somewhat uncomfortable with knowing that we have this big house for just the two of us when so many people have very little. I have also sometimes wondered how this house would feel if it had children in it, and whether sharing our home with children was a gift that we might be able to offer. At the beginning of my analysis, I recall that my analyst had asked me, if I were granted three wishes, what would they be? I listed: (1) become a writer, (2) run a small business and, (3) have a baby with my husband. I remember that at the time I did not think any of them were attainable. And yet, if one considers designing and building our home together to be a creative act equivalent to having a baby, I have come close to accomplishing all three.

I continued to think about Jessie from time to time, but it went no further until I began to focus on writing my dissertation proposal, and Jessie resurfaced in a rather indirect and unexpected way. I found myself struggling with letting go and trusting where the heuristic journey would take me. In spite of all the encouragement that there was value in exploring my experience as a parent of sexual minority children, I was having a difficult time finding my own voice and my own way to tell the story.

I suspect that some of this struggle was unconscious resistance serving a protective function because embedded in the taking of a journey is its ending, and endings always contain some degree of loss, no matter how happy the ending may be. Endings and loss are experiences that are still extraordinarily painful and difficult for me, and I know that I still have the tendency to deny this pain. However, as my understanding about the negative impact of disenfranchised grief has increased, so has my awareness of the importance of recognizing, rather than denying, this grief and working to integrate it back into my psyche. Several key phases of my life (including analysis, school, and work) were moving toward a place of transition or completion at approximately the same time. It was likely that these transitions would generate deep feelings of loss and grief, as *all* endings will. Had I failed to recognize this potential and failed to be attentive to myself through this process, it is likely that I would have missed the key lessons embedded within this loss.

With this in mind, I chose to try and just sit with the resistance I was experiencing and see where it took me. I had a feeling that I might be in the incubation phase of the heuristic process (Moustakas, 1990), and tried to just let go and trust that the current was taking me where I needed to go. It should be noted that, at least for this researcher, the act of letting go and trusting the current, which sounds so great in the abstract, is not so easy in practice. I began to understand why heuristic inquiry might be a road less traveled–letting go of the known generates anxiety and anxiety is experienced as distress. Letting go of the known also involves a loss and the accompanying experience of pain. If most people, as I suspect, carry some degree of disenfranchised grief as a result of the inability of their parents or other important attachment figures to respond empathically to their distress experiences in childhood, it is likely they did not learn how to manage their distress, but instead repressed it in an unconscious attempt to protect themselves from pain that was feared might be overwhelming. As a child, the experience of not having distress empathically witnessed by your parents *was* overwhelming. Therefore, it doesn't appear likely that a person whose parents reacted to his or her childhood distress by denying or distancing from it would willingly enter into a distress-inducing activity such as heuristic inquiry.

I became increasingly aware of my own distress during this incubation period. I was doing a great deal of reading and re-reading of the research on attachment. The more I read and understood the critical role that attachment and attunement serve in the development of an infant's mind and in the quality of the parent-infant relationship, the sadder I felt. I was realizing that motherhood could be a profound experience, if you were ready for it, and I had missed out. I also felt angry, because it seemed that I had missed out because of a lack of knowledge about mothering. I felt like I had been robbed.

It has been very difficult to sit with that feeling at times. I suspect that is one reason why I avoided it for so long. I felt deeply angry about the injustice of not getting to have the experience I should have had. I thought about how much it has affected my life and the lives of my children. I have sometimes felt afraid of my anger because it has felt overwhelming at times. I have also felt guilty because I think, who am I to expect that things should go the way I want? Other people have suffered far greater injustices and I am complaining about minor concerns. Why do I have such privilege? And why do I think I deserve even more privilege? I still tend to feel guilty about my anger, but I also continue to try to understand it.

The search to understand my anger led me to the discovery of two books by Nel Noddings, Education and Happiness (2003) and Critical Lessons: What Our Schools Should Teach (2006). I found myself deeply resonating with this educator who argues that we are *all* suffering from a lack of relevant information because the U.S. educational system is approaching education from the wrong perspective. Noddings contends that schools in the U.S. are focusing on test scores, fundamental skills, and the number of females and minorities in math and science, but are failing to recognize and educate the whole child. She advocates for a change in the *intent* of education to one that is focused on an "ethic of care" (2003, p. 67). Noddings writes:

> Those of us who work from an ethic of care regard moral life as thoroughly relational. We are, of course, individual physical organisms, but our selves are constructed through encounters with other bodies, objects, selves, conditions, ideas, and reflective moments with our own previous selves. A

relational view weakens and blurs the distinction between egoism and altruism, because much of what we do for others strengthens the relations of which we are part and, thus, our selves. (p. 158)

When I consider the underlying issues reflected in the current world situation and daily news headlines, the skills that appear to be required for the possible resolution of these issues are rarely the ones that are reflected in test scores. The common underlying element that I see embedded in the stories behind the news headlines, and in many of the current social issues we face, is a generalized failure on the part of humankind to relate to each other.

News headlines reflect very graphically how our youth, and many adults, are seriously deficient in the interpersonal skills that would help them to navigate the "encounters with other bodies, objects, selves, conditions, ideas" (Ibid.) without losing themselves in the process. The headlines also reflect society's lack of recognition and understanding of our youth, as well as the "abdication of adults who are supposed to love and protect our young and help them develop into healthy and productive citizens" (Pope, 2003, p. 44). And the casualties are mounting. As noted by authorities after the recent murder of thirty-two students and faculty by yet another "loner" student (with a history that included reports of feeling marginalized and ridiculed) at Virginia Tech, "It will happen again."

I am afraid it will continue to happen until we as a society stop and pay attention to what these incidents are telling us: we are not doing a good enough job with raising or protecting our children. It seems significant that, after a number of these incidents, there are individuals who come forward and disclose that they had seen something disturbing in the perpetrator years earlier and yet said or did nothing at that time. Why not? Why aren't the signals getting picked up sooner? Why aren't those who do see the signals making some kind of intervention? What prevents us from doing so? Why do we seem to be so "hands off" as a society?

I have to wonder if we have become such an individualistic society, and have taken privacy laws to such an extreme, that we have totally lost sight of the need for relationship and the fact that it really does take a village to raise our children and we all have to get involved. If we don't, we are seeing that there will be consequences. Winston Churchill (1874 – 1965) said:

There is no finer investment for any community than putting milk into babies. The potential for humanity lives inside every infant, *but healthy development is an effort, not a given* [italics added]. If we do not shelter that spark, guide and nurture it, then we not only lose the life within but we unleash later destruction on ourselves.

Lewis, Amini, and Lannon (2000), researchers studying the "psychobiology of love" (p. 4), echo Churchill's warning. They note, "although the nature of love is not easy to define, it has an intrinsic order, an architecture that can be detected, excavated, and explored" (p. 13). These researchers suggest that the intrinsic order of love is not random, rather it is "part of the physical universe" and therefore, "has to be *lawful*" (p. 5). If we violate these laws, or we are ignorant about them, there is a consequence.

We see the need for this knowledge every day, *and we see the bitter consequences of its lack.* People who do not respect the laws of acceleration and momentum break bones; those who not grasp the principles of love waste their lives and break their hearts. The evidence of that pain surrounds us, in the form of failed marriages, hurtful relationships, neglected children, unfulfilled ambitions, and thwarted dreams. And in numbers, these injuries combine to damage our society, where emotional suffering and its ramifications are commonplace. *The roots of that suffering are often unseen and passed over, while proposed remedies cannot succeed, because they contradict emotional laws that our culture does not yet recognize* [italics added]. (p. 13)

I found myself strongly reacting to this statement and wondered why. I realized that my reaction had to do with the understanding that important messages are being missed because we aren't paying attention, therefore, they are "unseen or passed over." I tried to recall how many times the important people in my life had failed to see me, or my messages were passed over, and how many times I had been badly hurt as a result. I realized that a great deal of my rage came out of having not been seen.

My colon cancer had remained "unseen" almost to the point of metastasizing to my bladder. It remained unseen because, according to the insurance industry, I was too young too be at risk. Therefore, diagnostic procedures, such as colonoscopies (which are very expensive, but are regarded as the most accurate for early diagnosis of colon cancer), are not covered by insurance until age fifty. The cheaper fecal-blood test, which is the approved screening for those under age fifty, is known to have only about twenty-five percent accuracy. So, despite the fact that I went to my family doctor three previous times with blood in my stool (one of the primary indicators of colon cancer), because my fecal-blood tests came back with a negative result, he didn't look any further. And he is a good doctor.

However, even the best doctor can miss something if he or she doesn't have accurate information. I wasn't able to provide my doctor with accurate information because I was ignorant about my family health history. My paternal grandfather died at age fifty-five when I was ten years old. My siblings and I had always thought that he died of leukemia. But after I was diagnosed, I learned that he actually died of colon cancer. Had I known that and passed that information on to my doctor, he might have thought to order a colonoscopy much sooner. I did not understand the significance of this until my family agreed to participate in a study of colon cancer patients and I discovered how little I knew about my family history, because there were many questions I could not answer. As I noted in the story about rediscovering my embodied voice, not only was I disconnected and clueless about my own body, I was also disconnected and clueless about my family history, which contributed to the cancer remaining unseen. Ignorance is *not* always bliss.

I began to get a sense as to the depth of meaning behind the ancient Greek aphorism, "Know Thyself." As noted earlier, one of the key lessons I learned as a result of my illness is that no one lives my life but me. If I don't make sure that I understand what is being done to me, I am the one who experiences the consequence, whether that consequence is positive or negative. I wondered about what it was that got in the way of my knowing myself. What skills or knowledge was I lacking? What was the best way to identify and learn those skills?

Noddings argues that these skills are developed through an educational curriculum that emphasizes critical thinking, which she notes:

> Refers not only to the assessment of arguments (that will certainly be included) but also to the diligent and skillful use of reason on matters of moral/social importance – on personal decision making, conduct, and belief. By including its application to personal belief and decision making, we extend critical thinking to every domain of human interest. . . To neglect critical thinking on topics central to everyday life is to make the word *education* virtually meaningless. (2006, p. 4)

Why is critical thinking not a part of the school curriculum? Noddings suggests that one answer to this question is ignorance. She notes, "people who have never explored these topics are unlikely to provide opportunities for others to do so; the notion never arises" (2006, p. 3).

When I consider Noddings' statement from the perspective of my own experience as a child and as a parent, I find myself getting angry again. I also find myself asking the question: how much pain do our children have to endure before we as a society decide that ignorance is no longer an acceptable response? Just as Luckmann (1978, in Martin, 2005) notes that "the job of science is to explain everyday life" (p. 212), the job of the educational system should be to provide our children with the skills they need in order to be able to live and to attain happiness in their every day lives. It could be argued that the 'No Child Left Behind' mentality of the second Bush administration is actually leaving the *whole* child behind.

I am troubled by Noddings' (2006) suggestion that, because those in educational leadership themselves lack experience with critical thinking concepts, this critical skill is absent from the school curriculum because either "the notion never arises" (p. 3) for these leaders or they do not recognize its importance. It is also disturbing to me that educational leaders, who are tasked with the development of a curriculum that should prepare our children to live happy, effective lives, are themselves apparently lacking the ability to objectively assess the environment, the educational process, the curriculum, or themselves as leaders. It would appear that our educational leaders might be out of touch with the real world.. As a product of this educational system, and as a mother, I am beginning to question why this is considered acceptable.

Reconsidering my parenting experience again in light of Noddings' suggestion, I began to realize that I am an individual, a mother, who has developed the ability to think and reflect critically about my own and others' behavior as a result of the hard work I've done during years of analysis. I thought that with all the experiences I'd had and all the mistakes I had made, perhaps I could bring a unique perspective and voice to the dialogue. I thought about how overwhelmed I felt at nineteen as a young and ignorant mother compared to how different mothering feels to me now. I mentally listed the credentials I could bring to such a dialogue. I have attained an advanced education that includes an understanding of child, adolescent, and human development. I have trained as a therapist and learned how to be able to sit with someone, listen empathically, and reflect back to them authentic regard. I have had the opportunity to undergo psychoanalysis to a greater degree than most people ever get to. And I have faced my own mortality. As a result, I have had the chance to have my disenfranchised grief empathically witnessed and integrated. After almost seventeen years of ongoing therapeutic limbic regulation with an empathic and attuned analyst, I have finally been able to attain what even fewer have, a re-regulated mind.

In other words, I have truly walked in both worlds and can directly speak to the need for the inclusion of critical thinking in the school curriculum. I have lived the experience of being an ignorant, overwhelmed mother and witnessed, first hand, the impact of that ignorance on the development of my children. I am now living the experience of being an empathic and attuned mother, and witnessing the impact of this kind of mothering on my children and grandchildren. Because of my lived experience in both situations, I can tell the difference. I prefer the impact of the latter, not only because of how it affects my children's experience, but also how it affects my experience as a mother. I thought that maybe this ability to tell the difference might not only be a great skill for a researcher to possess, it might also create an obligation for me to put it to good use.

It was at this time that I remembered Jessie again and his wish to be a part of a real family. In the time since I had first seen Jessie's photo, the idea of parenting again had been incubating, and I began to consider the idea of becoming a foster parent and potentially adopting children. I recalled a number of times when I had walked around my house and thought that maybe this house needed children in it. I enjoyed decorating the house for the different holidays, but often asked myself, "Who are you doing this for?" I thought about all the hard-won mothering skills I had developed, the solid relationship and beautiful home that my husband and I had built up over almost twenty years together, my developing ideas about the critical importance of the mother-infant attachment relationship, my social justice education, and the desperate need for good homes for foster children. I wondered if I was experiencing a call to mother again.

There were many, many questions that ran through my mind. Was I was feeling this impulse to raise another child out of some need to prove a point—that I really could mother well? At age fifty, was I too old? If I fostered and adopted an infant, I would be at least seventy years old by the time the child reached age twenty. Was I really willing to trade all the freedom I had come to enjoy for all the responsibilities that I now clearly understand go with parenthood? What would my husband, who is eight years older than I am, say about another family? Was I possibly trying to start over with a new family, rather than take my newfound knowledge and engage in the clearly longer and more challenging effort of reshaping my relationships with my adult children? Wasn't it enough to be a grandmother? Was I rushing into another major commitment as a reaction to nearing the completion of the intense experiences of analysis and earning a doctoral degree?

I also thought about the social justice emphasis of my education and the idea of using one's gifts or privilege to give back to the community. My husband and I had always said that we built our home to share with others. At the time, we had intended that sharing to be with family and friends, but perhaps we had also unconsciously meant sharing with children, too. And who needed good, experienced parenting more than children in the foster care system? The idea resonated very strongly with me, and to my surprise, it resonated with my husband as well. I told my husband that the only way I knew how to answer the question was to go through the process and see what happens. A colleague recommended a permanency placement foster care program through which she had adopted two foster children. She'd had a good experience with this agency and thought it would fit our situation.

I made contact with the agency. My husband and I were interviewed and invited to complete a thirty-two hour training program, one of the requirements for certification as a foster parent. The training, as it was explained to me, was designed to prepare potential foster parents to appropriately handle all the various situations and issues that can arise when dealing with birth parents, traumatized children, and the court system. It was also explained that the training was intended to help potential foster parents make sure that it was the right program for them. Therefore, the training was spread out over an eight-week period to allow time for questions or issues to arise. My husband and I agreed that we would go through the training to be certified as potential foster parents, and would make a decision as to the next step at that time.

I also sought out the advice of a number of people, including my parents and several female mentors, about my idea of becoming a foster parent and mothering again. I tried to intentionally seek out a range of opinions so I could make sure I wasn't manipulating the feedback to hear what I thought I wanted to hear. The feedback, as expected, ranged from "What a cool thing to do" to "Are you crazy?" There were those who supported the idea for similar reasons of social justice, or they enjoyed parenting, or they themselves were older parents. Several people told my husband that we "thought young" and would be able to relate well with children. One surprising supporter was my father, who I had expected would respond with, "Are you crazy?" Instead, he shared that he had once considered the idea of adopting or fostering but had not pursued it. He also agreed that it would be lovely to have children in our home. My father's response really took me by surprise and revealed a nurturing aspect of him that I didn't get to see very often when I was a child. That was a lovely moment for me as a daughter.

The individuals who questioned my idea of parenting again raised a number of valid questions or points to consider. Many had been free of child-raising responsibilities for a period of time and enjoyed it. They were not inclined to give that up to raise another child. They viewed parenthood as one phase in a linear process that is one's life, and felt that there is an order or progression from one life phase to another and you don't go back and repeat the experience. Some framed their counsel within a context of having a responsibility to something larger than oneself. They suggested I had a story that made an impact on people and gave them a way to think differently about LGBTQ issues. They argued that, if one has been given a particular skill or gift, do they not have a responsibility to the larger community to do what they have the ability to do? One of my mentors pointed out that I had worked very hard to develop myself and attain a high level of knowledge and that I could use my knowledge and ability to influence a larger group of people, such as through teaching, rather than limiting my influence to the raising of one or two more children.

Each comment I received was thoughtful, respectful, and showed me how well these people knew me and cared about me. I felt pulled by each different perspective because these individuals are important to me. But at one point, I remember thinking that, although each of these individuals had my best interests at heart, they were still speaking through their own perspective and experience. They were not me, they were not living my life, and I was the only one who could really determine what was right. I asked myself, "Are you listening more to other people than you are listening to yourself?" My husband had a similar perspective. He told me that we were different from other people and making a choice to have a second family needed to be our decision.

It's interesting to think that an exploration of my experience as a parent would lead me to consider parenting again. I would not have thought I would want to parent a second time as I have also enjoyed my freedom. I experienced both hesitation as well as a strong attraction to the idea of raising another child. I was curious about what it would be like to consciously parent a child knowing what I now know. What would it be like to parent with someone truly interested in parenting with me? What would it be like to parent a child with an understanding of their context, their internal world? What would it be like to parent a child knowing I hold the incredible and awesome responsibility of shaping their mind? How would the experience be different? How would it be the same?

One experience I was able to draw upon for comparison occurred about twelve years ago and involved the two-year-old daughter of one of Kristin's co-workers. Kristin and I fell in love with Clarissa when she was only two days old. This was fortunate because Clarissa's mother was not particularly interested in her. It is likely that initially Clarissa was a "failure-to-thrive" baby as she gained very little weight her first six months of life and was frequently hospitalized her first year. I remember I was reading Schore's (1994) book, Affect and Regulation of the Self, which was my introduction to the idea of the "intent gaze" between mother and infant and its critical role in neurological formation. Based on what I was learning, every time Kristin brought Clarissa over, I would carry her around with me everywhere and look into her eyes, smile at her, and talk to her. I remember thinking: "I've got to get some positive reflection into this child."

One afternoon, when Clarissa was about two years old, Kristin brought her over for me to baby-sit. I had a dog, Woodrow, and Clarissa loved to play with him. I was finishing a task when Clarissa started to head toward the door to go out and play with the dog. I told her to wait a minute and I would take her outside. She kept heading toward the door, and I told her again to wait for me. Clarissa continued toward the door and I told her that if she didn't listen to me, I was going to have to give her a time-out. She slowed down a little, but she was determined to reach the door. When my own children were small, I had regarded this same behavior as a challenge to my authority and felt angry. But this time, I remember I looked at Clarissa and said, "Oh, I see what this is, you're just being two." Clarissa continued to ignore me, so I picked her up and sat her on a chair. She wailed and cried and I said to her, "It's okay for you to be mad and to cry. And when you're done crying and you're ready to mind me, you can get down and let me know and we will go outside and play with Woodrow." And I walked back to finish my task. In less than two minutes, Clarissa was standing beside me. I looked down at her and smiled and said, "Great! You're all done? Let's go see Woodrow." I marveled at how differently I both felt and acted toward Clarissa when I understood what she was doing. Sadly, Kristin and I lost touch with Clarissa not long afterward when her mother moved away. I still think about her from time to time and hope that she is okay.

My husband and I made the decision to take the first step toward certification as foster parents and attend the foster parent training. At the first class, we were given a very large notebook with articles and resource materials covering a number of topics including grief and loss; effects of drug and alcohol exposure; physical, emotional, and sexual abuse; dealing with birth parents; and attachment. Participants were expected to have read the materials prior to the training and several social workers facilitated discussion about the topic and answered any questions.

From my own observations, there were four primary objectives to this training, three of which appeared to be consciously acknowledged by the social workers. The first objective of the training was to provide the social workers with an opportunity to observe and assess the participants for suitability as foster parents. The second objective was to familiarize the participants with the information and resources that would help them to deal with the issues and challenges that were likely to arise as a result of dealing with traumatized children. The third objective was to provide an opportunity for potential foster parents to get a realistic perspective of the program and the process and hear from other foster parents, to make sure that it was the right program for them.

The fourth objective, which I believe was not consciously acknowledged by either the social workers or the agency, was to facilitate what Bennett (1998) refers to as an "inoculation." Bennett's concept of inoculation from a multicultural perspective is similar to the concept of inoculation from a medical perspective. The idea is that by exposing the body to a very small amount of a toxin, the body can adapt by developing antibodies to defend itself against the toxin. In the same way, if a facilitator anticipates that the introduction of a particular idea or concept is likely to elicit resistance or a strong negative reaction from the participants, he or she can minimize the intensity of the reaction by briefly introducing the concept at the beginning of the discussion and acknowledging that some people may have strong feelings about the material. Providing the participants with a "heads-up" before controversial information is presented increases the likelihood that the participants will stay engaged, open, and ultimately, will accept the concept. The belief is that participants are more likely to put up a defensive posture if they feel blindsided or overwhelmed by the information. It is a concept similar to the idea that if you drop a frog in a pot of hot water, it will immediately jump out. But if you place the frog in cool water and raise the heat slowly, the frog will not notice the change in temperature and will get cooked.

There are very appropriate uses for inoculation, when used consciously by individuals who have been properly trained. This technique is particularly useful when one is working with people and attempting to change behaviors or create a shift with respect to the values and beliefs that are collectively held about the world and what is or is not "normal." Breaking down what is perceived as a large change into smaller, less threatening segments helps the participant to digest or get used to an idea, just as cutting food into smaller pieces helps the body to digest it more easily. However, this technique can also be misused, even with the best of intentions. I believe this is particularly true if the individuals using it are operating with disenfranchised grief. I have heard it said that some of the most emotionally damaged people are practicing in the field of psychology, that they are drawn to the field to heal their own psychological wounds. My experience with the social workers in the parenting class has caused me to wonder if the same might said for some people drawn to social work.

I wondered whether the social workers facilitating the foster parent training knew they were using inoculation techniques, but I suspect that they did not. Two of the social workers said they had been working in the foster care system for over twenty years. I would have to describe them as being institutionalized in their thinking. I don't believe that either of them realized how many times they responded to a potential foster parent's expression of frustration or concern about the process by defending the foster care system or saying something like, "Well, the [foster care] system isn't perfect." I also don't believe that the social workers were very aware of the level of their own personal distress, but they were certainly reacting to it. Their behaviors suggested to me that their focus was directed internally on calming their own distress rather than outward toward the participants and being present to the participants' concerns.

On a number of occasions, when a participant raised challenging or particularly emotional issues or concerns in the training session, the social workers did even not allow the participant to finish their question or statement. Rather, they interrupted the participant with their own responses, which I noted appeared to be presented in a defensive manner. This was evidenced by such behaviors as raising their voices above the level of the participant's voice, their speech becoming more rapid, or talking over the participant such that the participant's voice couldn't be heard. On a couple of occasions, I also saw what appeared to be a panicked expression on their faces. I thought to myself, how many times do we not recognize this distress because we don't know what to look for?

Foster parenting is not an easy undertaking, and potentially adopting a child who has an unknown history regarding exposure to drugs, alcohol, neglect, physical, emotional, or sexual abuse is almost like playing Russian roulette. It takes a certain kind of person to be able to open your home and heart to a child not biologically related to you. There are not nearly enough people willing to do so and the need for good foster homes is desperate. However, given what I have learned with respect to what is being asked of foster parents and the shocking list of assaults to their self-esteem and psyches that they are expected to endure, I am beginning to understand why there aren't enough good foster parents.

It is this lengthy list of psychological assaults that I believe the social workers were attempting to inoculate the participants against. Potential foster parents are advised that the training is intended to provide them with a realistic overview of the foster care process and an awareness of the resources available to assist them in the care of their foster child. When I reviewed the sequencing of the topics that were presented during the training, it appeared to me that the less challenging topics were presented first and the more difficult issues came later in the training. As a trainer, it makes sense to sequence the material in this way. If I had been hit on the first day with the list of responsibilities and the almost total lack of voice or rights for foster parents, just as the frog immediately hops out of a pan of boiling water, I would not have come back the second week.

Instead, participants were drawn in with information about the overwhelming need and how special we were for even considering being foster parents. Early on, we also heard from two foster mothers who shared their experiences foster parenting a child who was later reunited with the birth family as well as a child that they were later able to adopt. I recall that I told my husband that it was striking to me that both foster mothers had made some strongly negative comments with respect to the foster care system. One foster mother even told the group the first and last name of a social worker that she suggested, "we avoid like the plague." And yet, both foster mothers had said that they would go through the experience again. Therefore, despite our misgivings, we continued to attend the sessions. Each week, depending on the topic, my husband and I went back and forth as to whether we really wanted to take this challenge on.

I now believe that the panel of mothers was an inoculation tactic. The stories the mothers told were an indirect way to inform the participants that the process was going to be difficult to accept, Further, using *mothers* to relay the message created an emotional hook for the participants because they had what we wanted: a child. The effectiveness of this strategy is evidenced by the fact that every participant did return each week, even after the presentation of information that was highly charged or difficult to accept.

One of the most shocking realizations I experienced during the training was to learn that the court system, at least in the state of Washington, does not recognize either the voice or the rights of foster parents or the attachment relationship that develops between foster parents and the children they care for. According to the social workers, the attitude of the courts toward foster parents is that they are not a party to the matter of the child's welfare. Foster parents have no rights and are regarded by the courts as little more than live-in babysitters. This information came to light during a training session that focused on dealing with birth parents. At the time, I did not understand just how profoundly the information shared at this session was going to impact the direction and focus of my research.

During the class, we were told that the court upholds the rights of the birth parent with respect to visitation, decisions concerning care of the child, and even reunification, whether or not they are complying with their parenting plan. We were given one handout that noted a long list of rights and few responsibilities for the birth parent, and a longer list of responsibilities with virtually no rights for the foster parent. The *only* rights that foster parents currently have in the state of Washington are the right to attend hearings that concern the foster child and the right to prepare a written report for the judge about the foster child's day-to-day activities.

Despite the fact that many foster placements can last upwards of two years before a final determination is made as to whether or not the child will be returned to the birth parents, we were told that the court does not even recognize the existence of the attachment relationship that develops between foster parent and child. As noted earlier, the court's position is that foster parents "are not a party to the matter." We also learned that the court never even speaks directly with the children with respect to what they want to or whether they desire to live with the birth parents or the foster parents. We were told that the court subscribes to the belief that objectivity is best stance when making placement decisions, and objectivity is best achieved by not having interaction with the child. Yet this position regarding objectivity does not appear to be equally applied because the court *does* have interaction with the birth parents via court hearings. As a result, it has been suggested that judges develop empathy toward the birth parents, but not the child, leaving the child in an extremely vulnerable position.

I found myself strongly reacting to this information, but kept trying to suspend judgment, until the topic of potential placement with family members other than the birth parent came up. The social worker described a hypothetical situation in which a child had been living with a foster family in Seattle for over a year when a grandmother living in Omaha was located, and she was willing to take guardianship of the child. We learned that, in such a situation, it was possible for the foster family to get a phone call to get the child packed up because he or she would be leaving the next day. The social worker said that, although the ideal process would allow for a transition period to help the child and the foster family to adjust to the separation, if the grandparent was ready for the child, the grandparent's desires were accommodated over the interests of the child.

I remember something just went off in my mind, like a flashbulb, and I couldn't help but raise my hand. I said that it seemed to me that if the grandmother really wanted what was best for the child, then she should be willing to haul her butt from Omaha to Seattle once a month for a period of at least six months in order to help the child to get to know her, and feel comfortable with her and with the transition. I said that I could not understand why there wasn't a provision that stipulated that the child's needs and stability were the highest priority, and that the adults in the child's life were required to accommodate the child's needs instead of the other way around. I started to feel angry and found myself asking out loud, "*Where is the voice of the child here?*" An African-American woman attending that evening looked at me and said, "I am with you, Sister." Then it seemed as though the place erupted and, suddenly, everyone started talking and there was a lot of emotion in the room. This was one of those times when the social workers were talking louder, faster, and over the participants.

However, it was a simple statement made by one social worker in particular that began to crystallize this uncomfortable feeling I had been carrying. In response to a question about why a longer transition time wasn't mandated so the child had more time to adjust, the social worker said, "*I guess as adults, we forget what its like to be a child.*" That statement reverberated through me like a shock wave. I remember wondering why do adults forget what its like to be a child? What gets in the way of our remembering?"

Whether understood or acknowledged by the agency staff or not, it is my concern that one potentially damaging outcome of their inoculation training strategy might be the development or exacerbation of disenfranchised grief in potential foster parents by quashing what I experienced and observed to be natural, and appropriate, protests on the part of the participants to practices or policies that are intuitively understood to be psychologically damaging, particularly with respect to the attachment relationship.

The question comes up for me because it was my observation that, in most instances, the participants' protests seemed to be expressing a concern for both the foster child's attachment needs and their own. The response from the social workers each time these concerns were expressed was to reiterate the expectation that foster parents were being called upon to make the sacrifice to take on all the suffering and frustration of the process so the child wouldn't have to. I could have gotten on board with that concept, *if* it was evident that this expectation was being placed on *all* the adults in the child's life, not just the foster parents. However, in spite of the espoused values of the agency that the children's needs came first, it seemed that many decisions were made in consideration of the birth parent, or a policy or procedure, and not what was best for the child.

I began to feel as though my good intentions and I were being manipulated. Just as important information had been withheld or managed by my doctors when I was getting treatment for cancer, I believe the social workers were also managing the presentation of the information to the prospective foster parents. In the same way that a frog gets lulled into not realizing it is being cooked by slowly increasing the water temperature, it seemed as though we were being lulled into accepting what felt more and more like a toxic situation. By introducing the difficult material slowly and then responding to our natural protests by linking the pain we were protesting about to a higher calling, the social workers were able to keep us engaged in the process. In reflecting upon this experience, it occurred to me that corporate leaders practice a similar strategy on employees and for a similar purpose: compliance. (See also Lipman-Blumen, 2006)

It is important to state that I believe the social workers themselves are carrying significant disenfranchised grief. I cannot imagine how else they would be able to manage the effects of seeing so much pain and unfairness, especially concerning children. The concern for me is that not recognizing and dealing with this grief is likely to have desensitized them. Therefore, these social workers may not be as responsive to the dissonance between their ethics as social workers and the role they play in the mistreatment of both foster parents and, of greatest significance, the children they are supposed to be protecting. I believe that disenfranchised grief keeps them from fully seeing the impact of their decisions on the children they are supposed to serve. Until this is recognized and addressed, I am afraid the situation will not change for these children.

CHAPTER 5

RECONSTRUCTING THE MAP

Have patience with everything unresolved in your heart and try to love the questions themselves, as if they were locked rooms or books written in a very foreign language. Don't search for the answers, which could not be given to you now because you would not be able to live them. And the point is, to live everything. Live the questions now. Perhaps then, someday far in the future, you will gradually, without even noticing it, live your way into the answer.

-Rainer Maria Rilke

I have now arrived at the point in the journey where I am called upon to formulate the *creative synthesis* that is the last phase of the heuristic inquiry. In other words, what does it all mean?

According to Moustakas (1990), a creative synthesis is:

The unified picture of the person in his or her world. All the parts fit together in an integrated way, forming an integral theme or world view *that enables one to understand how this person sees himself or herself and his or her life* [italics added]. The external situation may remain the same, but an internal bodily shift has occurred. The person has moved from a self-defeating view of his or her place in the world to a sense of being competent to meet life's challenges, with an uplift of self-confidence and self-esteem that casts new light on both identity and destiny. (pp. 122–123)

I have thought a great deal about how to present what I have discovered as a result of having made the choice to let go and see where Roads' (1987, in Moustakas, 1990) heuristic river would take me. It is important that my experience is thoughtfully presented because, as I understand Moustakas, the purpose of developing a creative synthesis is to weave all the individual strands (or stories) of the heuristic journey together such that the reader will both be able to see me as I am now and understand how I got to be where I am.

It is also important that my experience be thoughtfully presented because it might serve as a guide for others who choose to engage in the heuristic process. From my own experience, I believe that it is a journey worth taking. However, it is also a challenging journey, and one most individuals have not been adequately prepared for. Without such preparation, it is possible to come to the conclusion that perhaps the journey should not be made. There would be a profound loss to such a conclusion because I believe the heuristic journey is one that we are intended to make. Therefore, those of us who began our journeys as wounded storytellers (Frank, 1995) and who have experienced the "internal bodily shift" (Moustakas, p.

122) that comes with heuristic inquiry each bear the responsibility to reach back and share (or witness) our stories to others. As Frank notes:

> People tell stories not just to work out their own changing identities, but also to guide others who will follow them. They seek not to provide a map that can guide others – each must create his own – but rather to *witness the experience of reconstructing one's own map* [italics added]. Witnessing is one's duty to the commonsensical and to others. (1995, p. 17)

Through the experience of reconstructing my own map, I have come to believe that life itself is a heuristic inquiry, much like the mythic journey in Joseph Campbell's (1949) <u>The Hero with a Thousand Faces</u>. Each individual is given a unique set of characteristics and the inner directive to go out into the larger world and attempt to create his or her life. No one really knows ahead of time how that life will turn out or what may, or may not, be learned as a result. The only way to find out is to begin the journey. The way to begin the journey is to ask a question.

I believe that the lesson Rilke was trying to communicate to his young poet was that it is through the process of accepting and *living with* (rather than avoiding or denying) the questions that are raised by the circumstances we encounter in our lives that we are ultimately led toward the fundamental answer that each of us seeks: *what is to be the meaning of my life*? Through this heuristic inquiry, I have come to understand just how profoundly the presence of disenfranchised grief affected or interfered with both my ability to recognize my own significant questions and to embrace the discomfort that comes with truly engaging with them as I have tried to live my way toward the answers.

When I began this heuristic inquiry, I wanted to understand my experience as a mother of sexual minority children. I wanted to understand why, unlike almost half of the parents of lesbian, gay, bisexual, transgender, or questioning children, I did not reject Julian and Kristin when they came out to me with respect to their sexual and gender identities. However, while I may not have rejected them outright, I struggled at times to be supportive or to even feel empathy for Julian and Kristin in their efforts to formulate healthy identities. I felt that both the outcome as well as the experience could have been much more positive, for all of us, if I had been better prepared as a parent. I deeply resonated with Noddings' (2003) call to educate children from an ethic of care and believed that an education focused more on the development of healthy interpersonal relationships was the answer.

However, as a result of this heuristic inquiry and what I have come to understand about the influence of disenfranchised grief upon one's perceptual lens or view of the world, I now realize that education by itself is not sufficient. I now understand that the presence of disenfranchised grief impaired my ability to access my intelligence, to accept the guidance of caring teachers, to feel like a competent and worthwhile person, to trust the wisdom of my own voice, to establish healthy relationships, and most profoundly, to experience the pleasure and satisfaction of mothering. It wasn't until I had the opportunity to experience the integration of my disenfranchised grief and the subsequent "reconstruction of my map" (Frank, 1985,

p. 17) through my therapeutic relationship with an attuned and empathic analyst that I realized the magnitude of what had been lost to me.

A Description of the Process

I did not realize the degree to which I have been conditioned by the society in which I have been raised until the heuristic process challenged me to let go of what I believed I knew. I found the process of letting go of what one knows can be very difficult, but it can be done. In my case, I had to trick myself into engaging in the process by believing that I could control it. Despite my initial confidence that I could both let go of the process and still maintain control, I finally came to the realization that letting go literally meant letting go. In this instance, what I had to let go of was my certainty about what I expected to find at the conclusion of this inquiry. It meant focusing my efforts on being present to the process rather than trying to direct it. When I finally did let go, I found that the current of Roads' (1987) heuristic river took me to a much deeper place than I had originally envisioned, a place where I really needed and wanted to be. After experiencing the journey, I have wondered why I fought so hard to hang on. This seems to be the way with heuristic inquiry.

The first instance where the heuristic river began to nudge me to let go occurred early in the process of writing the five stories that comprise the data presented in Chapter Four. I made the decision to take a leave of absence from my job in order to concentrate on writing the stories. For several months, I had been getting up very early in the morning and trying to write for two or three hours before I went to work. I was able to accomplish a considerable amount working in this manner. However, I reached a point where I was no longer making much progress. I discovered that there was a point in the heuristic journey that required me to direct my full attention to the process.

I understand this call for the heuristic researcher to engage their full attention to be somewhat like the difference between traditional Freudian psychoanalysis (where the client meets with the analyst anywhere between three and five times a week) and weekly therapy. Heuristic inquiry is deep inquiry, as is psychoanalysis, and it takes time to access information buried deep in the unconscious. It is like having to drill through miles of bedrock to reach a group of trapped miners: you will get to them much more quickly if you are drilling around-the-clock rather than once a week for fifty minutes.

As a heuristic researcher, you have to both create a heuristic space and then let yourself go within that space in order to allow the heuristic process to take over. As a therapeutic client, you have to both commit to show up to the therapy appointments and then allow yourself to regress in the presence of the analyst in order to allow the therapeutic process to take over. Both are difficult to accomplish and one has to be truly motivated to stay with the process. For as long as I can remember, I have been not just highly motivated, but driven to understand why things happen as they do. Over seventeen years of working with my analyst has further honed that inherent drive, contributing to my development as a heuristic researcher and my ability to stay engaged in the heuristic process.

Through my efforts to establish a daily writing routine, I believe I unintentionally created what I now regard as a heuristic ritual that opened up a pathway to the deeper unconscious data I was seeking. Each morning as I prepared to write, I attempted to suppress my preconceived ideas about what I was exploring and to open myself to whatever information would be presented to me. I believe the purpose of this heuristic ritual had been to hone my mind's ability to be open, aware, and focused. It occurs to me now that my mind *had* to be open, aware, and focused in order for me to truly be able to make the choice to let go of the known, as Roads (1987) suggests, and allow the heuristic river to take me where I needed to go. I have learned that one does not just fall into a heuristic journey. One consciously chooses to engage in the heuristic journey with eyes wide open.

As I became immersed in the writing, I made the decision, as recommended by Moustakas (1990), not to read or edit the stories until I felt that they were finished. I also considered that, by not reading or editing the stories prior to their completion, it could be argued that the data was presented in its purest form. Once the stories were completed, I read through each one with the intent of trying to understand what they had to tell me and where they would lead me next. After reading the stories, I felt compelled to read the entire research proposal again. I was surprised to discover how strongly each of the stories reflected a number of themes that were also woven throughout the writing and literature included in the proposal, themes that I had not previously been aware of. Further, it was striking to me that each story had been written about specific relationships or events, not about specific themes, yet the themes were there.

The Question Reframed

As I began to take a deeper look at the themes that were emerging from the stories, I was struck by two observations that felt very significant to me. The first was my growing sense that the heuristic current was taking me in a very different direction from the one I had initially intended.

I began this journey with the intent of examining my experience as the mother of fraternal twins who are sexual and gender minorities and the process I went through in coming to acknowledge and accept their sexual and gender identities. I had intended to focus on my experience of becoming a more empathic parent to my children as my understanding and acceptance of them increased. I had also intended to explore why I had been able to make this shift toward greater empathic acceptance of my children's identities when research indicated that almost half the parents of LGBTQ children either did not or could not do so (Ryan & Futterman, 1998). I was certain that empathy and empathic parenting were the central concepts I was trying to understand.

My reflections about the kind of parent I had been to my children, as well as how I had been parented as a child, had me convinced that the psychological wounds my parents had unwittingly inflicted upon me, and which I in turn inflicted upon my children, were not the result of a lack of love, but rather, a lack of knowledge and understanding *about* love. I believed that if we'd had access to more relevant information and greater wisdom, perhaps we would have parented differently. The issue, I thought, was primarily one of providing a better education. Particularly the kind of education, advocated by Noddings (2003), that is based upon an ethic of care and focused on helping children to develop the critical interpersonal skills that contribute to the primary source of human happiness: fulfilling relationships with others (See also, Lewis, et al., 2000).

I did not want to let go of that idea because it had made so much sense to me and seemed to fit so well with my own experience. My parents were good parents. But they were also young and had neither the kind of education that Noddings (2003) envisioned nor the life experience that would have enabled them to recognize and regulate the distress of their sensitive (and traumatized) first-born child. I wanted to believe that if my parents had known, they would have recognized my distress and helped me to manage it, just as I wanted to believe that I would have done the same for my children. It was a matter of parents not understanding what their children really need from them. I was certain that the focus of my heuristic search, and the source of empathy, was the quality of the attachment relationship between mother and infant. I thought that if parents were better educated about the attachment relationship and its importance in the emotional development of children, they would be better able to understand what their children need from them.

I was so certain about the focus of my heuristic search that I almost missed the second significant observation, which was the realization that Lenhardt's (1997) previously introduced concept of disenfranchised grief played a much greater role than I initially thought. However, analysis of a number of what I came to regard as synchronistic events led me toward the realization that the focus of my research question was expanding beyond the attempt to understand the role of empathic parenting on the development of a healthy identity in LGBTQ children. I realized that my research question was also a personal quest to discover and learn to love, as Rilke (1903) noted, "all that is unresolved in your heart" (in Mitchell, 1984, pp. 34–35). Somehow, I knew that this resolution was related to the understanding of disenfranchised grief.

Some of these synchronistic events were independent experiences of mine that I recognized were somehow interrelated, such as the stories presented in Chapter Four about the missing voices of the patient and the child. However, other synchronistic events did not become evident to me until after I had shifted into the creative synthesis phase of the heuristic process. It wasn't until I took a step back to reflect upon all of the stories as a whole that I began to see evidence of a sympathetic resonance between them. I also believe that it was through the process of pausing to reflect upon this sympathetic resonance that the emergence of the idea that disenfranchised grief might obstruct or interfere with a parent's ability to be empathic and to experience an attuned relationship with her child began to develop. Before presenting a more focused discussion with respect to what I have discovered as a result of my exploration of disenfranchised grief, it may be helpful to the reader to first describe some of the synchronistic experiences that directed my exploration.

Synchronicity

> *We've all had those perfect moments, when things come together in an almost unbelievable way, when events that could never be predicted, let alone controlled, remarkably seem to guide us along our path. The closest I've come to finding a word for what happens in these moments is 'synchronicity.' My quest to understand synchronicity arose out of a series of events in my life that led me into a process of inner transformation. As a result of this transformation I decided to follow a dream that I had held close to my heart for a number of years. It was the most difficult decision I had ever made, but the day I made it, I crossed a threshold. From that moment on, what happened to me had the most mysterious quality about it. Things began falling into place almost effortlessly, and I began to discover remarkable people who were to provide crucial assistance to me . . . Then I lost the flow and almost destroyed the dream I had worked so hard to establish. Ultimately I regained the capacity to participate in what I later came to understand as an unfolding creative order..*

> *-Joseph Jaworski*

As I continued to think about the development of my creative synthesis, I slowly began to notice another pattern or theme emerge out of the five stories. When I stopped looking at each of the stories as separate experiences and instead considered them collectively, I found that each of these experiences had contributed in some significant way toward my development. Regardless of how painful the experience may have been, I could not think of a single instance when I did not come away with some new or deeper level of awareness or understanding about myself. I also noted that these experiences, whether significant or relatively minor, were all serenity challenges in some way or another. Introduced in the first chapter, serenity challenges are experiences in which you are confronted with situations or problems that you have no ability or power to change, such as serious illness, divorce, the death of a loved one, or the sexual or gender identity of your child (J. Mavrelis, personal communication, August, 2002). Given the fact that you cannot change the situation, the only choice you do have is whether or not you are willing to go *through* it.

The writings of philosophers, psychologists, and poets suggest that humans are supposed to go through these experiences, or serenity challenges, because they are the necessary precursors to growth or transformation (Bridges, 2002; Frank, 2003; Frankel, 1984; Frick, 1990; Jung, 1963; Rilke, 1903). Serenity challenges are like those precisely placed blows by a diamond cutter that transforms a rough stone into a brilliant diamond. These challenges are the manifestations of Jung's (1963) metaphysical alchemical process whereby base matter is transformed into gold. Serenity challenges are also the equivalent of Frick's (1990) symbolic growth experiences (SGE), the outcome of which is said to be:

A sudden, dramatic shift in perception, belief, or understanding that alters one's frame of reference or world view. The internal change or revision is usually connected with an external event but the connection is synchronistic, an intentional or spontaneous happening rather than the result of a cause-effect relationship. The shift in perception and meaning launches in some measure a new attitude, a new process of learning, a character or personality shift in identity and selfhood. (in Moustakas,1990, p. 99)

As I reflected upon the many serenity challenges I had encountered in my life, it appeared to me that they had not only contributed to my development, they also seemed to have been specifically designed and orchestrated to bring me to a particular place and for a particular purpose. The most compelling sign of this synchronistic element was my recognition that two seemingly *different* experiences, a conference on care of the dying and a foster parent training course, led to my asking two very *similar* questions: "*Where is the voice of the patient?*" and "*Where is the voice of the child?*" I recall thinking that it seemed highly unlikely that this could be simply coincidence. There had to be a reason. So what was the reason? What was I supposed to learn or do?

I started to think more about the concept of synchronicity and went in search of my copy of Jaworski's (1996) work, Synchronicity: The Inner Path of Leadership. Jaworski presents two definitions of synchronicity: Carl Jung's definition and Arthur Koestler's. Jung defined synchronicity as "a meaningful coincidence of two or more events, where something other than the probability of chance is involved" (p. 88). Koestler, rather than seeing a connection between separate events, instead saw connections *within* them. Jaworski noted that Koestler "traces the idea of unity-in-diversity all the way back to the Pythagorean harmony of the spheres and the Hippocratics' 'sympathy of all things' – There is one common flow, one common breathing, all things are in sympathy'" (p. 88).

As I continued my consideration of the five stories as a collective body, it seemed that there was a sympathetic resonance between them. Further, I saw evidence of "one common flow, one common breathing" (Ibid.), given that the stories seemed to have been presented to me in a particular order and for a particular purpose. It seemed that Julian and Kristin's stories were presented first for the specific purpose of preparing both the researcher and the reader for the remainder of the heuristic journey. As the researcher, the purpose of beginning with Julian and Kristin's stories seemed to be a way to open me up, such that I felt I was being fully present to them for probably the first time. For the reader, the purpose of beginning with Julian and Kristin's stories was to bring the reader to a similar place as the researcher, so that the reader could then move through the remainder of the heuristic journey alongside the researcher.

Additional evidence that supports the existence of a sympathetic resonance between the stories made itself known through what I have come to understand as a number of *peak moments* in the heuristic process. Moustakas (1990) defines peak moments as those times when the researcher "recognizes the universal nature of what something is and means, and at the same time grows in self-understanding and as a self" (p. 90). I have been privileged to experience a number of peak moments during the course of this heuristic inquiry as well as during the course of my life. It seems that these peak moments have also been synchronistic and sympathetic in nature. They appear to have occurred in a particular order, they proved to play a pivotal role in my movement toward the next phase of the heuristic process, and each seemed to have been preparatory for the peak moment that followed.

The first peak moment I experienced is embedded in the first story, "Re-Discovering the Voice of my Body." I understand this story to be the foundation for the stories that followed in that it was during my illness with cancer that a number of key insights or choices occurred. The first key insight was my recognition of the interesting and ironic paradox that my body, which all my life I had regarded as an adversary, could become my ally and the instrument through which I would rediscover the lost voice of my body, and later, other lost voices as well. My experience with cancer created a situation in which I had to be both highly focused and attuned to my body, and for a considerable period of time, if I was going to survive. Further, the six months that I had to manage my bowel activity with an ostomy bag honed my ability to pay attention to and learn my body's cycles in order to determine the optimal times to change the bag. It also taught me that I could manage my distress, which at times felt overwhelming, when things didn't go well. I regard the ability to manage my distress as being critical to my ability to delve deeper into my own disenfranchised grief.

As I reflect upon it now, I cannot help but come to the conclusion that there had to be a synchronistic aspect to the erroneous delivery of clear rather than opaque ostomy bags (which provided me with a window to my body), as well as the many bag failures I suffered through. Each of these experiences played a significant role in directing my attention toward my body such that I began to literally *see* what was going on within me. I now believe that the development of this ability to see direct evidence of my embodied voice was, in effect, preparation for the next step, which was to connect the visual cues with the physical sensations in my body. I became familiar with these physical sensations and learned to recognize them as my body's "words." In time, I began to learn how to read my body in much the same way as I remember learning how to read a book.

I believe the development of this literacy with respect to my embodied voice proved to be a necessary step in preparation for the realization of two other significant insights that would emerge out of this foundational peak moment experience. These experiences occurred at a time when I had to undergo a series of additional surgeries and extended hospital stays due to complications from the treatment of my cancer. It was during this period that many of the previously recounted experiences when I had felt unseen or unrecognized as a human being by my medical caregivers took place.

These experiences helped me to realize that the actions of many of the medical professionals, despite their view of themselves as caregivers, were likely motivated by what was in their best interests and not necessarily what was in mine. I now believe that disenfranchised grief can interfere with a caregiver's ability to recognize the suffering of their patients, and sometimes, to even see their patients as human beings. I don't believe that caregivers can be present to or assist their patients with managing the distress that comes with serious illness or impending death unless and until they can recognize or acknowledge their own. From my experiences dealing with serious illness and with the sense of abandonment I sometimes felt after an interaction with one of my caregivers, I learned that I could not be just a passive actor in my own life, nor was it appropriate to pass authority for my life over to someone else just because they were identified as an expert or an authority. I could not just assume that my caregivers understood what I needed; I had to make sure they understood. My life was my responsibility and I had to be my own advocate and speak up on my own behalf. If I didn't speak up, I would be the one who suffered, not my caregivers. I was fortunate to be able to come to this realization and to be able to speak up. There are many who are not as fortunate.

The argument for a synchronistic relationship between my serenity challenge experiences was strengthened by my observation that these experiences appeared to be pivotal in sensitizing and refining my awareness. This sensitivity contributed to my awareness of the disenfranchised grief underlying the missing voice of the patient at a conference that was supposed to be dedicated to understanding the needs of the patient. It also contributed to my hearing the missing voice of the child in a system that was supposed to be focused on the protection of that child and charged with acting in his or her best interests. From my reflections about these experiences of feeling so vulnerable and so unseen, I not only discovered my own voice, I was also beginning to hear the countless voices of others who had been silenced as well.

A second peak moment is embedded within the title of the story; "Where is the Voice of the Patient?" When I first considered the question, I thought its significance had to do with its ability to convey the powerful emotional impact of my experience with cancer and the way I was sometimes made to feel by the people in whom I literally had entrusted my life. However, I came to understand that the peak moment was actually my recognition that there was a synchronistic relationship to another question that I would later ask about the missing voice of the child.

The synchronistic relationship between these two questions became evident to me when I recognized the striking similarity of the contexts in which the two questions came to me. The first question (Where is the voice of the patient?) came to me while in a setting that was supposed to be focused on the care and needs of the dying patient and yet the patient's voice was absent. The second question (Where is the voice of the child?) came to me while in a setting that was supposed to be focused on the care and needs of foster children. This time it was the child's voice that was missing. The recognition of this synchronistic relationship led to the next peak moment in my journey.

The third peak moment was my realization that these two strikingly similar questions had arisen out of a profoundly emotional response to something I experienced while in two different situations which, on the surface, would appear to have been unrelated events. I attended a conference on care for the dying because a friend asked me to go with her. I had seen information about the conference and it had not drawn my interest. But when my friend asked me to go with her, I thought that it might be a good experience for me. At the time of this conference, the idea of parenting again was not a conscious consideration for me. Any discussion between my husband and I with respect to parenting again would have focused on whether to adopt a child, not whether to become foster parents to one. In fact, I can recall saying to myself that I would never want to be a foster parent. I had had no idea at the time of the conference on care for the dying that I would be attending a foster parenting class less than a year later, and asking a strikingly similar question.

I felt a chill run through me as I thought about the similarity of these two powerful questions and began to recognize the common element whose absence I had so strongly reacted to—neither the presence nor the voice of either patient or child had been recognized in either situation. These were some of the most vulnerable members of our society and they had no voice. It was not simply a matter of having less of a voice; they literally had *no* voice. They were not seen. Despite the fact that both the medical professionals and the social workers stated repeatedly, and probably consciously believed, that the needs of the patient and the child were their primary focus, their actions suggested otherwise.

At the conference, the missing voice of the patient was evidenced by the lack of workshops dedicated to understanding the needs of the patient. Rather, the focus of the overwhelming majority of the workshops was on the needs (and the distress) of the caregiver and management of the health care system in which the caregiver had to function. The only activity that presented the experience of the patient was the film, Wit (2001), but the film was shown in the evening after a long day of workshops, and was never debriefed. The missing voice of the child in the foster care system was evidenced by three things: 1) the fact that a child is not allowed to speak to the judge with respect to custody or placement decisions that are being made on his or her behalf, 2) the fact that the courts do not recognize the voice of the foster parent or the importance of the attachment relationship that develops between foster parent and foster child, and 3) based upon its decisions, the court appears to place greater priority and accommodation toward the needs of the birth parent or adult caregiver over the needs or best interests of the child.

Another example that illustrates the extent to which the child's voice is missing in the foster care system described how the participants in the foster parenting class my husband and I had attended were prepared for the possibility that a foster placement could result not in adoption, but rather in the return of the child to the birth family or placement with another relative even if the child had been placed into foster care at birth and the foster parents were the only parents the child had ever known. If this forced separation occurred during the critical period when attachment bonds are being formed, or was just the latest in a series of abrupt separations from attachment figures, the impact could be devastating for the child. It could also be deeply painful or devastating for the foster parents. But foster parents are adults, which was the reason why we had to be advised. The children get no such consideration.

It feels deeply disturbing to me to consider that the courts and the foster care system do not appear to acknowledge the potential trauma and developmental disruption these children are likely to experience as a result of the loss of their primary attachment figures, particularly when it seems so obvious that much of this trauma and disruption could, at the very least, be significantly reduced through a more gradual transition of custody. A simple six-month transition plan that allows time for the child to develop a relationship with her new guardian, while in the familiar setting of her foster family, would help make the transition easier. A gradual transition could also increase the likelihood of identifying potentially unsuccessful placements *before* the child is put through the trauma of a move.

Yet, according to the social workers facilitating the class, these concerns are rarely, if ever, even brought up. How is it that something so important is not even mentioned by those responsible for the welfare of these children, particularly given that these children have already experienced significant trauma or abuse? I wondered if this might be an example of Pope's (2003) assertion that many of the problems of our youth are "the direct result of the abdication of adults who are supposed to love and protect our young and help them to develop into healthy and productive citizens" (p. 44). Pope was writing about sexual minority youth. However, his assertion strikes me as being relevant for children in the foster care system as well. Further, Pope's assertion that "failing to create a safe environment for all children is criminal and unethical behavior" (Ibid.), also strikes me as applicable to those responsible for the welfare of children in foster care.

The more I reflected on this example, the more it seemed as though the voices of the most vulnerable members of our society were *deliberately* being overridden or left out and I could not understand how or why this could happen. A statement made by one of the social workers in the foster parenting class had captured my attention and pointed me in the direction of a possible explanation. She'd said, "I guess as adults, we forget what its like to be a child." When I'd heard her statement, I felt as though bells, alarms, whistles, and sirens were sounding off in my head. I remember thinking to myself, "That's it! As adults, we distance ourselves from what it was like to be a child! Why? Why would we need to distance ourselves?" It occurred to me that disenfranchised grief might not just be an individual phenomenon: it might also be a *societal* phenomenon.

I thought about the recent shooting incident at Virginia Tech as a possible indicator of this societal disenfranchised grief. Early news reports after the incident suggested that a number of people, apparently the shooter's parents among them, indicated that they had no idea that there was anything wrong with this young man. However, as the news media probed deeper into the suspect's background, as typically happens after such an incident, it was revealed that there were a few people who apparently *had* noticed something. But in interview after interview, these individuals stated that they had dismissed what they had seen because either they had been taught that feelings weren't a tangible basis for action or they did not believe that it was their place to speak up—and they let it go.

It appears that a primordial limbic alarm went off informing these individuals that a member of our society was in need of help. However, our culture has trained us to think, *"If it's not my direct responsibility, then it's not my problem."* As a result, we either fail to hear the alarm or we fail to recognize its importance. Further, if societal disenfranchised grief is present, such "alarms" from vulnerable or troubled people are likely to activate our individual levels of distress. Given that this distress or grief has, in effect, been banned from our conscious awareness, any experience that could potentially bring this distress back to our awareness is likely to be met with denial or fierce resistance. The societal response, as Pope (2003) has pointed out, is to turn our collective backs and abdicate our responsibility of protecting our young. But as the increasing violence in our society painfully illustrates, it *is* our problem and too many people die because we simply aren't getting the message.

I began to consider that there might be a connection between these two questions: 1) Why is it that as adults we forget what its like to be a child, and 2) Why don't more people recognize when someone is troubled and intervene sooner? I wondered whether societal disenfranchised grief might be the connection and the explanation. If so, it seems appropriate to suggest that developing an understanding of disenfranchised grief might be a significant step toward discovering the answers to questions such as these. Further, these situations suggest to me that there could be another way to understand disenfranchised grief that is possibly distinct from, or at the very least, expands upon Lenhardt's (1997) definition. Therefore, it seems appropriate to move into a deeper exploration of the concept of disenfranchised grief.

Disenfranchised Grief Reconsidered

I was first exposed to the concept of disenfranchised grief, defined by Lenhardt as resulting from "experiences that are not or cannot be openly acknowledged by peers or society" (in Bracciale, et al., 2003, p. 4), because it had been proposed as one of the reasons why parents reject their LGBTQ children. For a long time, that was the only meaning the term held for me. But as I have come to understand and trust through my journey, the heuristic river keeps nudging you until you let go of old ideas so that new ones can emerge. I kept coming across references that pointed to this concept of disenfranchised grief and I finally took a closer look. The more I learned about this concept, the more *familiar* it felt to me.

As I learned more about disenfranchised grief, I began to suspect that it might exist on a much broader scale than previously defined or understood. My childhood experiences were a validation of the notion that disenfranchised grief was operating on an individual level. My experiences with my medical caregivers as well as the social worker's statement about how adults forget what it's like to be a child triggered the possibility in my mind that disenfranchised grief might also be operating at a societal level. If this were true, then the current definition, as well as the overall understanding, of disenfranchised grief must be incomplete. I began to believe that that the definition (and source of) disenfranchised grief could not be limited to simply "those experiences that are not or cannot be openly acknowledged by peers or society" (Ibid.). Disenfranchised grief might also result from loss experiences that are not or cannot be openly acknowledged *by or to one's own Self* as a result of attachment or attunement failures with the mother (primary caregiver or attachment figure) early in childhood.

Because the impact of the disenfranchised grief I saw appeared to be both individual and societal, it made sense that the source of the grief or loss would have to be something universally experienced, such as the experience of being parented. The fact that this societal grief is disenfranchised also suggests an association with the presence of shame as a result of how one was parented. This association is supported by Karen (1994), who argues, "the very fact of not being attuned to... is in itself a shame-inducing experience" (p. 239). Further, shame, as Karen notes below, is not an emotion that humans manage well.

> Built into the very nature of shameful self-feelings *is a desire to ignore them.* [italics added] Indeed, we often construct our lives in such a fashion as to keep them out of consciousness and away from the view of others. So it is not uncommon, even in adulthood, to be burdened with unexamined and hateful self-concepts first incorporated at a young age. (p. 206)

The potential consequences of carrying these unexamined and hateful self-concepts into adulthood as well as into the role of parenting can be profound. It does not seem unreasonable to suggest that the presence of disenfranchised grief, to a greater or lesser degree, obstructs, damages, or in some instances, can destroy a parent's ability to be an attuned emotional regulator of her children's distress and to provide her children with a secure attachment experience. According to Karen:

> The first emotions that the parent deals with are the attachment emotions themselves – the baby's desire for connection, his need to be taken care of, his need to be responded to when hungry, when in pain, when wanting love or attention. *Many parents, because their own dependency needs were rebuffed as children, still live in unresolved pain over them. But the pain is not felt, it is dissociated, and they structure their lives to keep it that way.* [italics added] An avoidant boy who is ashamed of being needy may grow up to be a man who is a caricature of independence, unable to ask for help or closeness or *even to feel those longings within himself* [italics added] without risking the disintegration of his self-respect. Will he be warmly receptive to moments of clinginess or dependency in his own little boy? (p. 243)

Karen goes on to state:

> Clinical evidence suggests that parents cannot tolerate seeing their unmet needs expressed by their children, and they cannot tolerate the anger and distress the child expresses when those needs go unmet again. They either overreact or become dismissive, with the result that the child's attachment feelings – *as well as his anger and distress* [italics added] – are either walled off from his consciousness or revved up to the point where they overwhelm him. His ability to communicate his attachment-related feelings is gradually shrunken and distorted *until it demands misinterpretation* [italics added] (Ibid.).

This distortion and misinterpretation by the child of their attachment-related feelings is experienced or expressed as a form of insecure attachment (Ainsworth, 1978). To help refresh the reader's memory, Lewis, Amini and Lannon (2000) described secure and insecure attachment as follows:

> A mother who had been consistently attentive, responsive, and tender to her infant raised a *secure* child, who used his mother as a safe haven from which to explore the world. He was upset and fussy when she left him and reassured and joyful when she came back. A cold, resentful, rigid mother produced an *insecure-avoidant* child, who displayed indifference to her return by turning his back or crawling away to a suddenly fascinating toy in the corner. The baby of a mother distracted or erratic in her attentions became an *insecure-ambivalent* toddler, clutching at his mother when they were together, dissolving into wails and shrieks when the two were separated, and remaining inconsolable after their reunion. (p. 74)

Therefore, children who experience their parents' unacknowledged resentment toward their dependency and attachment needs become wounded children who dissociate from their attachment feelings as well as their anger and distress. The experience for children with parents who are operating with unacknowledged distress is one of never being sure when their parents will be appropriately responsive to their dependency and attachment needs and when they will not. These children are often left questioning their own worth because humans, as meaning-making beings, require an explanation for that which they do not understand. Children are no exception. If the expectation is that mothers always respond appropriately to their children, what happens when they don't? According to Karen:

> The mothers of insecure children hung back, *giving no assistance even when it was needed,* or *got involved in ways that the child couldn't use* [italics added], with the result that some passive children never got the push they needed and others became so frustrated that the experience was ruined for them. In either case their confidence could only have been undermined by such experiences. (p. 182)

In examining my own experience, I now believe that children with otherwise good parents who carry *both* unacknowledged resentment and unacknowledged distress (from their own disenfranchised grief) face the greatest challenges. These children experience and attempt to articulate the painful impact of their parents' unacknowledged resentment. However, parents with disenfranchised grief are not likely to be able to tolerate awareness of either their resentment or their distress. It is likely that these parents will either deny the child's experience or project it back onto the child. Further, if the parents are good parents in most other respects, it increases the likelihood that these children may ultimately misinterpret or accept that they are to blame. I believe this because I consider myself as having been one of these children.

A Legacy of Disenfranchised Grief

My father didn't get to have much of a childhood. Born in 1935, his formative years occurred during the ending of the Great Depression and beginning of World War II. During his early years, my father's cultural influences must have included rationing, deprivation, and sacrificing for the greater good. These were serious times. Like many families of that era, my father's family was relatively poor. These circumstances contributed to my father, as the oldest child, developing a strong sense of responsibility. One of the family stories I recall hearing as a child was about my father, at age six, hunting for rabbits in a field in order to help put meat on the table. From comments I have heard my father make over the years, I believe that his way of dissociating from the painful loss of his own childhood was to regard childhood itself as frivolous.

I also believe that my father's dissociated grief came out as an unacknowledged resentment toward his own children for having the childhood that he was denied. As the sole provider for a wife and four children, I think there were times when my father resented all the responsibility he had to carry. His job was demanding and stressful and it seemed that he was often angry. He was also a strict disciplinarian and I remember being afraid of him. I can now appreciate how difficult it must have been for my father to manage all the responsibility and stress and also be expected to provide a myriad of enriching experiences for his children, experiences that he had missed out on himself. I can also now appreciate that he provided these experiences for us in spite of his resentment.

I believe my mother also carried unacknowledged resentment and distress into adulthood. Like my father, my mother didn't get to have much of a childhood. Her parents both worked and, by the age of nine, she was expected to care for her younger siblings, clean the house, and have dinner ready when her parents came home. In addition to not having much of a childhood, my mother also didn't get to have much mothering. My siblings and I had a different experience because my mother stayed at home with us. About her choice to be a stay-at-home mother, I remember her telling me, "You don't get close to someone who is not around." In addition to not being physically present for her children, I believe that my grandmother was not emotionally present to them either. I suspect that she too must have also carried significant unacknowledged resentment toward her children.

One example that illustrates this unacknowledged resentment was the way my grandmother responded to my mother's first menstruation. My mother was the fifth of seven children and the fourth daughter. So, my grandmother was an experienced parent by the time my mother came into her adolescence. Yet, my mother went to her older sister, not her mother, when she saw blood on her underwear. She said that she "confessed" (being raised Catholic) to her sister because she thought she must have done something wrong and felt ashamed. It was her sister, not her mother, who explained menstruation to my mother and showed her what to do. Later, my aunt approached my grandmother and asked her why she hadn't talked to her daughter about menstruation. My grandmother's dismissive response was, "Why should I tell her? My mother never told me."

When it was my time to learn about menstruation, my mother made sure that I had the information I needed. She was not able to tell me herself, just as her mother had not told her. Instead, my mother took me to a lecture about sexual reproduction and menstruation given by a medical doctor. I can still remember the name of the lecture and the small booklet the participants were provided, <u>A Doctor Talks to Nine Through Twelve Year Olds</u>. It was clinical, and a male doctor presented it, but it was information. Later on, when my own children came into adolescence, I was able to be the one who talked with them. A little at a time, the legacy is changing.

There were times when my parents were able to transcend their disenfranchised childhood distress and were able to recognize and respond to my dependency needs, such as when my mother took me to the lecture on menstruation. But there were other times when I believe that this unacknowledged distress created an obstruction or barrier and it seemed that I had to use drastic measures to get my parents' attention. I was the last girl in my class to get a bra in the sixth grade. I remember waiting for my mother to notice that my breasts were developing so she could take me to get a bra. But she never said anything and the girls in my physical education class had started to make fun of me. One Sunday morning, I decided I had to take matters into my own hands. My parents were sitting at our dining room table with a cup of coffee, which was their post-church ritual. I approached the table, pulled up my shirt and asked, "Am I ready yet?" My mother took me out to get a bra that afternoon.

I now believe that I felt deeply angry that I had to work so hard to get my parents to notice me, to recognize my developmental needs, and to help me with them. But how could I get mad at the people upon whom I depended for my survival for not being attuned to me? How could I have known that the reason why I felt such overwhelming pain and frustration was because I needed the help of my parents to develop and I wasn't getting it? I didn't know and I took the blame upon myself. I thought that I must not be worth noticing. I thought that I must be bad and I felt ashamed. I carried that self-hating message for many years. How could I have known that my mother would likely have difficulty recognizing my developmental needs, not because I was defective and not worth it, but because she had never had her needs recognized by her mother? This appears to be the way in which this form of disenfranchised grief is transmitted from one generation to the next.

My father unknowingly reinforced my belief that I was a bad kid with a casual comment he made to me on my tenth birthday. The entire family was going to see the Ice Capades for my birthday. I was sitting in the front seat of our car next to my father. I remember that he looked down at me and told me that I had started out as a lump of indigestion. I don't recall my father's facial expression or the tone of his voice when he said that, but I interpreted his comment to mean that I was a disappointment to him—that I had started out as something bad and things had not changed. I can remember attributing his disappointment to the fact that I had not been born male. But because it was said on my birthday, I started to question whether my father was telling me that I shouldn't have been born at all. At age ten, I was not able to consider that my father *must* have been glad that I was born because he was spending what little discretionary income he had available to take the entire family to a special event on my birthday. All I heard was that I shouldn't have been born.

Recently, on my 50th birthday, my parents spent the evening with my husband and me. They brought over a very nice bottle of champagne and made a toast to my birth. It was a particularly meaningful toast for me, as I was very glad to see my fiftieth birthday after my illness with cancer. As we were sipping the champagne, my father looked at me, smiled and said, "You know, you started out as a lump of indigestion." He took my mother's hand and told me that one night, shortly after they were married, he had to take my mother to the emergency room because she was having severe abdominal pain. He was terrified that my mother might have appendicitis and that he might lose her. He was 21 years old and my mother was 18. My father said the doctor examined my mother and came out to reassure him that she would be okay. The doctor then asked my father how long he and my mother had been married. When my father responded that they had only been married for a couple of months, the doctor told my father that he wanted him to bring my mother in to see him the following week. My father looked at me, smiled again and said, "That is how we found out that you were on the way."

I remember feeling stunned when he said that. I looked at my father and said, "Dad, do you have any idea what I have been carrying around about that story?" He looked at me with a somewhat surprised expression. I went on, "When you said that I started out as a lump of indigestion, I thought you were telling me that I had started out as a pain in the ass and that I still was one. I thought you were telling me that you were sorry that I had been born, because it was my birthday." My father just shook his head.

I found it interesting to consider that the same comment from my father, heard at age ten and understood to mean that I shouldn't have been born, would be heard again at age 50 and understood to mean something very different. My father is a natural storyteller and he was sharing with me the story about when I came into his life. Hearing the story at age 50, I could now see my father as a young man, newly married and with a very sick wife. I can imagine him feeling helpless and terrified. I can imagine his relief upon learning that he wasn't going to lose his wife, but instead, was going to become a father. I can now hear the gladness in his voice. You hear stories very differently at age ten than you do at age 50. One of the reasons why, I believe, is the presence of disenfranchised grief.

Unlike my siblings and I, my children were very vocal with respect to their dependency needs and their distress when those needs were not met. I now recognize that when my children did express or act out their distress, my own disenfranchised grief manifested as a sense of feeling overwhelmed and resentful. I felt overwhelmed and resentful a lot. I recall sometimes feeling that way when my children wanted my affection, touch, or attention; it felt as though I was being held hostage. I think I felt like a hostage because acknowledging my children's needs would mean I would have had to acknowledge my own. I wasn't able to do that because my distress had been disenfranchised and split off, and I didn't know why or how. It is sometimes frightening to consider how long this unconscious battle had been raging within me without my even being aware of it. I now know that the cost of dissociating from my distress in order to protect myself was high. Splitting off from the distress or pain meant also splitting off from the pleasure that comes from existing in attunement with myself and with others (Lewis, et al, 2000). It was a bargain with the devil that I had not even realized I had made.

Disenfranchised Grief and the Wounded Child

It might be expected that the current focus in the U.S. on improving the overall statistics concerning child development and education would indicate a shift with respect to the culture's value of children. Statistics can provide valuable information regarding the existence of a problem, and, possibly, who is affected. However, statistics alone cannot tell us why the issue exists, what it means, or how to respond. Therefore, it could be argued that this increased focus has accomplished little more than to place additional stress upon already besieged parents to become increasingly more involved in the lives of their children. As a result, the schedules of children and parents alike are becoming increasingly filled to capacity with activities that, while of value, are likely not meeting the child's fundamental dependency or attachment needs. Fulfillment of these needs requires involvement with an attuned parent, which is something even the most interesting of extracurricular activities cannot provide.

Further, to the extent that parents are operating with disenfranchised resentments or distress, the additional stress created by unrealistic societal expectations could have a negative impact on how parents interpret their children's needs as well as their ability to be responsive to them. With little societal recognition, acknowledgement, or education with respect to the existence of these unacknowledged feelings of resentment or distress by a parent toward their children's dependency needs, the likelihood that parents are going to displace these ill feelings onto their children seems quite high (Noddings, 2003).

As a result, it is likely that many children are receiving inconsistent, conflicting, or deeply confusing messages from their parents. In one respect, children might feel very much the focus of their parents' attentions, particularly those children whose parents actually attend some their extracurricular activities. However, when it comes to "providing their children with examples of what to do when problems arise," what Wilson-O'Halloran (1996) describes as "the function of responsive parents" (p. 4), the societal denial and lack of education regarding this disenfranchised grief leaves parents unaware and unprepared to serve as healthy emotional role models for their children.

Mothers, socialized to expect to feel nothing but deep love for their infants, often feel blindsided and deeply ashamed when they find themselves sometimes feeling like they hate their babies (Lewis, et al, 2000). Because humans do not manage shameful feelings very well, these feelings are often repressed. As noted previously by Karen (1998), "Many parents, because their own dependency needs were rebuffed as children, still live in unresolved pain over them. But the pain is not felt, it is dissociated, and they structure their lives to keep it that way" (p. 243).

When parents structure the family environment to keep their distress and pain dissociated, I believe their children are often wounded as a result.

Children can also be wounded if their parents' reaction to their distress signals is one of distress and denial because, not only do they lose out on an opportunity to learn to work through their feelings, but their parents' distress and denial places the child in a difficult dilemma. If the child is experiencing distress and her parents deny her distress, the fact that the child is dependent upon her parents, both physically and psychologically, often means she has no alternative other than to dissociate from her reality or what she knows to be true in an attempt to maintain the connection to her parents. She does this in order to survive. However, the impact of this unconscious survival strategy is a double-edged sword. The child survives, but no longer has access to her innermost self. It follows then that she would also lose access to her voice. It becomes disenfranchised.

The recognition that there might be a society of wounded children made me realize that my research question had expanded beyond the need for better education about LGBTQ parenting. I began this heuristic inquiry with the belief that I could have had a more positive experience as a mother if I had been provided with more relevant information. However, through this heuristic journey, I discovered that access to even the most cutting-edge information might not have been enough. Therefore, while I continue to believe that Noddings' (2003) call to educate our children from an ethic of care is very important, what Noddings and other educational leaders may not recognize is the possibility that the presence of disenfranchised grief may prevent or interfere with a child's ability to take in or benefit from even the best education. How can a wounded child be educated if access to her innermost self has been cut off?

To better understand the impact that disenfranchised grief can have on a child's ability to be educated, it seems appropriate to begin with a definition of education. One definition of the phrase "to educate," refers to the development of an individual's *"innate capacities*, especially by schooling or instruction" (Source: www.thefreedictionary.com/educate). The word, *innate*, refers to something that is "possessed at birth; inborn" or "possessed as an essential characteristic; inherent" (Ibid.). Definitions of *capacity*, include both "the ability to receive, hold, or absorb," as well as the "innate potential for growth, development, or accomplishment; faculty" (Ibid.).

According to these definitions, to educate a child means to develop or bring forth those essential characteristics *contained within the child* that have been present in the child since birth. These innate characteristics are deemed essential because they are fundamental to the child's ability to realize her capacity or to achieve her growth potential. This definition sounds strikingly similar to the Ojibwa concept of the Red Road. The development of the child's capacity also includes the development of her ability to receive, hold, or absorb the necessary information that she will need in order to realize her potential. This idea, too, is evident in the Ojibwa community's practice of the ethic of non-interference. If the definition and purpose of education is to develop and bring forth that which is innate in the child but access to her innermost self has been cut off, it seems reasonable to conclude that the child's potential cannot be reached.

I don't believe that Noddings or anyone within the ranks of educational leadership has recognized the impact of an educational system designed for open minds operating in a sea of closed-off, wounded children. It seems not unlike my experience with the ostomy bag and the numerous bag failures with which I had to contend. Much of the anxiety, stress, and frustration I experienced as a cancer patient was the result of my trying to adapt a device that was designed to function properly on a flat, firm abdomen to work on my softer, less toned one. When I consider that the ostomy bag is most likely to be utilized by a population whose abdomens are in a similar condition to mine, it raises the question, why was the ostomy bag designed for ideal conditions rather than realistic ones?

I believe that the U.S. educational system, like the U.S. health-care system, may be operating in a state of disenfranchised grief. And it is likely to remain that way, because to acknowledge that societal disenfranchised grief exists would mean that we'd have to look at our own individual disenfranchised grief. But our internal alarm system, set in place to defend against re-experiencing the pain from the initial wounding, sends out a warning that it would be dangerous to do so, that it could open up a Pandora's Box. So, we hunker down and find a way to survive. However, survival does not necessarily equate to growth. As the following Confucian proverb suggests, perhaps opening up Pandora's box is precisely what we need to do.

> *To put the world in right order,*
> *We must first put the nation in order;*
> *To put the nation in order,*
> *We must first put the family in order;*
> *To put the family in order,*
> *We must first cultivate our personal life;*
> *We must first set our hearts right. (Confucius, 551-479 BCE)*

What I understand Confucius to mean by this quote is that, in order to deal with societal disenfranchised grief, we have to first deal with our own. Grief is about feelings of loss; it is emotional. The line, "We must first set our hearts right," suggests that we must first get our limbic brains right, particularly given that the limbic brain is considered "the center of advanced emotionality" (Lewis, et al., p. 51) and the heart is the symbol of emotionality. Secondly, the line, "We must first put the family in order," speaks to our existence as open human systems and our need for relationship and mutual regulation with others. The oft-repeated statement from Lewis, Amini and Lannon (2000), "Stability means finding people who regulate you well and staying near them" (p. 86), is applicable here. It could also be argued that the progression from putting one's own heart in order to the world putting its collective heart in order suggests that it is both the individual and society which will have to change. Finally, the line, "We must first cultivate our personal life," provides a clue with respect to what it is that the individual and society must do in order to change and get our hearts right. If one is a wounded child, I believe that the cultivation of one's personal life, whether individual or societal, requires the witnessing of one's disenfranchised grief by an empathic other. One powerful form of this witnessing, which has been presented in this work and utilized by the researcher, is the psychoanalytic process (Montgomery, 2003). The psychoanalytic process seems particularly relevant when considered in the context of the Confucian directive regarding the cultivation of one's personal life.

One definition of cultivation has to do with the tilling of the soil or the breaking up of the hard ground in preparation for the planting of crops. Another definition of cultivation describes a process of being made ready or suitable or equipped in advance for a particular purpose or for some use or event (Source: http://www.thefreedictionary.com). These definitions also serve to describe both the process and the goal of psychoanalysis: the excavation of the "unexamined and hateful self-concepts" (Karen, 1998, p. 206), or disenfranchised grief, that we have carried with us into adulthood as a result of early attunement failures. Through the experience of having this grief recognized and witnessed by an empathic analyst, the hard, barren soil of disenfranchised grief can be broken up and integrated, rigid defensive barriers are dissolved, and the two-way flow of limbic regulation is restored.

What led me to this realization was the recognition of how disenfranchised grief had been operating in my own life through an experience my younger sister shared with me about our high school English teacher. This teacher recognized the writer in me and tried very hard to influence me to go to college and major in journalism. She even went as far as to make me editor of the school newspaper, even though I had never asked to be considered for the position. She tried so hard to encourage me, but I just could not see the same potential in myself that she saw in me. My sister told me that when she had this same teacher several years later, the teacher continually referred to her by my name until my sister finally stopped responding. When questioned by the teacher as to why she wasn't responding when called upon, my sister replied, "Because I am not Denise." She said the teacher responded back to her, "No, you are not Denise. She understood things that other students didn't. But she could never believe in herself." (L. Berg, personal communication, May, 2006).

My sister shared this story with me at a very difficult and critical period in my life. I was experiencing deep grief at the death of my best friend and mentor, Nashid. My friendship with Nashid was not recognized or supported by my family for a number of reasons. Nevertheless, I came to understand that this friendship was authentic and deeply important to me. Nashid had facilitated my entry into a group into of educators who, in time, became my friends, colleagues, and community. Diagnosed with pancreatic cancer in July 2005, Nashid suffered through an aggressive regimen of chemotherapy and for a while it looked like he might survive. However, by the following April, his condition had begun to rapidly deteriorate. When it became evident that he was dying, I received a call informing me that our community was coming together to say goodbye to Nashid and I needed to be there. It was an agonizing decision because I knew a decision to go would cause tremendous conflict with my husband. But somewhere deep inside of myself, I also knew that I would regret it for the rest of my life if I didn't go. I went. The experience of being part of a community that came together to witness the death of one of its members was one of the most profound experiences of my life. From that experience, I have begun to develop an understanding as to what it means to have a good death.

When I returned home, my husband, feeling very hurt and angry, did not speak to me for almost seven weeks. It was a difficult and painful situation. I had tried to do what I believed was right and it seemed as though I was now being shunned. I was in deep pain and had never felt so isolated and alone. I even considered ending my life. In the midst of this situation, my sister shared the story of our teacher with me. It was the first time I had been able to actually hear what this teacher thought of me. I was, first of all, deeply comforted. In spite of my isolation, my sister had given me the message that I did have worth. Later, I realized that my sister had given me another gift: this story was the first time that my own disenfranchised grief was made visible to me. It was also the first time I began to understand the impact that it was having on my entire life.

I thought a great deal about that story. Why hadn't I been able to respond to my teacher's mentoring and belief in me? Why did it take over thirty years for me to finally see and become the writer that she had first recognized in the seventeen-year-old girl? Why, in spite of my intelligence, in spite of the recognition and support of a caring teacher, was I not able to see in myself what she was able to see? I now believe that it was the presence of disenfranchised grief that interfered with my being able to recognize and achieve my potential. Where did this disenfranchised grief come from and how did it come to play such a prominent role in my life? My attempts to answer these questions brought me back to the consideration of my experiences parenting and being parented as well as what meaning parenting held for me.

Disenfranchised Grief and Parenting

If asked, most people would acknowledge a desire to experience having children as well as a desire to be good parents to their children. Yet, as most people who become parents know all too well, the responsibility of raising children is extremely challenging and continues for many years. Given the level of difficulty and commitment required, why do the majority of people still express a desire to be parents? Do the majority of people really desire to experience parenting or are they simply responding to societal expectations? How does one know whether they want to parent? How does one learn how to be a good parent?

The research of Lewis, et al. (2000) and Schore (1994), among others, has provided strong evidence suggesting that, because the process of parenting a child was biologically designed to be *successful* to ensure continuation of the species, it was also designed to be *pleasurable*. It makes intuitive sense that the best way to reinforce desired behaviors, particularly those behaviors deemed essential to the survival of the species, would be to make them pleasurable. This certainly appears to be the strategy with respect to sexual reproduction. It makes sense that this strategy it would be true for parenting as well.

The brains of living beings to distinguish between behaviors conducive to survival from those that are not have long utilized the presence of pleasure and pain. For example, moving close to a fire to stay warm both feels good and is conducive to survival, in that it keeps one's body temperature elevated on a cold night. However, placing one's body directly into the fire would be excruciatingly painful and likely to result in injuries that prove to be fatal. With respect to parenting, it makes sense that the presence or experience of pleasure should serve to inform the mother and infant that they are getting it right, while the presence of pain or distress should have been an indication that a problem or continuing need for limbic regulation or attunement still existed (Lewis, et al., 2000). Therefore, pleasure should be associated with a state of attunement and pain with its absence. Further, when a mother is attuned to her infant's distress cues and responds in a consistent and nurturing manner, the result should be as positive and pleasurable an experience for her as it is for her child.

The idea that the accurate reading of pleasure and distress signals could be used almost as navigational instruments in one's efforts to not only raise children, but also to manage all of one's social relationships, brought me back to Lewis, et al.'s discussion of the limbic brain.

> The limbic brain is another delicate physical apparatus that specializes in detecting and analyzing just one part of the physical world – the internal state of other mammals. *Emotionality is the social sense organ of limbic creatures* [italics added]. While vision lets us experience the reflected wavelengths of electromagnetic radiation, and hearing gives us information about the pressure waves in the surrounding air, *emotionality enables a mammal to sense the inner states and motives of the mammals around him* [italics added]. (2000, pp. 62–63)

The existence of the limbic brain and its specialization in the detection and analysis of the internal emotional states and motives of other mammals appears to lend strong support to the idea that there is an optimal process for the parenting of children.

However, if it is true that the optimal development of the child is dependent upon good parenting, and the activity of parenting is biologically designed to be a pleasurable experience for both parent and child, and most people at least report having the conscious desire to be good parents, then why weren't there more good parents? Why aren't more children experiencing optimal development? Why were there so many examples of poor parenting and maladjusted children? If the interactions between parent and child were intended to be pleasurable, then why did it seem that these interactions were more often adversarial, dysfunctional or downright unpleasant? If there really was a "blueprint" for optimal parenting, then shouldn't the lineage of bad parents eventually disappear?

I came into this heuristic journey having had less-than-optimal experiences, both in terms of how I parented and how I had been parented. My question now was, why? If this was supposed to be a natural process, why did it seem that most of the people I knew had experiences similar to mine? Rather than experiencing pleasure with my children, I felt frustrated, ill prepared, and overwhelmed. I also have few childhood memories of times that I felt like I was the focus of my parents' attention, unless I was in trouble. What had gone wrong? What had gotten in the way of this process unfolding in the way that it seemed clearly designed to do? As I sat with this question, the heuristic current pulled at me once again and the idea of a connection or relationship between disenfranchised grief, the experience of pleasure and pain, and attunement began to develop.

Disenfranchised Grief and Attunement

One of the strongest themes to emerge from the stories presented in Chapter Four, as well as the review of the literature in the second chapter, was the importance of attunement in human relationships for optimal development and functioning. In the stories, attunement, which was briefly discussed in the literature review as a component of secure attachment, began to emerge as a significant element in its own right. Erskine (1998) notes that attunement,

> *Goes beyond empathy* [italics added]: it is a process of communion and unity of interpersonal contact. It is a two-part process that begins with empathy, being sensitive to and identifying with the other person's sensations, needs or feelings; and includes the communication of that sensitivity to the other person. More than just understanding (Rogers, 1951) or vicarious introspection (Kohut, 1971), attunement is a kinesthetic and emotional sensing of others, knowing their rhythm, affect and experience by metaphorically being in their skin, and going beyond empathy to create a two-person experience of unbroken feeling connectedness by providing a reciprocal affect and/or resonating response. . . . *Affective attunement, for example, provides an interpersonal contact essential to human relationship. It involves the resonance of one person's affect to the other's affect. . . . Symbolically, attunement may be pictured as one person's yin to the other's yang that together form a unity in the relationship* [italics added]. (p. 2)

The idea that optimal parenting was designed to be pleasurable for the *mother* as well as the child was becoming more and more apparent to me. I began to understand *why* it was important for a mother to know when she and her child are getting it right: because when the mother is attuned to her child's distress cues and responds to her child in a consistent and nurturing manner, the result is positive for both mother and child. As Lewis, Amini and Lannon (2000) noted:

> Secure attachment resulted when a child was hugged when he wanted to be hugged and put down when he wanted to be put down. When he was hungry, his mother knew it and fed him; when he began to tire, his mother felt it and eased his transition into sleep by tucking him into his bassinet. Wherever a mother sensed her baby's inarticulate desires and acted on them, *not only was their mutual enjoyment greatest*, but the outcome was, years later, a secure child. (p. 75)

I believe the outcome is also a secure mother. Therefore, "getting it right" between mother and child should both *feel* good and *be* good in terms of not only the infant's development, but the mother's development as well. Further, when this attunement between mother and child is lacking or inconsistent, it should be expected that both mother and child would be affected by the loss and experience distress. Therefore, the lack of pleasure or presence of distress should be an indicator to the mother that she isn't getting it right with her infant and that she should keep working to understand her child's needs. However, a mother operating with disenfranchised grief is not likely to recognize this distress because she has split off from that part of herself.

Somewhere along the way, something interfered with this natural or organic process of attuned communication between mother and infant and the appropriate interpretation of these pleasure and distress signals was lost. An argument could be made that social forces, particularly the advent of industrialization, imposed changes on the family that resulted in the sacrifice of the healthy development of children in exchange for economic gain. It could further be argued that this societal shift may be one of the underlying causes of disenfranchised grief.

The connection between disenfranchised grief and attunement became evident to me in a more personal sense when I asked Julian and Kristin to each read the stories I had written about my relationship with them. Prior to having them read their stories, I told both Julian and Kristin that I had three primary concerns. I said, "My first concern is that you are okay. My second concern is that we are okay. My third concern is that I have told the truth to the best of my ability." I wanted to make sure that they heard that their needs, desires, and comfort were as important to me as my own, which had not always been the case in their earlier experience with me. I wanted to do what I could to ensure that Julian and Kristin would be emotionally prepared for what they read and that they knew they could talk to me if anything came up for them. I also wanted to try to make sure that they knew that I was telling *my* story about my relationship with them. I was not trying to tell theirs.

Julian and Kristin were certainly in the position to provide me with the feedback that I sought. I felt that they were more than capable of managing such a conversation with me. We were already experienced with candid conversations of this nature because we had shared a number of them, particularly while I was hospitalized during my illness with cancer. Although initially difficult and painful, the possibility of my death provided the motivation for me to overcome my fear and reluctance, and those conversations with my children were some of the most amazing, healing, and treasured moments I have experienced with them thus far.

Despite my children's strength and experience with challenging dialogue, I still felt some anxiety about having Julian and Kristin read what I had written about our relationship. I was raised within a conflict-avoidant culture and I recall hearing numerous colloquial sayings during my childhood that carried some version of the warning, "*Some things are better left unsaid.*" However, as a result of this study, I have learned that cultural or societal norms that discourage conflict are also norms that serve to keep our societal grief disenfranchised, because what remains unsaid also remains unfelt and unseen. I also realized that this anxiety likely had more to do with my pushing up against this cultural programming than any real danger that I might be potentially harming my children. The reality is that my warning system had been programmed in error. My anxiety should have been associated with *silence* not dialogue; we are designed to be *open* systems.

It is important to stress that it is critical that my anxiety was recognized and examined, because the chance did exist that what Julian and Kristin read could open old wounds and create additional suffering for them. That risk had to be taken into consideration. However, my previous discussions with Julian and Kristen, as well as the research literature reviewed for this inquiry, all indicated that their suffering would actually be relieved by the chance to talk and to have their suffering and grief witnessed, particularly by me as their mother. I had been a contributor to my children's suffering through my ignorance. Now, through the knowledge gained as a result of this inquiry, I believed that I could be a contributor to their healing through this empathic witnessing. What is interesting to me now is that I didn't realize the extent to which I, too, would experience healing as a result of our dialogues. I did not even yet understand the extent to which my own grief remained disenfranchised.

I had been primarily concerned about Kristin's response to what I had written because of her tendency to internalize her feelings, which had proven to be dangerous for her in the past. However, it was Julian who raised an issue with what I had written. There were some rather strange occurrences that came up around Julian's story. The first strange occurrence was that I thought he *had* read it. Julian had read much of the first three chapters and we had talked numerous times about my research, particularly about how it might affect or influence our relationship. However, it wasn't until I was talking to Julian about Kristen's reaction to her story that he asked me when he was going to get to read his. I was very surprised because I thought he had. I had a copy of the story with me. I gave it to him and asked him to let me know what he thought. Several days went by and I had not heard from Julian. I finally called him and noted that he seemed to be uncharacteristically quiet. I asked him if he had read the story and he replied that he had. I asked him what he thought. He very quietly said, "Mom, you started it with the most painful memory that I have about my childhood." I had no idea what Julian was referring to and went looking for a copy of the story to see what he was talking about.

Reading through what I had written, I was confronted with the shocking discovery that Julian and I had significantly different memories of what I had referred to in his story as an Oedipus Complex incident. In my memory, this incident had occurred when Julian was about five years old. Julian stated that it happened when he was ten and in a completely different context than I remembered. I was deeply troubled that I could not recall *anything* with respect to Julian's memory of the incident. I now believe that the difference between Julian's memory and mine was direct evidence of my disenfranchised grief.

The most notable difference between Julian's memory and my own, and most painful for me to acknowledge, had to do with our differing perceptions or interpretations in terms of my reaction to Julian's expression of his distress and his need for closeness with me. In my recollection of the situation, I perceived Julian's need for touch and closeness as inappropriate behavior. I also believed that by refusing to respond to Julian's need, I was being a good parent who set boundaries for her child. Julian's recollection about that time was of experiencing a deep need for the touch, closeness, and attention of his mother that he was desperately trying to get filled. Julian was experiencing distress that I, as his mother, failed to recognize and failed to respond to appropriately. How different might the outcome of Julian's development have been if, in that moment, I had recognized his need to be close and pulled that child up onto my lap and just held him? Stroked his hair? Kissed his forehead and told him that I loved him? How might this experience have been different for both Julian and me if I had been aware of my disenfranchised grief and how it affected my ability to be attuned and empathic to my child?

According to Julian, not only did I fail to recognize his distress, I turned on him as well. Julian told me that after he reached out and touched me, the coldness in my look and in the tone of my voice made him pull back and he felt ashamed. I cannot find words that can adequately describe how difficult it was for me to hear this and to accept that I could have reacted in such a way to my own child. It felt like someone had kicked me in the gut and I couldn't breathe. I had to pull back and just sit with the idea for a while before I was finally able to look at it. I had to ease into it slowly, but I did it.

Throughout this time, Julian and I continued to talk to each other about the differences in our memories, why were they different, and what it all might mean. In time, I came to realize that Julian had given me a tremendous gift. His gift was providing me with the opportunity to get a glimpse of a part of myself that had remained unconscious and hidden from me for a long time. It was a snapshot of how I reacted to my children's expressions of distress or need for love; it was a glimpse of my disenfranchised grief. Just as significantly, within Julian's gift, I thought I also recognized a hint of a familial, or even a societal legacy of disenfranchised grief as well.

Disenfranchised Grief Recognized

Hearing Julian's description of my reaction triggered what I have come to regard to as a "flashback moment," which I distinguish from the flashback experience that can result from an experience of trauma. In a flashback moment, something that is happening in the present triggers a memory of a similar experience and an insight or connection is made, sometimes instantaneously. My experience of these moments has been a feeling that a shift has occurred within myself. Frick (1990) would likely consider my experience as a symbolic growth experience given that he also refers to "a sudden, dramatic shift in perception, belief, or understanding" (p. 99) that occurs as part of the experience. Julian's gift of this snapshot of my reaction to his distress triggered a flashback moment for me in which I recalled memories of similar reactions from my mother in response to my expressions of need or distress when I was a child.

It occurred to me that I had learned how to react to my children's distress from my parents as a child. I also knew enough family history to know that my parents had experienced a similar kind of reaction from their parents, and so it went back for generations. I also realized that my recognition of this legacy meant that I now had the opportunity to choose to change it. Rather than *react* to my children's distress as I had previously done, I could now choose to *respond* to it. I now understand that there is a significant difference. To react to the distress of one's child suggests that the mother's attention is directed internally on her own distress, rather than on the needs of her child. To respond to the distress of one's child suggests a style of mothering where the mother's focus is empathically attuned to *both* the need of her child to be cared for as well as her own needs. Thus, while the mother is consciously aware of her own distress, she is not overwhelmed by it. Her need to relieve or to manage that distress can be temporarily suppressed, or set-aside, allowing her to focus on responding to her child. When this occurs, the two-way flow of attunement between mother and child is unimpeded.

It is important to emphasize that temporarily suppressing or setting aside one's own distress needs is very different from sacrificing them. My experience has been that sacrifice at the expense of meeting one's own important needs may actually be an act of unconscious avoidance or manipulation rather than one of selfless nobility, providing little benefit for anyone. I suspect that individuals who have the tendency to sacrifice their needs are, in actuality, attempting to deny them in an unconscious attempt to avoid having to confront their disenfranchised grief. I further suspect this tendency stems from an unconscious fear of looking at one's needs because many people learned in childhood to relate need with distress, distress with rejection, and rejection with intolerable pain. It could be argued that this relationship developed in response to having had parents who were not able to adequately model the healthy recognition and management of distress.

Because our parents' unconscious reaction to our childhood expressions of distress was often panic and distancing, we too react to expressions of distress with panic and distancing. As our relationship has healed and evolved over time, Julian and Kristen have begun to share with me some of times when I distanced myself from or even denied their distress. It has been difficult for me to listen to these experiences and to hear about the impact of my reactions upon my children. However, I believe that it was critical that I do so. As a result of these discussions I have seen connections between my children's current struggles and my own childhood memories. Through the exploration of these connections I have been able to *feel* both my children's pain as well as my own. It has hurt like hell at times. But it is a *good* kind of pain. It is a breaking *free*.

It has been disturbing to realize that I have no memories of some the experiences that Julian and Kristin are beginning to share with me. It has caused me to wonder whether I was ever really present to my children when they were growing up. However, the more I consider what Julian and Kristin have shared with me, the more I realize that my lack of memory underscores the extent to which the presence of disenfranchised grief really *does* interfere with a parent's ability to be present and attuned to her child. In fact, I really *wasn't* there for my children. They often had to emotionally fend for themselves, just as I had to fend for myself s a child, and my parents before me, and we have all paid a high price. Because of this experience, I now believe that it is not only important, it is *critical* for parents to understand the extent to which they themselves may equate expressions of distress with panic and whether or not this panic can be consciously acknowledged.

These questions have particular relevance given the significant body of research that suggests that panic is not the response intended by nature (Lewis, et al., 2000; Schore, 2003). Rather, the research presented in the literature review points to the expression of distress as the primary mechanism the infant utilizes to communicate to her mother that there is a need. Infants were *designed* to signal distress to their parents, and parents (particularly mothers) were designed to be receptive and responsive to those distress signals. When this process unfolds as designed, there is attunement. When it doesn't, there is the likelihood of disenfranchised grief, and later on, the real possibility of pathology (Erskine, 1998; Lewis, et al., 2000; Schore, 1994). According to Erskine (1998),

> *The continued absence of satisfaction of relational needs may be manifested as frustration, aggression or anger* [italics added]. When disruptions in relationship are prolonged the lack of need satisfaction is manifested as a loss of energy or hope and shows up in *script beliefs* such as 'No one is there for me' or 'What['s] the use?' (Erskine & Moursund, 1988/1998). These script beliefs are the cognitive defense against the awareness of needs and the feelings present when needs do not get a satisfying response from another person (Erskine, 1980). (p. 3)

"*No one is there for me*" and "*What's the use?*" were both script beliefs with which I was quite familiar. My unconscious defense against these beliefs was to expand upon my natural tendency towards independence and to develop the stance that I didn't need anyone's care because I could take care of myself. I believe that a number of events in my life were also indicators of these script beliefs. My mother told me that I ran away from home at age three supposedly because my father would not build me a sandbox. I got my first job at the age of nine so I could have my own money. Each summer I insisted on paying for my own school coat no matter how little money I earned or what else I may have wanted. It was my defiant gesture of independence. Lastly, I held a deep conviction that I could not go to my parents for anything that was really important to me or controversial.

However, in addition to these script beliefs, I also carried a belief that I was a bad kid, in my own words, "a defective gene," and therefore I felt unworthy of my parents' care, or anyone's care for that matter. I suspect that this belief was the barrier to my being able to accept the mentoring from my high school teacher. It is painful for me to consider now, from the perspective of a 50-year-old woman, the idea of a child believing that she is not worthy of her parent's care and attention, possibly not even worthy of life. I still haven't fully placed myself as that child and continue to have difficulty accessing memories from parts of my childhood. I can now imagine myself feeling overwhelmed and shamed, but it is still from a distance, in my head rather than my heart. However, I get closer and closer to my heart every day. I can now appreciate the logic of needing to defend against that early pain, because the alternative was psychological disintegration. I am also now able to understand that the cost of defending against feeling that pain was the sacrifice of my ability to feel pleasure or joy. That is a terrible deal for any child to have to make.

I now understand that my unconscious defense against the script belief that I was defective and not deserving of care was to develop a public stance of independence. I didn't need my parents. I didn't need anybody. I could take care of myself. However, there were several problems with this defense strategy. One problem was that my independence wasn't authentic. I really *did* need my parents and I really could not yet take care of myself. Secondly, to defend against something means to create a barrier against it. In this instance, the barrier was intended to defend against the experience of overwhelming pain. However, pain is to pleasure what yin is to yang. A barrier created for the avoidance of one will also be a barrier to the experience of the other.

Even more troubling, given that emotionality is the "social sense organ" that enables one mammal to "sense the inner states and motives of the mammals around him" (Lewis, et al, 2000, p. 62-63), it seems highly improbable that an individual who, because of maladaptive script beliefs, is unable to access important survival emotions such as pleasure and pain will experience much success navigating his way in the social world. I thought about my own experience as someone in such a predicament and how I have been shaped by it. Although these emotions are still difficult to access, I believe that one reaction was panic. To not be able to discern whether another person is potentially harmful leaves one in an extremely vulnerable position. I remember being hurt a number of times because I had the tendency to take people at their word, and there were some who took advantage of me. I believe another reaction was anger at not having my distress appropriately recognized and regulated. As a result, I did not have what I needed (full access to my limbic brain) to successfully identify and build attachments with others who would be good regulators for me.

Montgomery's (2004) research on witnessing grief provides compelling support for the assertion that distress is the signal mechanism to which parents are supposed to respond in order to regulate and ultimately shape the minds of their children. It also supports the assertion that attunement is the natural outcome that results when there is a match between the child's expression of distress and the parent's empathic response. Finally, Montgomery's work suggests a possible source of both individual and societal disenfranchised grief: the absence of attunement due to the inability of parents to recognize and respond appropriately to their child's distress. This parental failure forces the child into an intolerable dilemma of having to choose between the truth of her distress or need (her limbic brain) and the reality of the feedback she receives from her parents, who are the central figures of her young universe, and upon whom she is utterly dependent for survival.

Survival almost inevitably wins out and dictates the child's accommodation of her parent's truth over her own. But in order to do that, she has to dissociate or disenfranchise herself from her truth, her distress, and her needs. In essence, she must cut herself off from a fundamental part of herself: the input from her limbic brain. In other words, her voice. Further, if this intolerable conflict occurs early enough in the child's development, her dissociation or disenfranchisement becomes deeply embedded into the very structure of her mind. Is it any surprise then that she learns not to trust herself and to close off from other influential or caretaking adults? Or, that her ability to intuit the distress, needs, or intentions of others is impaired? Montgomery writes,

> It appears to be instinct that sends a child in distress hightailing over to mom, dad, grandma, teacher . . . whoever is available to listen, understand, empathize, and in so doing, soothe and comfort. This is how we move from a state of fragmentation into a state of containment. *Empathic responses from another help us integrate painful emotional states without needing to defend against them* [italics added]. This capacity is essential before we can develop the more sophisticated capacity to ask, "Is there learning and meaning to be had from this misfortune?" What happens, though, when a child is met with a discounting response from caregivers? When the caregiver is the source of abuse? When there is no one available who is capable of witnessing the grief of another (2003, p. 4)

I believe that what happens is disenfranchised grief. Multiply this scenario by millions and there is now the possibility of disenfranchised grief on a societal scale. Just as this disenfranchisement gets woven into the structure of the child's psyche, it is possible that societal disenfranchised grief has been woven into the very fabric of the culture.

The following example may help to demonstrate how an attuned parent can regulate and interpret distressing events for her child. This example might also illustrate how a parent's interpretation can shift from one of disenfranchisement to one of greater attunement and the impact that such a shift can have on her child's sense of self-esteem, as well as her own. The protection that a parent provides for her child by buffering or regulating negative experiences so she won't become overwhelmed is very important. Equally important is the interpretive function that a parent provides for her child. The way in which a parent interprets her child's life experiences and projects them back to her, particularly distressing experiences, shapes how her child will interact in the world. Interpretations from an attuned parent should serve as a scaffold or support for the child, thus enabling her to be open to the exploration of the larger world and of different possibilities. However, interpretations from a parent operating with disenfranchised grief will likely result in a child who is locked into patterns of rigid defensive reactions.

This example, which was described earlier in Kristin's story, took place when Kristin returned to work after her hospitalization and her employer inappropriately attempted to bully her into taking a lower paying position or quit. Despite having previously experienced her mother as helpless and incompetent in her ability to protect her when she was young, in this situation, Kristin was able to see me as a strong mother who did step in and protect her. When Kristin told me that she had been reinstated to her previous job and that one of her co-workers commented that the company had picked on the wrong person to mess with, I realized that I had shown Kristin how to defend herself by observing me do it. She needed to see that her mother thought she was worth fighting for and defending. Having shown her, my task would then be to step back and let her do it on her own. And she has.

I know this experience was a pivotal moment for me and, I believe it was pivotal for Kristen as well. After that experience, I began to notice a shift in her behavior. Prior to Kristin's hospitalization, I believe her survival strategy had been to be accommodating to everybody, "just go along to get along." After the experience with her employer, it was as though Kristin, who had been stuck in place, suddenly broke free. She began to make decisions for herself and to express her own opinions, even when I didn't like them. There were changes in me as well. I remember feeling that it was important to let Kristen know that I wanted her to leave home when she was ready. I had not been ready and it had been disastrous for me. However, I also told Kristen that it was my job as a parent to prepare her to live as an adult member of society. Therefore, I needed to turn up the heat a little bit at a time, like raising her rent, because one day she really did need to grow up and be on her own. But it was most important to me that *she* determined when to make that step, not have it imposed on her. Within a year, Kristin found an apartment and moved out on her own. It was the right time.

This experience taught me that a parent's response to her child's needs could promote resiliency, rebellion, or resignation in the child. Which one gets promoted truly depends upon the kind of experience (or lens) the parent herself is interpreting through. And that depends upon the manner in which a person's own parents responded to her distress and the extent to which she may be operating with disenfranchised grief. According to Montgomery (2003),

> Children run to mommy when their body is hurt, when their feelings are hurt, or when their mind is confused. Many moms are mostly good enough, especially about the kinds of hurts that can be seen or those that can be straightened out with a logical and conclusive answer or action. *But what about the deeper issues of emotional attachment?* Children can't talk about the deeper issues of emotional neglect, abandonment, or, on the other hand, intrusiveness with their parents, *because often both children and parents are unaware of or in denial about the problem* [italics added]. A child can't talk about the pain incurred by a father's cynical, irritable, and humiliating lashing out, when the mother's role in the family is to protect the father. . . Family and friends may see and hear abusive interactions, but no one dares interfere. Many children are without a human witness to their trauma-producing grief, which involves unmet emotional and spiritual needs. *The most basic of these needs is to be acknowledged as a vulnerable person.* (p. 5)

Why is the need to be acknowledged as a vulnerable person so critical? What does it mean to be a vulnerable person? Erskine (1998) suggests that it has to do with our need for security, which requires the presence of attunement.

> Security is the visceral experience of having our physical and emotional vulnerabilities protected. It involves the experience that our variety of needs and feelings are human and natural. *Security is a sense of simultaneously being vulnerable and in harmony with another* [italics added]. (p. 3)

It could also be suggested that the ability to be vulnerable is an essential component of mutual regulation given that, for one to be regulated, one has to be open. To be open is also to be exposed, thereby placing oneself in a position of vulnerability. One cannot be vulnerable when disenfranchised grief is present.

Further, as noted by Lewis, Amini and Lannon (2000), mutual regulation is the process by which we maintain our emotional stability throughout our lives. Their observation, which has been repeated a number of times throughout this work, has begun to take on the feel of a mantra for me: "*Stability means finding people who regulate you well and staying near them*" (p. 86). If, when we are children, our parents do not lay down the foundation for appropriate mutual regulation, it seems unlikely that we will be successful in finding other individuals who are capable of regulating us well. That is because we are not likely to consciously know that we should be looking for good regulators. What *is* likely is that we will follow the pattern that was imprinted in us by our parents and society, which is embedded with disenfranchised grief.

I believe that significant changes need to occur within the educational system as well as in our cultural mindset with respect to understanding and valuing the importance of attuned relationships for healthy human development. These changes will require education on *both* the fundamentals of parenting and the importance of attunement and attachment in forming healthy attuned relationships between parent and child. It will also require education about disenfranchised grief and the impact of disenfranchised grief on the individual and on society, as well as what is required for someone to be able to work through and integrate this grief once it exists. Given that a number of researchers are coming to the same conclusion that integration of loss or grief experiences (disenfranchised grief) requires the presence of an empathic therapeutic witness (Lewis, et al., 2000; Montgomery, 2003; Schore, 1994), a shift in our culture's currently dismissive regard for mental health must also occur. Should these changes not take place, it seems highly unlikely that parents will become aware of their disenfranchised grief, children will continue to be wounded, and the cycle will continue on—that is, unless something significant happens that forces a parent to become aware of their disenfranchised grief, as happened with me. However, waiting for a significant experience is not an effective method for change.

Disenfranchised Grief Reconceived

Through this heuristic inquiry, I have come to believe that there is another manifestation of disenfranchised grief that should be added to Lenhardt's (1997) existing definition. This additional form of disenfranchised grief results when young children must psychologically defend against the overwhelming pain that arises when they do not experience attunement with their parents. It is further thought that this form of disenfranchised grief acts to obstruct or interfere with the natural state of limbic resonance between humans, particularly between parent and child. Experiencing this kind of pain without a fully developed emotional regulatory system feels so overwhelming to the child that she has to completely block or repress the feeling. This repression is likely to affect the child on multiple levels.

At the most fundamental level, attunement with the parent increases the likelihood of physical survival for the child. Therefore, a child affected by disenfranchised grief is likely to experience feelings of emptiness, pseudo-independence, shame, panic, or overall worthlessness. Secondly, both the content and the structure of the child's mind are developed through the attunement relationship with her mother. Young children require attuned interactions with the mother and important others for emotional regulation, which involves the accurate recognition of, and response to, the child's distress. If the child's emotional regulation is compromised because the presence of disenfranchised grief interferes with the mother's ability to handle her child's distress, there will be gaps or missing structure in the child's emotional system. The impact is profoundly painful and long-lasting because it has been built into the very foundation of the child's emotional system. If the child's emotional system has not yet matured to manage such distress, literally the only way she would be able to psychologically survive would be to completely repress the experience from consciousness.

So not only do we *not* learn how to manage distress appropriately, ultimately, we lose the ability to even know that we are distressed. Part of the complexity of disenfranchised grief is that it is likely to have initially served as a protective mechanism for the developing mind. A mother protects her child from accidental poisoning by placing toxic substances out of her child's reach, placing warning stickers on bottles, and teaching her child not to touch anything that has a warning sticker on it. In much the same way, it is thought that the purpose of disenfranchised grief might be to protect the Self from "emotional poisoning." Memories of experiences that might have proved to be overwhelming for an immature emotional system were repressed in an attempt to ensure the survival and integrity of the psyche. However, because a child's mind is being both formed and informed through the attunement relationship with her mother, memories and experiences stored as "off limits" in childhood are likely to remain "off limits" in adulthood because they have become a repressed part of the fabric of the mind.

Analysis further suggests that memories or experiences that have been stored or marked as "off-limits" in early childhood, later in life, often become obstructions or barriers that impede the flow of the limbic regulation we seek from our social interactions with others. When the flow of our limbic regulation is impeded, our social interactions are less likely to be fulfilling because we are operating with faulty programming. Even if we do become aware of this faulty programming, it is often extremely resistant to modification because it has been stored behind a locked door that has been wired with many alarms. Every time we get close to the door, the alarms go off and we run away in fear. The paradox is that our emotional warning system thinks that it is doing a *good* thing, protecting us from memories that would have overwhelmed us as children. However, we are no longer children in need of protection. We are now adults in need of a well functioning limbic system that will allow us to interact and navigate effectively within the social world that we inhabit.

A friend once described it to me in computer programming terminology, terminology that has been used extensively by the psychoanalytic community in their attempts to describe the functioning of the mind. Not having our infant distress accurately recognized and appropriately responded to by our mothers (parents) is like having a bug or virus introduced into a computer program; the program runs but it doesn't run well. The child interacts with others but she doesn't interact all that successfully. Initially, you cannot see the virus; all you can see is that things just aren't working the way they should. It is unlikely that a parent with disenfranchised grief would be able to recognize her child's need to have her distress managed (or her emotional state regulated), because her own infant distress went unrecognized and unmanaged. You cannot teach what you do not know.

In the therapeutic context, it takes time to identify the source of distress, witness it, and model (re-imprint) a different way to respond to it, just as it takes the computer programmer time to correct a program even after a virus has been identified. Because computer programs, like humans, are interactive, the initial bug is likely to be replicated in numerous other areas of the program. Therefore, it takes time to search through each area and to remove the virus, once found. This is a primary reason why psychoanalysis takes so long. The therapist is literally engaged in a "search and modify" operation within the client's mind. It took a certain number of years to complete the initial programming, and reprogramming takes even longer.

Societal Disenfranchised Grief

There are a number of ways that I see disenfranchised grief evidenced at a societal level, beginning with a highly individualistic U.S. culture that creates an ideal environment for disenfranchised grief to exist. One example is the overall societal attitude towards children. How many times has the comment been made, in response to a child's experience of a traumatic or painful event, "Oh, they're young, they won't even remember that it happened," or, "Children are so resilient, they'll get over it." I now notice that my body tenses up every time I hear comments such as these.

Other evidence pointing to the existence of disenfranchised grief on a societal level includes the U.S. culture's valuation of technology over relationship. There is an underlying societal script belief (Erskine, 1998) that we don't have to concern ourselves with respect to the state of our relationships with others or with our environment because we can fix with technology whatever we damage. Therefore, we can disregard the idea that humankind was intended to be stewards of the Earth rather than dominators. We don't have to worry about polluting our limited sources of fresh water, we'll just figure out how to convert seawater because there is plenty of that. As a society we devalue children, mothers and mothering, females or feminine characteristics, emotional expression, the elderly, the oppressed–*any* group that might remind us of our vulnerability.

It occurred to me that our societal culture has been operating as though we are insecure-ambivalently attached children who deny ourselves the very thing we most desperately want, the comfort of another human being's attuned response. But defended against pain and cut off from pleasure, we cannot experience our need, so we deny that it exists or we minimize its value. Consider the stigma and negative stereotyping associated with mothering, caretaking, and the "helping professions." Josselson (1996) notes:

> Because we tend to equate motherliness and care, our attitudes towards tending are fused with our attitudes toward being mothered. Tenderness is the ideal of motherliness, perhaps, but it is our very conflicts around the experience of being tended and nurtured that make this such a difficult topic to discuss. We are never more vulnerable than when we are in need, and it is our (vaguely remembered) and terrifying experiences of being helplessly untended that lead to our powerful defenses against and denials of our need for care. Luepnitz (1988) suggests that nurturance is a taboo topic of discussion under a patriarchy that is contemptuous and frightened of mothering. Balint (1959) years earlier, coming from a different continent and tradition, similarly wonders whether the neediness represented by the need for the mother is so primitive or dangerous that no language has words to describe it. Thus, defensively, we disown and depreciate, demean and devalue this dimension of experience. (See also Miller, 1986.) Caretaking jobs are usually the lowest paid and afforded the least respect. Those of us in the "helping sciences" (such as medicine and psychotherapy) publicly emphasize the "science" part of what we do; and we do not acknowledge too openly that we are in the business of taking care. (p. 196)

I believe that unless we, as a society, move to recognize how deeply we have been affected by unacknowledged societal disenfranchised grief as well as how deeply it has permeated every aspect of our culture, the damage to our children, and our society, will continue.

Implications for Educators and Parents

As a result of having engaged in this inquiry, my thinking as to what information or skills are needed in order to be able to parent empathically has shifted, and the shift has been profoundly meaningful to me. My initial thinking was that the educational system had to do a better job educating children about the interpersonal skills that have been shown to be necessary to achieve happiness in everyday life (Noddings, 2003). However, I now believe that there *also* has to be education about disenfranchised grief and how humans understand and manage distress, because this knowledge could profoundly impact one's ability to parent empathically. This is particularly true for parents of LGBTQ children, due to ongoing societal stigmatization.

As discussed previously, it is highly likely that most adults carry some level of disenfranchised grief. Given the negative impact that disenfranchised grief can have on a parent's ability to respond to their child's distress, there is a real need to develop educational programs to help parents recognize and work through this grief. It is also important to educate the professionals who interact with parents, as they are also not likely to recognize when disenfranchised grief is operating. Finally, if we are to have a societal goal to develop empathic parents, then this ability must be developed early on through the educational system. Otherwise, as Noddings (2003) asks, how will parenting ever change or improve? Just as Luckmann (1978, in Martin, 2005) asserts that "the job of science is to explain everyday life" (p. 212), I have come to believe that the job of schools should be to educate for everyday life and for the attainment of happiness in everyday life. This is not yet happening.

I have discovered that, through my process of psychoanalysis, I have been able to recognize, work through, and integrate my own disenfranchised grief. Through the course of being witnessed and re-regulated by an empathic analyst, I have developed the ability to recognize and better manage my own distress. The ability to manage one's own distress must be developed for a parent to then be able to bracket or set aside her distress in order to focus on the distress of her child. I discovered that the more I was able to recognize and manage my own distress, the more empathically I was able to respond to my children's distress. Further, how I *feel* when I am presented with my children's distress has changed significantly: the sense of panic is gone. More importantly, I have rediscovered the ability to experience and appreciate pleasure and joy.

I believe that parents with disenfranchised grief become panicked when their children express distress. When operating from a state of panic, parents with disenfranchised grief can focus only on their own distress. They cannot assist their children in the regulation of their distress because their attention isn't directed toward their children. Their attention is directed inward and focused on managing their own panic. Therefore, the child not only does not get help with her distress, she isn't even *visible* to their parents.

A recent experience provided me with an opportunity to witness this state of panic operating in my parents and to experience, as an adult, what it likely felt like as a child to be invisible to them. I was going through a very painful situation and had reached a point where I was beginning to ask myself whether it might be time to just give it up and acknowledge that I was a loser. I just wanted the comfort of my mother, or father, or someone in my family who cared about me, and no one was responding. It hurt so badly that I considered ending my life. But instead of ending my life, I took the risk of acknowledging my anger. I wrote a three-page letter and sent it to my family telling them exactly how I felt. I thought I had written an articulate and well-crafted letter. I felt that had finally found my voice. But I was also afraid, because if nobody heard me, what did it matter whether or not I had a voice?

Eventually my mother contacted me and we set a time to sit down together and talk about what was going on with me. When I met with her, I was emotionally depleted and raw. But I was there. My mother and I sat down together in my parents' living room and my father had promised to leave us alone. My mother reached over and took my hand, and, before I could begin to speak, she began talking about my younger sister and asking me why couldn't I just talk to her. She said that my sister worked so hard and was such a good person and she had so much respect for her. I remember feeling confused and then stunned. I remember that I quietly said, "Mom, my sister is a great person. But I don't want to talk about her right now." I remember that my mother then got very upset. My father rushed to my mother's side and told me that I had better leave. I did. I was in shock and I was hurt and I was angry. I remember that I drove home at about 85 miles an hour and seriously thought about just steering the car off the road. But I didn't.

I think that my state of shock and intense anger also put me into a state of hyper-awareness. As angry as I was, I was also thinking with what felt like extraordinary clarity. When I reflected back on what had taken place, I realized that my parents were so focused on their own distress that there was no way that they could help me with mine. They were so distressed they could not even see me. As much as it hurt, I also realized that it didn't have anything to do with me. It wasn't about whether they loved me or not; they did. It was about how they had learned to cope with distress. I had been given my first opportunity to witness a manifestation of disenfranchised grief in my parents.

For a child, I believe that the experience of not being seen by one's parents feels like abandonment, because that was my experience. Further, if this experience happens repeatedly, both the child's cognitive and emotional development are likely to be negatively impacted. As Tronick (1998) noted previously, "with continued failure and the structuring that that goes on around that failure, affective disorders and pathology may result" (p. 297). One can heal from that pathology and develop a more adaptive personality. I know because I have done it. However, it requires finding an empathic therapist and making a significant investment of both time and money. I was fortunate to have had access to both. Many people are not so lucky. Given that there is information and knowledge about how to help our children to develop appropriately the first time, it seems not only foolish but morally wrong as a society to not make a significant shift toward providing the kind of education and experience that will help parents to be successful at raising healthy and happy children. It is time for us to do so.

From Wounded Child to Empathic Mother

The question was once asked of me, "How did you move from being a wounded child to an empathic mother?" Hearing this question, I realized that it captured the essence of my heuristic journey. The original intent of this heuristic inquiry had been the exploration of my experience as a mother of sexual and gender minority twins and why I chose to struggle with accepting my children's identities when almost half the parents of LGBTQ children do not (Ryan & Futterman, 1998). I had Lenhardt's (1997) concept of disenfranchised grief in the back of my mind because it had been suggested as a possible reason why parents might reject their LGBTQ child. I thought that the problem was societal stigmatization, due to ignorance, which isolates parents of LGBTQ children. I believed the solution was better education.

I still believe that to be true. However, as a result of my choice to let go of the known and to trust that the heuristic river would take me where I needed to go (Roads, 1987), I now understand that I was intended to engage in a deeper exploration of disenfranchised grief. Initially, I approached this exploration with the motive of understanding my children. But as I delved further into the research on disenfranchised grief and then compared this research to my own life experience, it was as though a lens had been placed in front of me and suddenly, once-cloudy images came into focus.

I believe that the particular experiences of my life, and the ability I developed to reflect on them through psychoanalysis, were critical to shaping me such that I was able to recognize the presence of disenfranchised grief in myself, my children, my parents, my husband, and in society. Jonas Salk's quote, *"Evolution is picking yourself up one more time than you fall down,"* which provided me with so much comfort many years ago, also gave me the courage to look deeper into my disenfranchised grief. I knew from my experience in psychoanalysis that any pain experienced as a result of re-experiencing my disenfranchised grief would be worthwhile. I also knew, from both my experience with psychoanalysis and with cancer, that the only way to move forward was to move through the experience, and more importantly, I knew that I could manage it.

My heuristic inquiry had become a heuristic journey. It had become what Frank (1995) calls a quest story wherein the question to be answered is: How did I rise to the occasion?

> The genesis of the quest is some occasion requiring the person to be more than she has been, and the purpose is becoming one who has risen to that occasion. *This occasion at first appears as an interruption* [italics added] but later come to be understood as an opening.

> A woman . . . expresses what is said in almost every quest story: "I would never have *chosen* to be taught this way but I like the changes in me. I guess I had to go to the edge to get there." What started the illness is secondary to the effect of going "to the edge." [Her] purpose is coming back from that edge to become the person she is, someone who is changed. Illness was an interruption she would not have chosen, but she now accepts it as the cost of changes she likes. Losses continue to be mourned, but the emphasis is on gains. (p. 128)

Like this woman, I would not have chosen to have cancer or to be the mother of children who are sexual or gender minorities. Yet, I like the changes I see in myself as a result. Initially I *did* regard having to deal with cancer and with my children's sexual and gender identities as unwelcome interruptions. I now regard them as some of my greatest learning experiences because they were the channel as well as the motivation for me to come face-to-face with my disenfranchised grief, to embrace it, and ultimately, to begin to integrate it. I, too, came back from the edge. As I continue to learn how to embrace and integrate this disenfranchised part of myself, I am finding that my sense of wholeness and attunement is being restored. I now know that this, too, is part of the heuristic journey.

Finding Beauty in the Beast

> *Everyone carries a shadow, and the less it is embodied in the individual's conscious life, the blacker and denser it is. To confront a person with his shadow is to show him his own light . . . to penetrate the darkness we must summon all the powers of enlightenment that consciousness can offer. The hero's main feat is to overcome the monster of darkness: it is the long-hoped-for and expected triumph of consciousness over the unconscious.*
> *-Carl Gustav Jung*

Through this heuristic inquiry, I believe that another form or manifestation of disenfranchised grief has been identified which should be added to Lenhardt's (1997) existing definition. This additional form of disenfranchised grief results when young children must psychologically defend against the overwhelming pain and shame that arises when they do not experience attunement with their parents. It is further thought that this form of disenfranchised grief acts to obstruct or interfere with the natural state of limbic resonance or attunement between humans, particularly between parent and child. Experiencing this kind of pain without a fully developed emotional regulatory system feels so overwhelming to the child that she has to completely block or repress the feeling in order to psychologically survive.

Erskine (1998) notes that "Symbolically, attunement may be pictured as one person's yin to the other's yang that together form a unity in the relationship" (p. 2). I believe this aspect of unity, which is represented by the symbolism of yin and yang, exists within the individual, within the dyadic relationship (most profoundly between parent and child, but also between intimate partners), and within society. In a state of attunement, the distance between the yin element and the yang element is very small and the flow of limbic resonance is unimpeded. However, when disenfranchised grief is present, we can visualize that its presence would be reflected through a wider distance between the yin and yang elements. The greater the gap, the greater the level of disenfranchised grief and the more it is likely that the flow of limbic resonance will be blocked or distorted. It should be noted that it is appropriate that there should be some distance between the two elements, as each is a separate entity. However, that gap should be small.

As I have drawn closer to the ending of this heuristic journey, I have wondered how to best sum up my experience and represent what I have learned as a result. As has happened many times throughout this journey, the answer seemed to come to me in the form of yet another synchronistic encounter. At a recent diversity event, a casual acquaintance came up to me and said that she had something she thought would be of interest to me. What she had to show me was a beautiful image titled, <u>Beauty and the Beast</u>, by artist Mercer Mayer (1978), based upon the fairy tale of the same name. In this image, a beautiful young woman, Beauty, is cradling the head of the Beast in a tender embrace. The Beast is a lion. His eyes are closed and his expression appears to me as one of utter surrender. Beauty's eyes are also closed and in the corner of each eye there is a single tear. The moment I looked at the face of the Beast, I thought, *"Oh my God, this is disenfranchised grief!"* What I saw in the face of this Beast was the face of the wounded child who had finally found the comfort of his mother's loving embrace. I saw within this image that I am *both* the mother and the wounded child. For me, it is a beautiful and bittersweet image.

I was also struck by the realization that the overall image of Beauty embracing the Beast appears to be that of a complete circle, suggesting to me integration or wholeness. I also noted a similarity between this image and numerous images I have seen of the yin and yang symbols and of mother and child. This similarity seemed to validate my initial recognition of disenfranchised grief in the face of the Beast and of myself as both mother and child. This validation appears to be strengthened when I consider that, like the other images, the image of Beauty embracing the Beast also appears to represent what is required in order to integrate the disenfranchised parts of ourselves and achieve wholeness: we have to empathically embrace it, which requires that we recognize it, engage with it, struggle with it. Or, as Rilke (1903) noted, we have to learn to live with it. It was clear to me in this image that there had been a tremendous struggle between Beauty and her Beast, and there had been tremendous suffering. But I also now saw deep connection and peace between them: there was now empathy. The integration that I saw in Beauty's embrace of the Beast was hard won. To me, the image and the message are now clear.

Implications for Leadership

> *To be free is not merely to cast off one's chains, but to live in a way that respects and enhances the freedom of others.*
>
> *-Nelson Mandela*

Over a period of several years, poet Rainer Maria Rilke (1875-1926) wrote a series of ten letters to a young student who sought Rilke's advice about whether to pursue his dream of writing or his duty to join the military. Mitchell (1984), in his translation of Rilke's correspondence, referred to these ten letters as a how-to manual of what it takes to become an artist and a person. In response to the young poet's request to critique his writing, Rilke (1903) wrote:

> Always trust *yourself* and your own feeling, as opposed to argumentations, discussions, or introductions of that sort; if it turns out that you are wrong, then the natural growth of your inner life will eventually guide you to other insights. Allow your judgments their own silent, undisturbed development, which, like all progress, must come from deep within and cannot be forced or hastened. *Everything* is gestation and then birthing. To let each impression and each embryo of a feeling come to completion, entirely in itself, in the dark, in the unsayable, the unconscious, beyond the reach of one's own understanding, and with deep humility and patience to wait for the hour when a new clarity is born: this alone is what it means to live as an artist: *in understanding as in creating* [italics added]. (in Mitchell, 1984, pp. 23–24)

What I understand Rilke to mean by this quote also speaks to what I believe are the significant implications of this research not only for each individual, but also for parents, for educators, and for leaders most of all.

Through this heuristic journey, I have learned that there is an *art* to being a mother (or a parent). There is an *art* to being a teacher. There is an *art* to being a healer. And there is an *art* to being a leader. To be an artist, a leader has to be willing to give up the illusion of control. One has to be willing to open oneself up to the heuristic river and trust that the river will take you where you need to go. To be an artist, to quote Rilke (1903), requires that a leader be willing to "let each impression and each embryo of a feeling come to completion, entirely in itself" and "with deep humility and patience to wait for the hour when a new clarity is born" (Ibid.). To be an artist-leader, it seems to me, is very similar to being an attuned parent. I know of few leaders willing to take on such a challenge.

I believe that the most powerful and compelling evidence I can offer to leaders with respect to the absolute necessity to develop *both* the artist and the technician in those who will ultimately come to lead can be found in psychoanalyst René Spitz's description of the fate of orphaned children reared in foundling homes or institutions, as well as babies separated from young mothers in prison (in Lewis, et al., 2000).

> In deference to the newly validated germ theory of disease, institutional babies were fed and clothed, and kept warm and clean, but they were not played with, handled, or held. Human contact, it was thought, would risk exposing the children to hazardous infectious organisms… Spitz had rediscovered that a lack of human interaction—handling, cooing, stroking, baby talk, and play—is fatal to infants. (pp. 69–70)

The impact of the loss of this human interaction for these babies, which later on came to be referred to as "failure to thrive," is powerful proof that technology alone will never be sufficient to develop healthy human beings. Relationship is to technology what the heart is to the mind, and what the soul is to the body. Without relationship, human beings cannot survive. Without relationship, leaders cannot truly lead.

It is Time for the Voice of the Mother

Noddings (2003) states that it is time for the voice of the mother to be heard in education. As I come to a pause in the heuristic journey that is my life, it is my hope that adding a mother's voice to the dialogue by sharing the journey through which I rediscovered my voice and my capacity for empathy will offer hope and encouragement to others who continue to struggle with how to love their children and themselves.

At this point, it is important for me to acknowledge that I have used the words "mother," "father," and "parent" somewhat interchangeably throughout this work. However, my voice *is* that of a mother, this mother. While there is much of my experience that I believe is reflective or applicable to the experience of all parents, it does not reflect the totality or the complexity of what it means to parent a child. As I was recently and graciously reminded by a man who attended a presentation I gave on my research, "There is a father looking at the baby too" (D. Alexander, personal communication, September 20, 2007). He is absolutely right. Of his experience as a single father, he wrote:

> I was so much the mother and father to my child that she often referred to me as "mom." Even the school . . . put me down as "mother." She had a rather disconnected biological mother who eventually left. It is a long story, and one not yet over either. *It makes me sensitive to the importance of male, female, family, and community energy in raising children –especially male energy* [italics added]. . . As I mentioned in my feedback, the relationship of daughter to father is the single strongest influence for girls to become independent women. If the father is absent (emotionally, physically or both), adolescent girls are at much higher risk of losing themselves to a man. This is well emphasized in the area of prostitution. The way recruiters succeed is by looking for attractive girls with weak or absent father figures; they then meet that father-need in a twisted way. I discovered this when working with at-risk middle-school girls. (Ibid.)

The voice of the father is one that deserves to be explored and understood in future research. Another desire for this researcher is to explore the possibility of a dialogue between the voice of the young mother and the voice of the grandmother.

To me, Rilke's (1903) words both echo and validate the thoughts of the single father who took the time to share his experience with me.

> Don't be confused by surfaces; in the depths everything becomes law. And those who live the mystery falsely and badly (and they are very many) lose it only for themselves and nevertheless pass it on like a sealed letter, without knowing it. And don't be puzzled by how many names there are and how complex each life seems. Perhaps above them all there is a great motherhood, in the form of a communal yearning. The beauty of the girl, a being who (as you so beautifully say) "has not yet achieved anything," is motherhood that has a presentiment of itself and begins to prepare, becomes anxious, yearns. And the mother's beauty is motherhood that serves, and in the old woman

there is a great remembering. And in the man too there is motherhood, it seems to me, physical and mental; his engendering is also a kind of birthing when he creates out of his innermost fullness. And perhaps the sexes are more akin than people think, and the great renewal of the world will perhaps consist in one phenomenon: that man and woman, freed from all mistaken feelings and aversions, will seek each other not as opposites but as brother and sister, as neighbors, and will unite as *human beings*, in order to bear in common, simply, earnestly, and patiently, the heavy sex that has been laid upon them. (in Mitchell, 1984, pp. 39–41)

At the beginning of this heuristic inquiry, I noted that circumstance made me the mother of sexual minority children. It was not an experience I would have willingly chosen any more than I would have wanted to go through the experience of surviving cancer. And yet, I like where I am and who I am becoming: a wise woman, a grandmother. And there is an important place for grandmothers, as evidenced in the natural world. A friend recently shared with me that, in the dolphin community, first-born dolphins have a significantly higher mortality rate. The reason is that the inexperienced mother doesn't know to push the infant to the surface for air. However, if there is a grandmother dolphin in the vicinity, she swoops in and pushes the infant to the surface, and the mother learns through observation. I like the idea of being a grandmother dolphin.

As I reflect on the completion of this journey and await the journey to come, I have wondered, why me? What was the purpose for my having been led through this heuristic process? I have come to believe that the reason was simply to be a witness for what is possible. Having been through the experience of "learning to live my questions," as Rilke implored us to do, the answer I realized I have been trying to live my way into was simply learning how to love my children, my husband, my parents, and, mostly, myself. In fact, I learned that learning how to love *requires* that I begin with myself, with the disenfranchised part of myself, and to embrace that disenfranchised part of me as Beauty embraces the Beast. This is the lesson I am asked to witness.

NOTES

[1] It should be noted that much of the discussion throughout this work makes reference to the role of the mother in the parent-child relationship. Much of the research to date has focused on the mother as the primary caregiver, and my own research focused on my experience as a mother. This in no way negates the significance of the role that fathers serve in their children's development, particularly for adolescent girls. I believe that what applies to mothers in this work, also applies to fathers and that much more research is needed to capture the voice of the father.

[2] It should be noted that, in order to protect their safety and privacy, I have not used the real names of the individuals presented in this work.

[3] http://www.glsen.org/cgibin/iowa/all/library/record/1278.html

[4] Julian will be referred to as both "he" and "she" in this story in order to indicate for the reader Julian's gender identification at a particular point in time.

REFERENCES

Ainsworth, M., Blehar, M., Waters, E., & Wall, S. (1978). *Patterns of attachment: A psychological study of the strange situation.* Mawwah, NJ: Erlbaum & Associates.

Aksan, N., Kochanska, G., & Ortmann, M.R. (2006). Mutually responsive orientation between parents and their young children: Toward methodological advances in the science of relationships [Electronic version]. *Developmental Psychology, 42*(5), 833–848.

Balser, R. B. (1980). *Parental empathy.* Unpublished Doctoral Dissertation. New York University.

Barber, J. G., Bolitho F., & Bertrand, L. (2001). Parent-child synchrony and adolescent adjustment [Electronic version]. *Child and Adolescent Social Work Journal, 18*(1), 51–64.

Barnett, M. A., King, L. M., Howard, J. A., & Dino, G. A. (1980). Empathy in young children: Relations to parents' empathy, affection, and emphasis on the feelings of others [Electronic version]. *Developmental Psychology, 16*(3), 243–244.

Bennett, M. (Ed.). (1998). *Basic concepts of intercultural communication: Selected readings.* Boston: Intercultural Press.

Berreby, D. (2005). *Us and them: Understanding your tribal mind.* New York: Little, Brown and Company.

Bowlby, J. (1988). *A secure base: Parent-Child attachment and healthy human development.* London: Basic Books.

Bracciale, M. T., Canabria, S., & Updyke, E. J. (2003). *Assisting Parents of Gay and Lesbian Youth.* Paper presented at the American Counseling Association Conference, Anaheim, CA, March 21-25, 2003.

Brems, C., & Sohl, M. A. (1995). The role of empathy in parenting strategy choices [Electronic version]. *Family Relations, 44*(2), 189–194.

Bridges, W. (2001). *The way of transition.* Cambridge, MA: Da Capo Press.

Brokaw, C. (Producer), & Nichols, M. (Director). (2001). *Wit* [Motion picture]. United States: HBP Home Video.

Buchholz, E. S., & Helbraun, E. (1999). A psychobiological developmental model for an alonetime need in infancy [Electronic version]. *Bulletin of the Menninger Clinic, 63*(2), 143–158.

Campbell, J. (1949). *The hero with a thousand faces.* Princeton, NJ: Princeton University Press.

Capper, C. A. (1993). *Educational administration in a pluralistic society.* State Albany, NY: University of New York Press.

Chng, C. L., & Wong, F. Y. (1998). Gay, lesbian and bisexual (GLB) children: Implications for early childhood development professionals [Electronic version]. *Early Childhood Development and Care, 147*, 71–82.

Davidov, M., & Grusec, J. E. (2006). Untangling the links of parental responsiveness to distress and warmth to child outcomes. *Child Development, 77*(1), 44–58.

Denzin, N. K., & Lincoln, Y. S. (Eds.). (2003). *Collecting and interpreting qualitative materials.* Thousand Oaks, CA: Sage Publications.

Dewey, J. (1916). *Democracy and education: An introduction into the philosophy of education.* New York: MacMillan.

Donald, T., & Jureldini, J. (2004). Parenting capacity [Electronic version]. *Child Abuse Review, 13*(1), 5–17.

Douglass, B., & Moustakas, C. (1985). Heuristic inquiry: The internal search to know. *Journal of Humanistic Psychology, 25*(3), 39–55.

Eisenberg, N., Schaller, M., Fabes, R. A., Bustamante, D., Mathy, R. S., & Rhodes, K. (1988). Differentiation of personal distress and sympathy in children and adults. *Developmental Psychology, 24*(6), 766–775.

Eisenberg-Berg, N., & Mussen, P. (1978). Empathy and moral development in adolescence [Electronic version]. *Developmental Psychology, 14*(2), 185–186.

REFERENCES

Erskine, R. G. (1998). Attunement and involvement: Therapeutic responses to relational needs [Electronic version]. *International Journal of Psychotherapy, 3*(3).

Etherington, K. (2004). Heuristic research as a vehicle for personal and professional development [Electronic version]. *Counseling & Psychotherapy Research, 4*(2). Retrieved March 26, 2007, from http://proxy.seattleu.edu:2678/ehost.html

Fonagy, P., Steele, M., Steele, H., Moran, G. S., & Higgitt, A. C. (1991). The capacity for understanding mental states: The reflective self in parent and child and its significance for security of attachment [Electronic version]. *Infant Mental Health Journal, 12*(3), 201–218.

Frank, A. W. (1995). *The wounded storyteller: Body, illness, and ethics.* University of Chicago Press.

Frankl, V. E. (1984). *Man's search for meaning.* New York: Washington Square Press.

Frick, W. (1990). The symbolic growth experience: Paradigm for a humanistic existential learning theory. *Journal of Humanistic Psychology, 27,* 406–423.

Gruen, R. J., & Mendelsohn, G. (1986). Emotional responses to affective displays in others: The distinction between empathy and sympathy. *Journal of Personality and Social Psychology, 51*(3), 609–614.

Halverson, E. R. (2005). InsideOut: Facilitating gay youth identity development through a performance-based youth organization. *Identity: An International Journal of Theory and Research, 5*(1), 67–90.

Jaworski, J. (1996). *Synchronicity: The inner path of leadership.* San Francisco: Berrett-Koehler Publishers.

Jeltova, I., & Fish, M. C. (2005). Creating school environments responsive to gay, lesbian, bisexual, and transgender families: Traditional approaches for consultation [Electronic version]. *Journal of Educational and Psychological Consultation, 16*(1/2), 17–33.

Josselson, R. (1996). *The space between us: Exploring the dimensions of human relationships.* Thousand Oaks, CA: Sage Publications.

Jung, C. G. (1963). *Memories, dreams, reflections* (A. Jaffé, Ed., R. Winston & C. Winston, Trans.). New York: Pantheon Books.

Karen, R. (1994) *Becoming attached: First relationships and how they shape our capacity to love.* New York: Warner Books, Inc.

Kochanska, G., Friesenborg, A. E., Lange, L. A., & Martel, M. M. (2004). Parents' personality and infants' temperament as contributors to their emerging relationship [Electronic version]. *Journal of Personality and Social Psychology, 86*(5), 744–759.

Leerkes, E. M., & Crockenberg, S. C. (2006). Antecedents of mother's emotional and cognitive responses to infant distress: The role of family, mother, and infant characteristics. *Infant Mental Health Journal, 27*(4), 405–428.

Lewis, T., Amini, F., & Lannon, R. (2000). *A general theory of love.* New York: Vintage Books.

Lipman-Blumen, J. (2005). *The allure of toxic leaders: Why we follow destructive bosses and corrupt politicians—and how we can survive them.* New York: Oxford University Press.

Lipsitt, N. (1993). *Development of empathy in children: The contribution of maternal empathy and communication style.* Unpublished Doctoral Dissertation, Case Western Reserve University.

Martin, P. (2005). Sturdy roots for the graceful eucalyptus: The parallel process of integrating counseling around a client's needs and aligning research paradigms with methodology [Electronic version]. *Counseling Psychology Quarterly, 18*(3), 207–213.

Maslow, A. (1943). A theory of human motivation [Electronic version]. *Psychological Review, 50,* 370–396.

McNab, S., & Kavner, E. (2001). When it all goes wrong – challenge to mother blame: forging connections between mother and daughter [Electronic version]. *Journal of Family Therapy, 23,* 189–207.

McNeil, K. (2005). *Through our eyes: The shared lived experience of growing up with attention deficit hyperactive disorder.* Unpublished Doctoral Dissertation, Seattle University.

Montgomery, G. A. (2003). *Grief needs a witness.* Unpublished Doctoral Dissertation, Pacifica Graduate Institute, CA.

150

Moustakas, C. (1990). *Heuristic research: Design, methodology, and applications.* Newbury Park, PA: Sage Publications.

Noddings, N. (2003). *Happiness and education.* New York: Cambridge University Press.

Noddings, N. (2006). *Critical lessons: What our schools should teach.* New York: Cambridge University Press.

Peña, R A., Guest, K., & Matsuda, L. Y. (Eds.). (2005). *Community and difference: Teaching, pluralism, and social justice.* New York: Peter Lang Publishing.

Pope, M. (2003). *Sexual minority youth in the schools: Issues and desirable counselor responses* [Electronic version]. *Information analyses.*

Redmond, D., & Flauto, P. (2001). *Gender identity disorder in children. Information analysis* [Electronic version]. OH: Kent State University.

Rilke, R. M. (1984). *Letters to a young poet* (S. Mitchell, Trans.). New York: Random House.

Roe, K. V. (1980). Toward a contingency hypothesis of empathy development [Electronic version]. *Journal of Personality and Social Psychology, 39*(5), 991–994.

Rudacille, D. (2005). *The riddle of gender.* New York: Pantheon Books.

Ryan, C. (2003). Lesbian, gay, bisexual, and transgender youth: Health concerns, services, and care [Electronic version]. *Clinical Research and Regulatory Affairs, 20*(2), 137–158.

Ryan, C., & Futterman, D. (1998). *Lesbian and gay youth: Care and counseling* [Electronic version]. Retrieved from www.safeschoolscoalition.org

Schore, A. N. (1994). *Affect regulation and the origin of the self.* Hillsdale, NJ: Lawrence Erlbaum Associates.

Schwaber, E. (1981). Empathy: A mode of analytic listening [Electronic version]. *Psychoanalytic Inquiry, 1,* 357–392.

Slesneck, J. D. (1995). *Psychotherapy and parenting: Parallels and shared processes.* Unpublished Doctoral Dissertation, Widener University.

Spiegel, D. (1992). Effects of psychosocial support on patients with metastatic breast cancer. *Journal of Psychosocial Oncology, 10*(2), 113–120.

Strayer, J., & Roberts, W. (2004). Children's anger, emotional expressiveness, and empathy: Relations with parents' empathy, emotional expressiveness, and parenting practices [Electronic version]. *Social Development, 13*(2), 229–254.

Tesch, S. A., & Cameron, K. A. (1987). Openness to experience and development of adult identity [Electronic version]. *Journal of Personality, 55*(4), 615–630.

Tronick, E. Z. (1998). Dyadically expanded states of consciousness and the process of therapeutic change [Electronic version]. *Infant Mental Health Journal, 19*(3), 290–299.

Wilkinson, S., & Kitzinger, C. (1994). The social construction of heterosexuality [Electronic version]. *Journal of Gender Studies, 3*(3), 307–316.

Wilson-O'Halloran, H. A. (1996). *The transmission of empathic capacity from maltreating and nonmaltreating parents to their children.* Unpublished Doctoral Dissertation, University of Toronto, Toronto, Canada.

Wood, A. R. (2001). *Portray me in silence: A heuristic inquiry and journey home.* Unpublished Doctoral Dissertation, Arizona State University, Tucson, AZ.

Yunger, J. L., Carver, P. R., & Perry, D. G. (2004). Does gender identity influence children's psychological well-being? *Developmental Psychology, 40*(4), 572–582.

Printed in the United States
149069LV00002B/1/P